007

JOHNNIE JOHNSON

Spitfire Top Gun

Part One

JOHNNIE JOHNSON

Spitfire Top Gun

Part One

Dilip Sarkar

Ramrod Publications

Contents

Dedication

For
AVM JE Johnnie Johnson
Sqn Ldr J Danforth Browne
& my father, Mr TC Sarkar JP
Sadly none of these fine men lived to see this work in print

Other books by Dilip Sarkar:-

SPITFIRE SQUADRON: 19 Squadron at War, 1939-41.
THE INVISIBLE THREAD: A Spitfire's Tale.
THROUGH PERIL TO THE STARS
ANGRIFF WESTLAND
A FEW OF THE MANY: A Kaleidoscope of Memories
BADER'S TANGMERE SPITFIRE'S: The Untold Story, 1941
BADER'S DUXFORD FIGHTERS: The Big Wing Controversy
MISSING IN ACTION: Resting in Peace?
GUARDS VC: Blitzkrieg 1940
BATTLE OF BRITAIN: The Photographic Kaleidoscope, Volumes I, II, III & IV
FIGHTER PILOT: The Photographic Kaleidoscope
SIR DOUGLAS BADER: An Inspiration in Photographs

Dilip also contributed a chapter on historical accuracy to Robert Rudhall's best-selling BATTLE OF BRITAIN: The Movie.

Johnnie Johnson: Spitfire Top Gun, Part One.
© Dilip Sarkar, 2002
ISBN: 0-9538539-4-2

First published 2002 by Ramrod Publications, Bayhouse, 16 Kingfisher Close, St Peter's, Worcester WR5 3RY, ENGLAND. Tel & Fax: 01905 767735. Email: anita@ramrodbooks.u-net.com.

Layout & design by Ramrod Publications.
Printed & bound in Great Britain by Aspect Design, 89 Newtown Road, Malvern, Worcs WR14 1PD

Acknowledgements

This book could not have been written without my special friendship with Air Vice-Marshal JE 'Johnnie' Johnson CB, CBE, DSO**, DFC*, DL, who sadly did not live to enjoy publication. Thanks must also go to Johnnie's family, especially Jan Partridge and Chris Johnson.

The following veterans all flew in Johnnie's first Canadian Fighter Wing, and all kindly provided assistance: Dr HC Godefroy DSO, DFC, MD (all quotes from whom have been extracted, with kind permision, from 'Lucky Thirteen'), Wing Commander CM Magwood DFC, Wing Commander R Middlemiss DFC, (the late) Squadron Leader JD Browne DFC MID and Flight Lieutenant R Booth. I would also like to thank cANDACE & James Beistle, Mrs Roberta Chevers, Miss Eileen G Steel & Mrs G Gavim.

As ever, a number of fellow authors and enthusiasts kindly gave freely of their time and information, including Andy Long, Larry McHale, Dr Bernard-Marie Dupont, John Foreman, Mark Postlethwaite, Ernie Hardy, Rob Van Den Nieuwendijk, Don Caldwell, Michael & Richard Parry, and Paul Lambon (who read through the original draft).

Collectively, all researchers owe a special debt to the Keeper & Staff of the Public Record Office for preserving and providing access to essential wartime documents, and likewise the Commonwealth War Graves Commission.

Finally, without my wife, Anita, who is 'Ramrod Publications', this book would not have been such a pleasure to produce.

Bibliography

My own research revolved mainly around the relevant squadron Operations Record Books (ORB) and Personal Combat Reports (PCR), the relevant sections from Air Vice-Marshal Johnson's Pilot's Flying Logbook (PFLB), and my extensive taped interviews and correspondence with Johnnie and his former pilots.

The following published sources were also of assistance, and all titles listed are recommended reading.

Wing Leader, AVM JE Johnson, Chatto & Windus Ltd., 1964.

Full Circle, AVM JE Johnson, Chato & Windus Ltd., 1956.

Winged Victory, AVM JE Johnson & Wg Cdr PB Lucas, Stanley Paul & Co Ltd., 1995.

A Few of the Many, Dilip Sarkar, Ramrod Publications, 1995.

Bader's Duxford Fighters, Dilip Sarkar, Ramrod Publications, 1997.

Bader's Tangmere Spitfires, Dilip Sarkar, Haynes (PSL), 1996.

Aces High, Christopher Shores & Clive Williams, Grub Street, 1994.

Aces High Volume II, Christopher Shores, Grub Street, 1999.

Lucky Thirteen, Hugh Constance Godefroy, Croom Helm, 1983

Prelude to Overlord, Humphrey Wynn & Susan Young, Airlife, 1983.

RAF Squadrons, Wg Cdr CG Jefford, Airlife, 1987.

RAF Fighter Command, Norman Franks, PSL, 1992.

Spitfire: The History, Eric B Morgan & Eric Shacklady, Key Publishing, 1987.

The Mighty Eighth, Roger A Freeman, MacDonald, 1970.

The JG 26 War Diary Volume I, Don Caldwell, Grub Street, 1996.

The JG 26 War Diary Volume II, Don Caldwell, Grub Street, 1998.

The Luftwaffe War Diaries, Cajus Becker, MacDonald, 1967.

Foreword

J ohnnie Johnson and I met for the first time during early 1943, when I joined 403 Squadron at Kenley. We immediately became friends, remaining so until that sad day on January 30th, 2001, when Johnnie passed away.

Whoever assigned Johnnie to the Canadian squadrons based at Kenley made a match from heaven. There was an instant rapport and the Canadians followed him like wolves in a pack. We pilots had complete trust in and respect for our leader, who was clearly destined for great things.

Let us look at a typical sortie from Kenley at that time, led by Johnnie.

Generally, hot steaming tea was brought to the pilots' bedside tables with the words "Briefing in 15 minutes". Those words would shock us into action. We went to the briefing hut, and there would be the clean-shaven 'Wingco' standing in front of a large map. The day's targets and routes would be indicated thereon by red ribbon, and key times would be noted as to when our Merlins would cough and settle into a smooth drone of power. We then went to breakfast, which consisted of sluggish, steaming porridge and kippers, which hopefully stayed put until we returned safely from the 'show'. Invariably we had to cross the Channel, sometimes at wavetop, or climbing to Angels 390, depending on the strategy involved.

During WW2, the 'Wingco' repeated this scenario a total of 700 times, surviving every attempt to kill him and the pilots flying with him. He was never shot down, despite having started operational flying in 1940, and still being there on May 8th, 1945. During this period he destroyed 38 enemy aircraft, a score which officially made him the top RAF fighter pilot. All of his victories, remember, were German fighters, the most difficult opponents of all.

In my opinion, Johnnie was *the* epitome of a warrior, *the* outstanding leader, in fact, of both the RAF and RCAF fighter forces throughout WW2. He is rightly ranked as one of England's great military heroes. He was truly a giant amongst men. From a personal perspective I feel that I received the best award of WW2, however: 58-years of Johnnie's friendship.

Dilip Sarkar, I know, shares my positive views about Johnnie. Dilip too knew

Johnnie well, and has spent many years studying our mutual friend's career. Dilip and Johnnie frequently 'formated' on tape and once I was able to contribute to one of those sessions, the result of which is included in this book. What Dilip has done since is weave together the official texts with the recollections of Johnnie himself and other survivors, in the process producing as definitive a record that time now permits and which will, I am sure, stand the test of time.

So, Johnnie may now be gone, but in this book his spirit lives on, together with the ghosts of those far-off days when we all fought, side-by-side, high over Europe. We are proud of having done so, and that the English speaking and other free peoples of the world decisively defeated the deranged leaders of the Axis powers.

Squadron Leader J Danforth Browne DFC MID

Postscript

On December 29th, 2001, 'Dan' Browne was killed in a tragic flying accident when his Cessna 210 crashed, due to a mechanical fault, near Atlanta. This august survivor of many an air battle was aged 81.

Introduction

B ack in the 1960s, making scale plastic model kits was a popular pastime for schoolboys and adults alike. Of course then, as now, the Supermarine Spitfire was everyone's favourite. Airfix manufactured and marketed a Spitfire Mk IX in 1/72nd scale. The parts were moulded in pale blue plastic and came in a clear bag together with some instructions bearing an artist's representation of the particular aircraft depicted. In this case the picture was of a green and grey camouflaged Spitfire with a maple leaf painted below the windscreen, and the initials 'JE-J' on the fuselage. The instructions provided written data on Spitfire 'JE-J', which was apparently the mount of Wing Commander James Edgar 'Johnnie' Johnson, the top scoring RAF fighter pilot of WW2. The first time that I made this kit was probably at the age of eight-years old, the same age that I had read Paul Brickhill's best-selling book *Reach for the Sky*, concerning the legless Group Captain Douglas Bader. The name of Johnnie Johnson was already familiar to me, therefore, although over the years ahead I would lose count of how many examples of 'JE-J' I made. Duelling Spitfires, *Focke Wulfs* and *Messerschmitts* hung from my bedroom ceiling, my parents frequently on the warpath due to glue and paint marking my clothes and bedroom furniture! The point is, however, that even then, at that early age, I found the story of Johnnie Johnson inspirational. Never did I then dream that one day I would meet and become close friends with this truly great man, and indeed research and write this book. The experience of both has been a privilege.

When I grew up, the schoolboy fascination gave way to being deeply moved by the stories of casualties, young men whose names are now largely forgotten by all but their families. This was my initial motivation, to research and collate as much information about these poor souls as was possible, before it was too late. This work brought me into contact with their relatives and surviving wartime comrades. Circulating amongst the survivors, it was clear that although the stories had been told of the famous pilots, there were many 'also rans' out there who had not received or sought recognition. On their behalf I worked too, recording and publishing their memories whilst time still permitted.

It became clear that Douglas Bader, due to the widely distributed book and film *Reach for the Sky* of the 1950s, was *the* icon, so far as the general public were concerned. Knowing many other pilots who flew with him, however, I resolved, in 1995, to write my sixth book, *Bader's Tangmere Spitfires*, to tell the overall story of the Tangmere Wing in 1941. Although Air Vice-Marshal JE Johnson and I had corresponded over the years regarding a variety of research projects, we had not met. When I contacted him and described my Tangmere Wing project, however, Johnnie was immediately enthusiastic and invited me to The Stables straightaway.

Andy Long, my friend and photographer, were soon heading north, driving across the Derbyshire peaks and past the gurgling becks. As we approached Hargate Hall, near Buxton, The Stables was obvious: a large brass Spitfire could be seen perched on a windowsill. We pulled up the car and got out, smartly dressed and not a little nervous at the prospect of meeting such a personality, *the* top scoring RAF fighter pilot in WW2. Johnnie answered the door to our knock, and we were warmly welcomed. Inside, The Stables was exactly what I had pictured Johnnie's home to be in my mind's eye. Original Taylor and Shepherd paintings hung on the walls, and Johnnie's conservatory office was the perfect enthusiast den. Within minutes we were engrossed in conversation with the tape running, as Johnnie took us back to those heady days of summer 1941.

My immediate impressions, despite being slightly overawed, were that here was a tremendously warm and gregarious man with enormous charisma. Had Johnnie Johnson not lived up to my expectations it would have been shattering. Little did he know, that morning he surpassed them and some! We had connected, we shared an interest, a common bond. Over the next few years, in what was sadly the winter of Johnnie's life, I got to know him well. We would, in fact, spend many hours together in that office, and at enthusiast gatherings and book signings all over the country.

On a number of occasions, Johnnie gave presentations at my symposiums in Worcester. At one of these, shortly after publication of *Bader's Tangmere Spitfires*, the idea occurred to me to write *Johnnie's Kenley Spitfires*, the idea being that as the Tangmere book had looked at 1941, the Kenley Wing book would examine the middle-of-the war period in an ongoing chronicle. I put the idea to Johnnie, whose response was immediately positive. Over the next two years we therefore spent many sessions together going over the records that I had obtained from the Public Record Office and taping interviews. The frustrating thing was that I had to fit this work in around my full-time job as

a police officer, a young family and commitment to existing publishing projects.

Having survived and responded to a heart bypass in November 1996, Johnnie's health was fine for some time. By the late 1990s, however, it had deteriorated significantly and to the extent that Johnnie, apart from very rare appearances at, for example, Mark Hannah's Memorial Service and Duxford's 'Johnnie Johnson Airshow', he retired from public life. Unfortunately, although the material for this book had largely been collated, as Johnnie was unable to participate further in the project it was mothballed. In January 2001, the 'Boss' finally lost his long dogfight with cancer and passed away.

During his active retired life, Johnnie Johnson, as an author, historian and lecturer was an extremely popular personality amongst enthusiasts the world over. He would frequently attend major air shows all over the world, signing autographs and generally enjoying the opportunities and lifestyle that his status provided. Johnnie helped and befriended many would-be WW2 authors, historians, artists and enthusiasts. Mark Postlethwaite, John Foreman and I are but three who have occasion to be grateful for Johnnie's kindness, knowledge and enthusiasm. If Johnnie knew that you were sincere, and that your project was worthwhile, he would help. If he thought you were a fool, he would probably say so, in forthright and often colourful language!

After he retired from the RAF, Johnnie founded the 'Johnnie Johnson Housing Trust', by whose staff he was mostly affectionately and respectfully referred to the 'AVM', or, on those more frustrating occasions, 'Captain Chaos'. The Chief Executive, Jim Lunney, tells an amusing tale about Johnnie, in ruthless businessman mode, chopping down a surveyor's bill in 30 seconds flat, then selling the astonished man one of his most expensive Robert Taylor Spitfire prints – personally signed of course!

On April 25th, 2001, my wife, Anita, and I joined other personal guests of the Johnson family at 'A Service of Thanksgiving for the Life and Work of Air-Vice Marshal James Edgar 'Johnnie' Johnson DSO** DFC* DL', held at St Clement Danes Church in the Strand. It was a moving experience, the church was packed with people even standing in the aisles. Although with Johnnie departed I felt a personal loss that had blunted my motivation and enthusiasm to write the Kenley book, in that church I decided what must be done: the book *must* be written, as a tribute to Johnnie. Furthermore, the scope would be broader, not just concerning the Kenley Wing, but looking at the period from when he became CO of 610 Squadron in July 1942, until rested as a Wing Leader in September 1943. This mid-war period was, I knew, very interesting for many reasons, such as the appearance of the Spitfire Mk IX and the first blows struck by the Eighth Air Force, so it just had to be done.

Johnnie and I had also spoken at length about a sequel to our proposed Kenley Wing book, concerning the D-Day period, which Johnnie always referred to as the 'Great Adventure'. To tell the whole Johnnie Johnson wartime story, therefore, another book would be required, covering the period March 1944 – May 1945. And so it was that this book, *Johnnie Johnson: Spitfire Top Gun Part One* was born, in St Clement Danes Church, and the seeds sewn too for *Part Two* (which will be released in 2004). What, I wonder, would the little boy making models of 'JE'J' have thought if he had looked into the future all those years ago?

Of course Johnnie himself was an excellent writer, and has a number of classic books to his name, not least amongst them *Wing Leader* (see Bibliography), his flying autobiography. Readers familiar with that work may question why this book and its proposed sequel were considered necessary. There are, in fact, a number of reasons. Firstly, *Wing Leader* is purely Johnnie's personal account, and as such does not include the experiences of other pilots involved, detailed historical day-by-day data or analysis of combats fought. Furthermore, *Wing Leader* was not illustrated. The book that Johnnie later co-authored with Wing Commander PB 'Laddie' Lucas, *Winged Victory* (see Bibliography), was punctuated by photographs, but these were mostly from general and widely available sources. This book, however, draws largely upon photographs from Johnnie's personal photograph albums, to which I also had unlimited access during the production of my *Bader's Tangmere Spitfires*. What I have aimed to do, therefore, is fill a large gap in the information currently available concerning the Johnnie Johnson story, and place this data firmly between the covers of two books. These, together *with Wing Leader* and *Winged Victory*, ensure that the saga of the RAF's top scoring fighter pilot in WW2 is as well documented as it possibly can be.

Those readers who also knew and loved Johnnie will appreciate that my dedication comes from the heart. The void in our world created by his loss will never be filled.

So, whether you personally knew this great man, or admired him from a distance, read on, and be *inspired*.

Dilip Sarkar, Worcester, December 2001

Chapter One

Prelude to Excellence
September 1940 – July 1942

"Well, I don't hunt, Sir, I shoot."

James Edgar 'Johnnie' Johnson was born on March 9th, 1915, at Barrow-upon-Soar, near Melton Mowbray in Leicestershire. The son of a policeman, of Welby Lane, Melton, young 'Jim', as he was then known, was a bright lad who attended Loughborough Grammar School, then University College, Nottingham. From there he graduated in civil engineering, first working as an assistant to the Borough Surveyor, Mr WH Jarvis, at Melton Urban Council, before taking an appointment at Loughton in Essex. He was then 22-years old, and the year was 1938: the time of Munich. Like many other young men, Johnnie rightly considered that war with Germany was inevitable. Being very much a 'press on' type (a keen rugger player, he was playing for Chingford at the time) he had started learning to fly at his own expense and applied to join the Royal Auxiliary Air Force. As Johnnie later told me:-

I went along for this interview and the senior officer there, knowing that I came from Leicestershire, said "With whom do you hunt, Johnson?"
I said "Hunt, Sir?"
He said "Yes, Johnson, hunt; with whom do you hunt?"
I said "Well, I don't hunt, Sir, I shoot".
He said "Oh, well thank you then, Johnson, that will be all!"
Clearly the fact that I could shoot game on the wing impressed him not one bit. Had I been socially acceptable, however, by hunting with Lord so-and-so, things would have been different, but back then, that is what the Auxiliaries were like, and do not forget that many members were of independent means, which I certainly wasn't!

As the RAF Volunteer Reserve was not such an elitist organisation, Johnnie applied. Unfortunately the VR was inundated with applications, and his was amongst many put on hold. Disappointed but still keen to play his part, Johnnie consequently joined the Leicestershire Yeomanry (Territorial Army):-

Yes, but it was all very well being on the back of a bloody great horse! One day two Spitfires flew overhead and I thought 'Christ, that's more like it, get me out of the saddle of this bloody great thing!' Fortunately upon my return to Loughton, there was a letter from the Air Ministry informing me that my application was being reconsidered, given plans to expand the VR. That was great news and after I was accepted, I later began flying training at Stapleford Tawney.

Following Hitler's invasion of Poland, and refusal to remove forthwith his forces therefrom, Britain and France declared on Nazi Germany on September 3rd, 1939. On that day, Sergeant JE Johnson, RAFVR, was called up to full-time service 'for the duration of hostilities'. In the war ahead, like other men with whom he later rubbed shoulders, Johnnie would fulfil his true destiny and potential. Had the war not happened, then Johnnie Johnson may well have remained a civil engineer, albeit no doubt a successful one, for all of his working life. For Johnnie, along with the rest of the world, the Second World War would change everything.

By July 1940, Nazi Germany had occupied France, Luxembourg, Belgium and Holland, Denmark and Norway. Britain stood alone to defy the anticipated seaborne invasion of these islands. America was not yet in the war, and her journalists gave Britain just a matter of weeks before the Germans marched down Pall Mall. Between this ghastly scenario and reality, however, lay the young pilots of RAF Fighter Command, whose task was to deny the *Luftwaffe* aerial supremacy as a prelude to a seaborne invasion. As this aerial conflict, now called the Battle of Britain, started, Sergeant Johnson was himself learning to fly a Spitfire at No 7 Operational Training Unit (OTU), Hawarden. At the end of August, by which time he had been commissioned, with 23 hours on Spitfires proudly recorded in his Pilot's Flying Log Book, Pilot Officer Johnson was posted to No 19 Squadron at Fowlmere, the Duxford satellite. He arrived on September 3rd, 1940, one year exactly after the declaration of war.

No 19 Squadron was a regular unit of high repute, not least due to having been the first to receive the new Spitfire in 1938. The Squadron had first engaged the enemy *en masse* over the French coast on May 26th, 1940, during which combat Pilot Officer Watson was killed and the Commanding Officer (CO), Squadron Leader Geoffrey Stephenson, was captured. After being temporarily commanded by the popular Flight Lieutenant Brian Lane DFC, Squadron Leader Phillip Pinkham AFC, formerly a Chief Flying Instructor, arrived to command. Unfortunately, however, 19 Squadron was equipped with the troublesome Spitfire Mk IB, which had no machine-guns but two 20mm cannons, and it was with these trials that the new CO found himself committed. Eventually, the Commander-in-Chief, Air Chief Marshal Sir Hugh Dowding himself, flew to Fowlmere to talk to the pilots first-hand regarding the problems experienced (see *Spitfire Squadron*, also by this author). Fighter Command was naturally very keen to correct what was a serious oversight by not having armed the Spitfire, unlike the Me 109, with both cannon and machine-guns, but clearly it was unacceptable that trials should be conducted in actual combat. Dowding therefore arranged for the Mk IBs to go to an OTU, whilst 19 Squadron received that unit's machine-gun armed Mk IAs. So it was that, despite having joined the Squadron two months previously, Squadron Leader Pinkham was unable to lead 19 into action until September 5th. Sadly, it would be the only occasion: the 25-year old career officer was shot down over Kent and killed by an Me 109.

It was on the day of Squadron Leader Pinkham's death that Pilot Officer Johnson and the two other young pilots who had also joined 19 from Hawarden were posted to 616 Squadron. Many years later, Wing Commander Bernard 'Jimmy' Jennings remembered:-

We pilots of 19 Squadron had been absorbed with the problems caused by the experimental cannon, and we were all a bit frustrated. All we wanted to do was get into action without a gun stoppage. We were just not in a position to train new pilots, so when Johnnie Johnson turned up we had to turn him and the others around sharpish to go elsewhere where, hopefully, they could gain a bit more experience before having to meet the enemy.

No 616 'South Yorkshire' Squadron had been withdrawn from Kenley, in 11 Group, where it suffered horrendous casualties in just a few days in August, to Coltishall in 12 Group. There, away from the combat zone, 616 received and trained replacement pilots before returning to the line. As Johnnie told me:-

And so it was ironic, really, that I should join an Auxiliary squadron after all! The situation had changed by then, however, as casualties had been inflicted and replacements were required – from whatever stable!

The Squadron's new Commanding Officer was Squadron Leader HF 'Billy' Burton, a former Cranwell Sword of Honour man destined for high office. It was at Kirton that Johnnie would meet pilots with whom he would later fly with in fierce action: Lionel 'Buck' Casson, Hugh 'Cocky' Dundas, and Ken Holden amongst them. But there was a problem, as Johnnie recalled:-

When playing rugby before the war, I was tackled hard and broke my shoulder. It had not been set properly and when I crashed during training at Sealand it took a bit of a bashing. Flying a Spitfire needed two strong arms, so it was now starting to concern me a bit. The doc had a look at it and arranged for an x-ray, but the Station Commander gave me a choice: fly light aircraft, as I had during training without any problems, or have an operation to put it right. Naturally I jumped at the chance to have the knife, as this meant that I could stay on the Squadron, where I was starting to be accepted. It was a good job that I made the choice I did, because I could otherwise have been accused of 'Lacking Moral Fibre'!

So, off Pilot Officer Johnson went to the RAF hospital at Rauceby, Lincolnshire, to have his shoulder 'fixed up'. During Johnnie's enforced but necessary absence, 616 Squadron, having moved by then to Kirton-in-Lindsey, began contributing to the so-called 12 Group 'Big Wing', based at Duxford. It is important to study the 'Big Wing' controversy, if only in passing, to understand the birth, development and application of the Wing concept.

In 12 Group at that time was probably the most single-minded and forthright squadron commander in the service: Douglas Bader. Between the wars, Bader, a Cranwell graduate, had been a gifted sportsman and aerobatic pilot. Unfortunately, he crashed whilst performing unauthorised low-level aerobatics at Woodley Airfield in 1931, as a result of which he became a double amputee. Although he mastered artificial legs, the service would not let him fly again, so he resigned his commission in 1933. Having initially rejected the offer of his flying services after the Munich Crisis of 1938, however, the Air Ministry relented when war was declared, providing that he could pass the necessary flying test. Flying Officer Bader promptly did so, and by early 1940, was flying Spitfires at Duxford with 19 Squadron. By the spring of that year he was promoted to Flight Lieutenant and given command of 'A' Flight in Squadron Leader 'Tubby' Mermagen's 222 'Natal' Squadron. Having opened his account as a fighter pilot over the Dunkirk beaches during Operation DYNAMO, the aggressive and gutsy Bader was given command of 242 Squadron. A Hurricane squadron comprising mostly Canadians, 242 had suffered during the Battle of France, moral being low. The swashbuckling Squadron Leader Bader soon inspired his pilots, however, and had then formed up right behind him in every respect. Based at Coltishall, the energetic Bader soon became frustrated with the monotonous round of convoy protection patrols and the interception of lone raiders. He was desperate for some of the action being enjoyed by the fighter squadrons in 11 Group, covering London and the south-east, some of which, hopelessly outnumbered, were in action several times a day during that fateful summer of 1940.

Another chore endured by 12 Group's pilots was providing protective patrols over 11 Group's airfields whilst its squadrons were engaged further forward. For Bader, who craved to be in the thick of it, this was completely unacceptable. On August 30th, 1940, however, 242 Squadron intercepted a raid on the aircraft factories at Luton and Radlett. Some damage was inflicted on the enemy, but, in their excitement, 242 Squadron believed that theirs were the only RAF fighters present. This led Bader to argue that if he had more fighters in the air then more damage could be executed. His theory was that, being further back, the 12 Group squadrons could be scrambled when radar (or more correctly at that time 'Radio Direction Finding' or 'RDF') plots indicated a build up of enemy aircraft over the Pas-de-Calais. Such early warning meant, Bader argued, that 12 Group could arrive at height and *en masse*. The problem was that such a tactic was completely contrary to the System of Air Defence laid down before the war (and now used in earnest) by the Commander-in-Chief, Sir Hugh Dowding, and his Senior Air Staff Officer, Keith Park, now the AOC 11 Group. Simple mathematical calculations prove that, taking into account time over distance, Bader's idea was not actually feasible. Furthermore, on August 30th, 1940, the day that the 'Big Wing' theory was born, 242 was not, in fact, the only RAF fighter squadron engaged. Combat reports preserved today at the Public Record Office prove that several 11 Group units were also involved (and shot down enemy aircraft). So it was that the 'Big Wing' was, in fact, flawed from the outset.

Douglas Bader nevertheless found an ally for his theory in his adjutant, Flight Lieutenant Peter MacDonald, a Tory MP, who later used his political position to raise the matter of tactics with the Prime Minister, Winston Churchill. His Station Commander, Group Captain 'Woody' Woodhall, who was also Duxford's 'Boss Controller', also agreed with Bader's views which, in turn, attracted the support of the AOC 12 Group himself, Air Vice-Marshal Trafford Leigh-Mallory. The ambitious 'LM' was already unhappy that Keith Park, who was his junior in terms of seniority, had been given command of the prestigious 11 Group whilst he was forced to take a back seat defending the industrial Midlands and the north, not to mention, adding insult to injury, Park's airfields. Young Bader's theory seemed to be the answer, thus providing a means of getting both men into the battle.

Air Vice-Marshal Leigh-Mallory allowed Bader to fly at the head of 242 and 310 Hurricane so-called 'Big Wing' first saw action on September 7th, 1940, but despite positive interpretation by 12 Group at the time, it was not a huge success. In that and subsequent actions, however, the Wing claimed many enemy aircraft destroyed, the majority of which appear to have been confirmed with little or no cross-reference. On the basis of this apparent success, two more squadrons were added to the 'Bader Wing', namely 302 (Hurricane) and 611 (Spitfire) Squadrons.

The problem was, in fact, that the more fighters are engaged then the more confusing combats become. Given the speed and numbers involved, time after time several or more fighters attacked the same enemy aircraft, all pilots later submitting a claim for its destruction. It can now be categorically proved, through cross-referencing RAF combat claims with *actual* German losses over England (many of which actually crashed on English soil) that the Wing was not as effective as it was first believed. In fact, the contrary appears to be the point of fact. Nevertheless, 12 Group HQ appeared to accept Bader's pilots' claims on face value (that the majority were Canadian may have been a contributory political factor). These impressive figures soon attracted the support of the Chief of the Air Staff, Sholto Douglas, and others of influence.

From September 19th onwards, 616 replaced 611 Squadron in the 'Big Wing', and Squadron Leader Burton subsequently led up to 14 Spitfires from Kirton to operate from Fowlmere on a daily basis. This gave his pilots a chance to experience operations, but the enemy was rarely met. That having been said, these were important, confidence-restoring sorties for young men who had either yet to fire their guns in anger or, like Hugh Dundas, had already survived the traumatic experience of having been shot down. Unfortunately, Pilot Officer Johnson missed all of this due to hospitalisation.

By September 30th, 1940, the German bomber force could no longer sustain such heavy losses in daylight, and was forced to largely switch to bombing by night. Although the Battle of Britain is officially considered to have concluded on October 31st, and despite German historians arguing that the matter was undecided until May 1941, the fact is that the attempt to bring Britain down through air power alone had failed by that last day in September. The *Luftwaffe* was not a strategic air force, lacking as it did a long-range heavy bomber, and its fighters were short-range defensive, as opposed to long-range offensive, machines. The RAF had therefore fought at an advantage given that the Spitfires and Hurricanes were being used in their intended role as a defensive interceptor.

It is perhaps surprising that whilst young pilots risked their lives in action against the enemy, behind the scenes a bitter battle went on involving both officers of Air rank and politicians. Today, survivors' recollections and impressions of the 'Big Wing' make interesting reading:-

Air Marshal Sir Denis Crowley-Milling:-

Subsequent study suggests that Sir Keith Park's 'penny packet' formation attacks were actually the sounder. He used smaller numbers to break up the attacking formations, so disrupting their concentration of force over the target area and the effectiveness of their attack. It also enabled him to retain some aircraft for the defence of their bases during that most vulnerable operation: refuelling and re-arming.

Wing Commander Frank Brinsden:-

The constraints of Bader's ponderous formation was a disaster in my opinion, a retrogressive step. Nothing was achieved by arriving en masse because the Wing disintegrated almost immediately battle was joined.

Wing Commander David Cox:-

Was the Big Wing a success? I doubt it. Its best effort was on the afternoon of September 15th, 1940, when I remember the words of Bobby Oxspring, then a flight commander in an 11 Group Spitfire squadron, saying what a wonderful sight it was to see 60 friendly fighters suddenly appear. No doubt it was a bit of a shock to the *Luftwaffe*!

Wing Commander George Unwin:-

The Big Wing was a perfect combination between Spitfires going for the escorting fighters and therefore protecting the inferior Hurricanes, which it was, no matter what loyal Hurricane pilots might say, which were able to go for the bombers relatively unmolested. The drop in Hurricane casualties when we operated like this would support this argument.

What must be remembered, however, is that fast monoplane fighters were still relatively new. The Spitfire, for example, had only been delivered to 19 Squadron just two years before the Battle of Britain. Military thinking in Britain and France had advanced little since the First World War, still revolving around relatively slow moving or static ground warfare. The prospect of France falling within just a matter of weeks, and therefore putting London within the range of German fighters, was unthinkable. Before the war, Fighter Command's tactics had understandably been formulated in anticipation of attacks by lone or small numbers of German bombers. The tacticians foresaw orderly queues of fighters lining up to shoot down these slower and less manoeuvrable aircraft. They did not envisage either massed raids or the provision of fighter escorts. As Wing Commander Unwin told me:-

Hitler's modern ground tactics took his armies to the Channel ports in an unprecedented advance. Once London was within range of the 109s, everything changed literally overnight.

So, given, this sudden and 'unprecedented' situation, it was a case of learning the hard way, in actual combat. There was no time to re-evaluate tactics and re-write the book, the experience was gained during actual raids on this island. Mistakes would inevitably be made, but what must not be forgotten is that Air Chief Marshal Sir Hugh Dowding and Air Vice-Marshal Keith Park had both been fighter pilots during the Great War, and ranked amongst the most experienced fighter leaders in the world. Together they had developed the System of Air Defence, which far-sightedly integrated the new science of RDF, and knew exactly what they were doing. Air Vice-Marshal Leigh-Mallory, on the other hand, had never been a fighter pilot and the evidence proves conclusively that he did not truly grasp the (sound) principles of the 'System'. That having been said, Leigh-Mallory did what he thought was right, although ultimately the blame must lie at Dowding's feet. He had delegated too much autonomy to his Group commanders, and whilst aware of the developing situation between 11 and 12 Group, he took no action until it was too late. What he should have done, in retrospect and with the benefit of hindsight as he himself agreed, was got both the commanders together and spelt out in crystal clear terms what was required of them. This especially applied to Leigh-Mallory who was acting contrary to the orders of his Commander-in-Chief (it is interesting to ponder that the scene from the 1969 film *Battle of Britain*, in which Dowding, Leigh-Mallory and Park discuss the 'Big Wing' did not actually take place. Had it done so, then things might have turned out differently. See *Battle of Britain: The Movie* by Robert Rudhall, Ramrod

Publications, 2000).

Air Marshal Sir Denis Crowley-Milling:-

The relative merits of the two methods were argued openly by the circulation of correspondence on the subject between the two Groups. Many of us felt that this was a diversion of mental effort from the main aim of defeating the *Luftwaffe* and was not entirely becoming of the authorities concerned.

Behind the scenes, the 'Big Wing's' influential supporters campaigned to have the concept adopted as standard operating practice. On October 15th, 1940, in what has since become known as the 'Meeting of Infamy', Dowding and Park were called to the Air Ministry and literally had to account for their tactics. Soon afterwards the two real victors of the Battle of Britain were 'got rid of': Air Chief Marshal Sir Hugh Dowding was retired, having been given 24 hours to clear his desk, and Air Vice-Marshal Park was shunted off to *Training* Command. An absolute disgrace. Their places were taken respectively by 'Big Wing' protagonists Air Marshal Sholto Douglas and Air Vice-Marshal Leigh-Mallory.

Infamously, however, on January 29th, 1941, Air Vice-Marshal Leigh-Mallory conducted a paper exercise using the exact circumstances of an actual attack on the Sector Stations of both Kenley and Biggin Hill (which had occurred on September 6th, 1940). The new AOC 11 Group totally mismanaged this exercise which had actually been orchestrated to prove the supposed great worth of large fighter formations in the defensive role. The 'enemy raid' was not intercepted whilst inbound, and had bombed both target airfields before the AOC's fighters got off the ground!

Nevertheless, Fighter Command's new Commander-in-Chief, Air Marshal Sholto Douglas, had immediately set about formulating an offensive policy for the year ahead. The intention was that Fighter Command would go onto the front foot by 'Leaning into France'. Air Vice-Marshal Leigh Mallory summed-up this newly found offensive attitude:-

We have stopped licking our wounds. We are now going over to the offensive. Last year the fighting was desperate. Now we are entitled to be cocky.

Fighter Command had ended 1940 with 1,243 pilots, this figure increasing to 1,655 by early 1941. Help continued to arrive from abroad, as an increasing number of trained pilots escaped from the occupied lands, more came from the

Commonwealth countries and, indeed, volunteers from the still neutral United States. Lord Beaverbrook, the Minister for Aircraft Production, had swiftly organised the production of fighter aircraft, in particular Spitfires at Vickers' Armstrong's huge Castle Bromwich Aircraft Factory. Although the more traditionally built Hurricane was more numerous during the Battle of Britain, the Spitfire, now being manufactured in large numbers, became the front-line fighter squadron's mainstay.

The new offensive fighter operations were code named 'Rhubarb', being primarily intrusions over enemy territory by single aircraft or formations of up to six, using cloud cover. Such sorties were only possible if the cloud base was at 2,000 feet or less, the purpose being 'to attack and destroy enemy aircraft, or, if impractical, suitable ground military objectives'. The first of many, highly dangerous, Rhubarbs was flown on December 20th, 1940, by Flight Lieutenant Christie and Pilot Officer Bodie of 66 Squadron. The Spitfire pilots subsequently reported having successfully attacked an enemy airfield on the French coast.

During that same month, December 1940, Pilot Officer Johnson returned to 616 Squadron at Kirton, his shoulder repaired and fully fit. As the foregoing indicates, whilst Johnnie had been in hospital for those three months, things had changed considerably.

On January 15th, 1941, Pilot Officer Johnson took off with Flying Officer Dundas to intercept an 'X-Raid'. The pair intercepted a Do 17 over North Coates, which they subsequently shared as damaged. As Johnnie said to me many years later, "Well, it was a start!"

On February 26th, 1941, 616 Squadron flew south to Westhampnett (now Goodwood Motor Racing Circuit), the satellite of Tangmere Sector Station on the south coast, near Chichester in West Sussex. The other Spitfire squadrons in that Sector were 610, also at Westhampnett, and 145 at nearby Merston.

Building upon the cornerstone created by the Rhubarb, Fighter Command devised a comprehensive list of more offensive operations, the names of which will appear frequently throughout this book and would become familiar indeed to operational fighter pilots from 1941 onwards:-

Circus: An attack by a small force of bombers heavily escorted by
               fighters, intended to provoke a reaction from enemy fighters.
Rodeo: A straightforward fighter sweep over enemy occupied territory.
Ramrod: A small-scale but aggressive attack by fighters or fighter-
               bombers against a ground target.
Ranger: Another fighter sweep intended to harry the enemy.
Rover: An armed reconnaissance behind enemy lines.
Roadsted: An attack by heavily escorted bombers on shipping or coastal
               targets.

Johnnie:-

It was amazing really to think that only a year before Fighter Command had been up
against it during the Battle of Britain, defending our very homeland, but there we
were 12 months later looking to go on the offensive and take the fight across to
France.

HQ Fighter Command had also decreed that Sector Stations would become
home to Wings comprising three fighter squadrons. There would be no
Hurricane only Wings, but, until their Spitfires arrived, certain Hurricane
squadrons were included to operate alongside Spitfire units. Although each
fighter squadron would still have a Squadron Commander, it was recognised
that one man should exercise overall control of a Wing (of three squadrons) in
the air. Consequently the new post of 'Wing Commander Flying' was created.
The Wing Leader's task in the air was to lead his pilots into action in such a
way that the most damage would be executed against the enemy whilst at the
same time retaining control of the Wing during an engagement. Considering
the prevailing facts of speed and the natural confusion of fighter-to-fighter
combat, the latter was the hardest task. If the Wing scattered as combat was
joined (as had so often happened in 1940), then it's true potency and destructive
potential was lost. At the same time, the Wing Leader had to keep his own
casualties to a minimum. All of this could be achieved through not only a
high standard of flying ability but also strict aerial discipline and radio drill.

In March 1941, the first 'Wing Leaders' were appointed: Harry Broadhurst
got Hornchurch, Victor Beamish North Weald, Johnnie Peel Kenley, 'Sailor'
Malan Biggin Hill, and Douglas Bader Tangmere. The latter had chosen
Tangmere, because it was 'far enough away for the flesh-pots of London not
to distract his pilots'.

With the apparently tireless Wing Commander Bader at the helm, the Tangmere Wing was soon in action, sometimes several times a day. The Wing Leader chose to base himself at Westhampnett, with Billy Burton's 616 Squadron, which he knew from the 12 Group 'Big Wing' days of 1940. As 'Wing Commander Flying' was a new post there were no precedents, and Wing Commander Bader chose not only to always lead with 616, but also flew with the same pilots in his section: Sergeant Alan Smith, Flying Officer Hugh 'Cocky' Dundas and Pilot Officer Johnnie Johnson. The latter recalled:-

Yes, it was a very exciting and inspiring time down at Tangmere that summer, Bader the great man, Wing Commander DSO, DFC, legendary and so on, and of course by comparison I was just a Pilot Officer. But he treated us all as equals, he was a great leader. I learned a great deal from him regarding the qualities of leadership. You can, in fact, learn 90 % of the skills required to be an acceptable leader, man management, being straightforward with your subordinates and so on, but that last 10%, which wins the hearts and minds, is an indefinable gift given to but a few, such as the gift of a great writer or artist. Bader had that gift, make no mistake. When my turn to lead came later, I modelled myself upon him really.

Prior to going down to Tangmere, we of 616 were not flying in the usual 'vics' but in pairs. This may have been due to the terrible battering that 616 had during the Battle of Britain whilst flying from Kenley. It may have been that the survivors had realised the danger of flying in tight vics, where pilots had to concentrate more on formation flying than on the all-important search for the enemy. When we got to Tangmere we were told that we were going to fly in three sections of four in line astern, but sometimes 'weavers' were put up over the squadron. These were always the first to go, just picked off and never seen again. Then Douglas Bader arrived and at first we flew in the three fours, being loose fours in line astern, but then Dundas, who of course had already survived being shot down during the Battle of Britain, suggested that we should fly the fours in line abreast. Consequently, after a little experimentation, we adopted this in May 1941. This formation was identical to the German *Schwarm*, which we had of course seen, their fighters being spread out and stepped up like the four fingers of an outstretched hand. There was sufficient sky between each aircraft to make collision very unlikely, meaning that you could search for the enemy. When battle was joined, the four crossed over, hence the 'Cross Over Four' by which name it was also known, and split into two fighting pairs, comprising leader and wingman. Whilst the leader went for the kill, it was the No 2's job to cover his tail. This remains the basis of fighter tactics even today, it was and is absolutely right. Douglas was the first man to talk to us about tactics, he had the ability to dissect an air battle and learn from it.

Air Commodore Sir Archie Winskill flew with 41 Squadron (which replaced 145 Squadron in the Tangmere Wing):-

Three sections of four, each aircraft well spread out, made up the squadron of 12 aircraft. Thus 12 pairs of eyes could cover the squadron, lookout being in all directions. The Wing's component squadrons were 400 - 500 yards apart and stepped up in high altitude.

Had Fighter Command used such a formation during 1940, there is no doubt whatsoever that Spitfire and Hurricane losses would not have been so high. The reader might legitimately ask why the RAF lagged so far behind the enemy in tactical thinking but the answer is straightforward. During the mid-1930s, having swept aside the restrictions of the Versailles Peace Treaty, Nazi Germany had not only re-armed but also had developed superb ground and aerial combat tactics during the Spanish Civil War. It was over Spain that many of the German fighter leaders, including the exceptional Adolf Galland and Werner Mölders, learned their trade.

On June 22nd, 1941, Nazi Germany invaded Soviet Russia. This changed everything. Suddenly Stalin, who had previously been content to have a 'devil's alliance' with Adolf Hitler, was clamouring for assistance from the Allies. As there was no chance whatsoever of liberating Europe during the summer of 1941, especially considering that America had still yet to enter the war, the only way that Churchill could hope to alleviate the pressure on Russia was by increasing the tempo of the aerial campaign in the west. As RAF Bomber Command attacked the Reich by night, so the 'Non Stop Offensive' gathered in momentum by day. On June 26th, for example, the Tangmere Wing operated from Redhill, in Surrey, on Circus 24. Pilot Officer Johnson reported that:-

I became detached from Wing Commander Bader's Section at 15,000 feet through watching three 109s above me. I saw them dive away to port and almost immediately afterwards saw an Me 109E coming from my starboard side and which flew across me about 150 yards away, turning slightly to port. I immediately turned inside the enemy aircraft (E/A) and opened fire, closing to 100 yards. After two one-second bursts the E/A jettisoned its hood, rolled over and the pilot baled out, his parachute opening almost immediately. I then broke away as there were other E/A about. I estimated that I was over Gravelines when in combat. On landing I heard that several pilots of 145 Squadron had witnessed this. After the combat I joined up with Flying Officer Scott of 145 Squadron and we landed at Hawkinge to refuel, returning to Westhampnett at 13.25 hours.

That victory was Johnnie's first enemy aircraft confirmed as destroyed. It would be the first of many.

Despite such successes, however, the Non Stop Offensive proved to be a costly business for Fighter Command, which lost a number of experienced leaders whilst operating over France that heady summer. These were men that could not be replaced. Johnnie Johnson:-

Eventually they got Douglas. It was inevitable, really, he was tired and, characteristically, would not give in. Eventually fatigue and a hunger for personal kills over-rode his better judgement and he was lost over St Omer on August 9th, 1941. He disappeared in a confused fight after we were led into a trap and bounced by a large force of 109s. I have never been so frightened in my life, never! Afterwards there was silence on the R/T, which we knew was a bad sign as he always kept up a stream of chatter on the way home. As is now widely known, and as you wrote about in your book *Bader's Tangmere Spitfires*, he was safe, although a prisoner of war.

The loss of Wing Commander Bader was a great blow for the Tangmere Wing as a whole, and 616 Squadron in particular. For Hugh Dundas, the thought of Bader dead was 'utterly shattering'. Although he led 'Dogsbody Section' on an Air Sea Rescue search of the Channel, the endeavour was fruitless. At the Bayhouse, the bungalow that the Wing Commander and his wife, Thelma, rented near Bognor Regis, the mood was desolate. There Thelma, her sister Jill (who later married another fighter 'ace', Wing Commander PB 'Laddie' Lucas) and Jean Burton, wife of 616's CO, waited patiently for news. Eventually it came: Douglas was a prisoner! Although safe, the loss of experienced men like Wing Commander Douglas Bader DSO DFC were serious blows indeed.

Wing Commander David Cox, of 19 Squadron:-

Of course the brass hats knew all about the true impact or otherwise of what we were doing, due to ULTRA intercepts, but they couldn't let it become general knowledge. It would have been disastrous for morale.

The morale factor may also be why the claims of RAF fighter pilots were often allowed despite there being no corroborating evidence (in the absence of a witness, bear in mind that the Intelligence Officers had no wreck lying on British soil to examine). The claims were made in good faith, but again as with the 'Big Wing' of 1940, we are back to the confused situation caused by the sheer volume of fighters in the air. The situation was further compounded by the fact that the Me 109, with its fuel injected engine, would habitually dive when taking evasive action. As the enemy pilot rammed forward his throttle, the engine would momentarily eject a plume of black smoke. Frequently these combats were fought above cloud, and the 'stricken' 109 would be seen trailing black smoke and plunging down vertically, at high speed, into the cloud. Understandably, the RAF fighter pilot was left in no doubt that he had destroyed the 'E/A', when in reality the 109 had merely taken successful evasive action and levelled out below cloud. So, when studying RAF combat reports today, reports of black smoke must be treated with caution (unless the enemy aircraft was seen to hit the ground, of course. Streams of white glycol, however, were a different matter, indicating that the coolant system had definitely been damaged).

Air Commodore Sir Archie Winskill:-

After I was shot down over France, I was hiding out at a safe house when visited by a British agent. He asked me why there were more Spitfires crashing in France than 109s. I had no answer for him.

The main reason for the RAF's high losses was that 1941 was a reversal of 1940, the RAF fighter pilots now having to make two Channel crossings in fighters that were not designed for offensive operations. Conversely, the Germans were using their fighters in their intended role, i.e. as a short-range defensive interceptor. Because none of the targets involved were vital to the Germans, the enemy was also able to choose how, when and where to attack, basically in conditions favourable to them. Often this would be when the RAF fighters were turning for home with limited fuel available for combat.

By August 1941, Air Marshal Sholto Douglas himself expressed grave doubts regarding the wisdom of continuing these daylight operations. Unfortunately, however, the invasion of Russia had, as already indicated, placed a greater emphasis on these sorties in order to indicate positive action by the Allies in support of Stalin. Fighter Command's operations could not, therefore, be discontinued. Although RAF claims were high, there was clearly no reduction in the fighter forces available to the Germans. This led some RAF fighter pilots to believe that the *Kanalfront* had been reinforced, which was after all their objective, i.e. to draw westwards units previously sent to the east. Unfortunately this was not the case. The Channel coast remained defended by just two *Jagdgeschwader*, JG 2 *Richthofen* and JG 26 *Schlageter*.

The fact of the matter was that, again as previously indicated, although made in good faith, the RAF claims were in no way related to the *actual* German losses. The Germans, however and like it or not, subjected their pilots' combat claims to a rigorous process of verification. German claims were only submitted if supported by a witness, in any case, in direct contrast to those of Fighter Command. The point is illustrated by the fact that by early September, Air Vice-Marshal Leigh-Mallory claimed that his pilots had definitely destroyed 444 enemy aircraft, probably destroyed 192, and damaged 240. In reality, German losses, from *all* causes, amounted to no more than 200 for the whole year! Although some people still have difficulty in accepting this, the German figures involved were not produced for propaganda purposes but for internal audit. They can therefore be considered reliable. By comparison, German victory claims were nearly 100% accurate, and losses were 2:1 in the Germans' favour.

For the Wings at Tangmere and elsewhere, however, there would be no respite from the constant sweeps. Johnnie Johnson:-

We are talking about the period immediately Bader had been brought down, by which time I had been in the Tangmere Wing for some time, certainly all that spring and summer, and I had shot down at least four enemy aircraft. Soon after Bader disappeared I was awarded the DFC and made up to Flight Lieutenant on the same day, which I think was one of the highlights of my career, because when the CO told me that I had got the DFC together with a chap called Whaley-Hepple from Newcastle, and another guy called Jeff West from New Zealand had got the DFM, and then the Squadron Commander said "Oh, and by the way, I'd like you to take over 'B' Flight". My feet, I don't think, touched the ground for about two days, a feeling of great elation to have these two things. Winning the DFC and being promoted means that you are at last out of your apprenticeship and were now an experienced flight commander with upwards of 100 offensive sweeps under your belt.

I always thought that the fighting in 1941 was harder than it was in the Battle of Britain simply because of the two way Channel crossing. We had to cross it on the way out, then re-cross it on the way home, and a lot of good men dropped into the Channel, and don't forget that we were often doing it twice or even three times a day. However, Douglas was replaced by a man called Woodhouse, who I don't think was in the same calibre as a leader, and shortly afterwards, on October 6th, we were taken out of the line.

Our CO, an admirable little man called Billy Burton who had won the Sword of

Honour at Cranwell, was posted away too and the squadron was taken over by a chap called Colin Grey, a New Zealander, who was a very able and successful fighter pilot, but he did not have the same qualities of leadership as Billy Burton did, he was rather a rough, aggressive, sort of man. Anyway, he took us back to our original base at Kirton in Lincolnshire where we settled down to a winter of training new pilots, of convoy patrols off the east coast, a little night-flying over Hull and the industrial cities which were being bombed during that winter, but we couldn't do much from a Spitfire because of its limited vision at night and it was a tricky aeroplane to land at night because of that narrow undercarriage.

Our Honorary CO was a man called Lord Titchfield, and all Auxiliary squadrons had honorary COs, and he had a big estate not far away at Welbeck Woodhouse which had one of the best pheasant shoots in the country. He knew that some of us were very keen on shooting, so every week or so four or five of us were invited to shoot at Welbeck, which was very enjoyable, and I loved every moment of it myself. As I say, we trained a lot of pilots, we sent a lot of pilots overseas, got a lot of new ones to replace them, and trained them too.

In January 1942, we left Kirton and went to Kingscliffe, which was a Wittering satellite, and there we were re-equipped with the Spitfire Mk VI, which had extended and pointed wingtips, meant to operate at 40,000 feet, which was very high in those days. In fact I took one up to 42,000 feet from Kingscliffe. So there we were at Kingscliffe with these high altitude aircraft designed to operate in the desert and shoot down those high flying Ju 88s etc, and what do they do – put us on convoy patrols at 500 feet! So that was really a waste of a good aeroplane and not very pleasant because, as they were pressurised to some extent, the hood was locked down and had to be unlocked by the groundcrew, although you could blow it off if there was an emergency. It wasn't such a nice feeling as the old hood, which slid back, so I often took to flying with no hood at all, especially on comparatively low-level convoy patrols over the sea. You still suffered, though, as it was so noisy without the hood that you couldn't hear the R/T very well.

In November 1941, 616 Squadron flew down to West Malling, in Kent, from where it flew a sweep with two Canadian Spitfire squadrons. An engagement took place over the French coast with unfamiliar German fighters. Flying Officer 'Nip' Hepple insisted that they were not 109s and had radial engines. All agreed that the enemy fighter encountered was superior to their own Spitfire Mk V in every respect. The new menace in the sky was the Focke-Wulf 190, appropriately known by the Germans as the 'Butcher Bird'. The 190 had, in fact, first appeared in small numbers during September 1941. The radial engine caused confusion, and the possibility of an awesome new German fighter was at first dismissed by RAF intelligence, which stated it more likely to be a Curtis Hawk (some airworthy examples of which had been captured by the Germans in 1940). In October, however, cine-gun camera film definitely confirmed that this was no obsolete Hawk but was indeed a potent new enemy fighter. If things had not gone to plan for Fighter Command's Non Stop Offensive so far, they were about to get much worse.

The FW190 was powered by a 1,700 hp BMW 801D-2 14 cylinder radial engine. This provided a maximum speed of 312 mph at 19,500 feet; with a one-minute override boost it could accelerate to over 400! The 190's operating ceiling was 35,000 feet, and it could climb to 26,000 feet in 12 minutes. Furthermore, it was extremely manoeuvrable. By comparison, the Spitfire Mk VB, with which Fighter Command's squadrons were most commonly equipped at this time, could reach 371 mph at 20,000 feet, but could not operate much above 25,000 feet (359 mph), and took some 25 minutes to reach that height.

The Spitfire Mk V was essentially a Mk II airframe coupled with a more powerful Rolls-Royce Merlin 45 engine. This extra power was needed in part due to the increased weight caused by the eventual successful inclusion of two 20mm Hispano-Suiza cannons in the Spitfire's armoury. The 'B' wing had been found to be the answer to this problem and provided the Mk V with a total of four machine-guns and two cannons. The difficulties experienced by 19 Squadron during 1940 had been caused by the Spitfire's thin wing section, meaning that the cannon had to be mounted on its side. This led to frequent jamming as shells were either fed into the breach or cases were ejected. The 'B' wing allowed the cannon to be mounted upright, meaning that ammunition feed and shell ejection could take place in the attitude intended by the manufacturer. This was possible due to the addition of streamlined blisters on the upper and under wing surfaces, thus allowing for the height of the cannon and ammunition to exceed the actual wing's thickness. Initially, the Mk V was seen merely as a stop-gap, to provide a fighter with a better high altitude performance than the Mk II (the 'B' type variant of which enjoyed cannon armament but without any extra power). Although 94 examples of the Mk VA were built, which retained the full complement of eight machine-guns without cannon, production of this version ceased completely in favour of the cannon-armed Mk VB. During 1941, production at Castle Bromwich, Supermarine and Westlands switched over to mass producing the Mk VB, which was really our response to the Me 109F, a great improvement upon the original 'E' and which had outclassed, in certain respects, the Spitfire Mk II.

By October 1941, over 100 FW190s had been delivered and began engaging on an increasing basis. Initially, however, the first pilots to fly the new fighter, II/JG 26, were forbidden from operating further than the French coast for fear of being brought down over or close enough to England for an example to be captured and examined by the British. The German pilots were impressed with the 190s rate of roll and acceleration, but significantly it was unable to out-turn a Spitfire Mk V.

On December 7th, 1941, however, the Japanese awoke the sleeping American giant by successfully executing a perfect surprise attack on the American fleet at Pearl Harbour. The attack was made in advance of any declaration of war, and could therefore be considered the first of a long list of atrocities committed by the Japanese during the Second World War. Interestingly, America's immediate response was to condemn the attack and declare war on Japan. The United States surprisingly did not, however, declare war on Nazi Germany. Hostilities between America and Germany arose as the result of Hitler declaring war. Whatever, America was now in the fight for democracy alongside Great Britain. Although a tough and arduous road lay ahead for the Allies, Britain was no longer alone and had been joined by the world's greatest power. FW 190 or not, therefore, in the long-term, the Axis's fate was sealed that momentous day of 1941.

As the weather began to improve during 1942, Fighter Command continued with its offensive policy. During April 1942, 616 Squadron participated in seven major sweeps over France. From Kingscliffe, 616 flew down to West Malling in Kent, and operated from there in concert with 609 and 412 Squadrons. Little action was, in fact, found, however, although on April 15th (Ramrod 52) Flight Lieutenant Johnson winged a 190, which he claimed as 'damaged'. The squadron's casualties were disproportionate: two Spitfire pilots were lost.

The 190 threat had caused so much consternation to the High Command in England that plans were hatched to capture an airworthy example. A commando raid was to cross the Channel and steal a 190, which would then be flown home by Jeffrey Quill, the Supermarine test pilot. Fortunately such a hazardous undertaking became unnecessary when on June 22nd, 1942, *Oberleutnant* Armin Faber (of *Stab* III/JG 2), disorientated after combat with the Exeter Spitfire Wing, mistook the Bristol for the English Channel and landed at RAF Pembrey in South Wales. The quick thinking Duty Pilot leaped on the wing and shoved a Very pistol under the Faber's nose, the German unaware until then of his catastrophic mistake. Thus did Sergeant Jeffries capture the first intact FW 190, an A-3, *Werk-Nr* 5313. The enemy aircraft was rapidly evaluated at Farnborough, which included comparison against a Spitfire Mk V. The essential information gained was rapidly fed into the Spitfire development programme, the result of which would eventually put the Spitfire back on top when the Spitfire Mk IX eventually emerged.

The Mk IX, in fact, started to reach the Squadrons from June 1942 onwards. The first were received by 64 Squadron at Hornchurch, followed by 401 and 402 (Canadian) Squadrons in August, and 133 (US Eagle) Squadron in September. Production output increased slowly, however, and so for some time the majority of RAF fighter squadrons had to sally forth with the obsolete Mk V, with tragic consequences.

Back at 616 Squadron, changes were afoot; Johnnie:-

We were then posted to Kenley on July 8th, 1942, but it was being whispered at the time that I was going to get command of a squadron. I was getting telephone calls from staff officers asking me how many operational hours and when did I last have a rest and so on. No sooner had we got to Kenley than I was posted to Ludham, a satellite on the Norfolk Broads, to take over 610 'County of Chester' Squadron. At that time I was 27-years old.

Clearly Johnnie's potential, not just as a fighter pilot but equally as a leader, had not been overlooked by those on high. He continues:-

My 1942 diary says that I left 616 on July 10th, 1942, and that we had a farewell party in the 'Greyhound' at Croydon with all 'B' Flight pilots (I was commanding that flight) and all the groundcrews, including my fitter old Fred Burton. I had been with the squadron almost two years and had seen a great many changes amongst the pilots, but the groundcrew had remained constant, and we had become very attached to each other.

On the way to Norfolk, I spent the night with 'Cocky' Dundas at Newmarket, he was at a place called Snailwell, commanding the first Typhoon squadron, No 56, which was having a lot of teething troubles and killing a lot of pilots. He kept the morale up, he was a very good leader, 'Cocky', and had also been down there with us in the

Tangmere Wing. We then set course for the big Wittering summer party, calling in at the 'Bridge' at Huntingdon, and the 'Haycock' at Wansford. We had lots of beer and spirits, and, oh yes, lobster and crab - we certainly lived well in those days!

The following evening, 'Cocky' organised a party to celebrate my promotion with his pilots, and this was attended by, amongst others, John Grandy, who went on to become Chief of the Air Staff, and Paul Richey, author of *Fighter Pilot*. We had a right old session, but the following day it was off to Ludham and 610.

The time had come for Johnnie to take on more responsibility, both in the air and on the ground. The ex-police inspector's son from Melton Mowbray was now about to start down another road, one that would see his qualities of leadership honed to perfection. One thing was for sure, his promotion had come about for no other reason than recognition of merit and potential.

Chapter Two

Squadron Commander
610 'County of Chester' Squadron

"Street fighting in Dieppe itself!"

Johnnie:-

First I went to the Sector Station, Coltishall, where I had an interview with the Station Commander, Group Captain Lees, and met the Wing Commander Flying, a chap called Prosser Hanks who had flown during the Battle of France with Paul Richey. Ronnie Lees told me that I would be taking over 610 (author's note: again ironically, an original Auxiliary unit!) from a chap called 'Scruffy' Haywood, a regular chap, but he said "I don't know whether you'll see him or not because I haven't even seen him for several weeks. So far as I can make out he is shacked up with some society woman in a caravan just outside the airfield!" The 'society woman' was Lady Margaret Strickland, who had been a bit of a beauty in her day and still was, and achieved a certain amount of fame for anti-blood-sports and that sort of thing.

Then it was off to Ludham, hard by Hickling Broad, to meet the people of 610 who seemed to be a pretty good bunch. The squadron had been commanded by Ken Holden when in the Tangmere Wing, so I knew a bit about it. We had 11 pilots in 'A' Flight, and 11 in Crow's 'B' Flight. These included people from Canada, France, Belgium, Norway, and even a Rhodesian, people from all over the place. That was a big change from pre-and early war days.

When I got to Ludham, Denis Crowley-Milling, or 'Crow' as we called him, was a Flight Commander on 610, with whom he had flown during Tangmere Wing days. He was really senior to me, having been commissioned before me and won a DFC before me, and it put me in a bit of an invidious position to suddenly become his boss. I told the Group Captain, who lived at Coltishall, this when I took over the squadron, but he told me not to worry as 'Crow' would be getting his own squadron any moment now. In fact he got one of the very first Typhoon squadrons. He was a good little man, Crow, his Memorial Service in 1996 was packed, and you just couldn't get in.

One thing that caused Squadron Leader Johnson a certain amount of frustration early on during his time with 610 Squadron was that the 12 Group Wing Leader, Wing Commander Pat 'Jamie' Jameson, insisted that his squadrons flew in the outdated line-astern formation. This is an interesting point, given the work done on the south coast by the Tangmere Wing during 1941 to find a more acceptable alternative. As previously related, the outcome was the 'Finger Four' which proved highly successful. It is surprising, therefore, that given this formation's superiority, it had not been made standard operating procedure throughout Fighter Command. This indicates exactly what autonomy Wing Leaders had when it came to flying and fighting. Johnnie put to Jameson that the Wing should change over to the 'Finger Four' and stated a sound case for doing so:-

The thing was that in line astern it was OK for those up front, but the chap at the back was unprotected. Inevitably he was the first to go down, often unseen by everybody else. Our 'Finger Four' had everybody spread out in line abreast, so everybody had the same chances. 'Jamie' wouldn't agree to it, and insisted that when 610 was flying with the Wing, we did so in line astern. 'Crow', who was still one of my flight commanders and who had also been at Tangmere with us, agreed that the 'Finger Four' was the best, and so we hatched a plan that 610 would cross the Channel in line astern, but once at our operating height we would switch over to line astern. We were hoping that 'Jamie' wouldn't notice as we were usually Top Cover!

Had Wing Commander Jameson been aware of this disobedience to orders then Johnnie would have been for the 'high jump'. Fortunately, the Wing's squadrons operated together only on an occasional basis!

The following selected dates from Johnnie's time with 610 Squadron provides an insight into that period of his flying career and equally a snapshot of squadron life at that time. Unless otherwise indicated, all quotations are from the 610 Squadron ORB.

July 9ᵗʰ, 1942
F/O (A/F/Lt) JE Johnson DFC (83267) posted to this unit from 616 Squadron.

July 13ᵗʰ
F/Lt JE Johnson DFC appointed to the acting unpaid rank of S/Ldr on appointment to S/Ldr post.

July 18th

Johnnie:-

My diary for July 18th, 1942 says that I was lying in bed early on listening to the radio when it was announced that Wing Commander 'Paddy' Finucane, leader of the Hornchurch Wing, had been killed. He had been beating up a machine-gun post on the French coast but was hit, turned his Spitfire around but with the motor cutting he went straight in. His boys circled the spot for some time, but all they saw was a patch of oil on the surface. What a bloody end, another great pilot lost on another useless Rhubarb – for what? Although he may have shot a line at one time, since he had the Wing he had improved tremendously, proven by analysis of recent combat films.

July 24th

Duke of Kent had tea at Ludham after meeting the Squadron at 'A' Flight dispersal.

During the month of July, 610 Squadron had been completely re-equipped with the Spitfire Mk VB, with Merlin 46 engines. These particular machines were fitted with long range jettisonable fuel tanks, to extend the fighter's limited range (more of which later). From their base in Norfolk, the pilots of 610 Squadron would soon find themselves flying to Holland, far across the cold North Sea.

August 16th

The major part of the Squadron, 13 officers and 64 airmen, equipped with 18 aircraft moved on attachment to RAF Station West Malling for temporary reinforcement of 11 Group for Operation JUBILEE.

Before focussing on Operation JUBILEE, it is important to review the war in general at this time. In Russia, the *Wehrmacht* was rolling ever onwards to the Caucasus, having annihilated 300,000 Soviet troops at Kharkov and Kiev. The Japanese were over-running the Far East and were even threatening to link up with advancing German forces in Russia. In North Africa, things were also going badly: the British Eighth Army was in headlong retreat towards the Egyptian border as King Farouk prepared to welcome the Italian *Ducé*, Benito Mussolini, at Alexandria. In spite of demands made by the Soviet Dictator, Joseph Stalin, for the Allies to invade France, and therefore alleviate the military situation in Russia, such an enormous undertaking was impossible at this time. It was agreed, however, that the enemy's defences would be probed on August 19th, 1942: 'Operation JUBILEE', the proposed amphibious landing at Dieppe, represented the largest combined service operation of the war so far.

Dieppe, a thriving French coastal town, was protected by high cliffs, on which were situated heavy coastal batteries. Overlooking the town, it was necessary for commandos to destroy these guns prior to a seaborne assault by two brigades of the Canadian 2nd Army and a Canadian Tank Regiment. Of the 6,000 men involved, 5,000 were Canadian. The Operation's intention was to ascertain whether the harbour town could be seized and held for a day. Whilst on French soil, Allied troops would also destroy installations and any naval vessels moored in the harbour.

Air Vice-Marshal Leigh-Mallory, still AOC 11 Group which would bear the brunt of the Dieppe aerial fighting, saw the Operation as an opportunity to lure the *Luftwaffe* into action on a scale not seen since the Battle of Britain. The fighter force at his disposal comprised 56 squadrons, 48 of which were Spitfire-equipped.

August 19th

For Johnnie's 610 Squadron, 'Dieppe Day' started early with 'a breakfast of egg and chips in the wee sma' hours'. By 0300 hours, the Squadron was at Readiness: 'Pilots were very early astir, but ground crews were before them – busy as bees through this night, fitting long range jettisonable tanks to the Spitfires'.

At 0740 hours, Squadron Leader Johnson led 610 off from West Malling in Spitfire VB EP254, DW-B. As a part of the 12 Group Wing, with 411 and 485 Squadrons, 610's brief was to patrol Dieppe as top cover (10,000 feet). Some three miles off the French coast, Johnnie and his pilots found about 50 enemy fighters, both Me 109Fs and FW190s, flying singly, in pairs, or in fours. From Dieppe itself, the Spitfire pilots could see a heavy pall of black smoke rising. The ORB reports that the German fighters 'fought persistently'. A large-scale dogfight was already in progress ahead of 610 Squadron, into which Johnnie and his boys sallied forth, engaging the enemy at 7,000 feet. Not surprisingly, during the ensuing scrap the Wing, and squadrons, were split up, pilots fighting independently. 610 Squadron's CO reported:-

I saw 30-40 Me 109s and FW 190s 2,000 – 3,000 feet above the Squadron and manoeuvring to attack us. I climbed the Squadron fast and when the attacks commenced I broke in towards them. I climbed after a 190 and opened fire from astern, closing from 250-150 yards. The E/A turned to port and I closed in and attacked from the beam with both cannon and machine-gun. The E/A commenced smoking, its wheels dropped and it dived steeply to crash into the sea, as seen by Flight Lieutenant Crowley-Milling DFC, Pilot Officer Hokan and several others. We were then attacked three or four times and had to take violent evasive action.

I then chased an Me 109F and opened fire from astern, closing from some 250-200 yards with cannon and machine-gun. Two other pilots of my Section also fired at this E/A. Pieces flew off as he started to smoke heavily. I closed right in and the E/A half-rolled and dived vertically out of control. Pilot Officer Wright and I saw him crash into the sea. After we attacked, I saw one of my Squadron with glycol pouring from the aircraft but under control and heading for the emergency landing ground east of Dieppe.

This FW 190 was Johnnie's eighth kill and his first 'Butcher Bird'. The Spitfire streaming glycol was flown by an Australian, Flight Sergeant 'South' Creagh:-

At approximately 4,000 feet, whilst doing a climbing turn to port I was then attacked from below and behind, receiving hits in the engine and fuselage behind the cockpit. The cockpit became filled with liquid glycol and smoke. I was temporarily blinded and on recovering found that I was diving at 280 mph. I wiped the windscreen and pulled up, then seeing white smoke issuing from the starboard exhausts I decided to bale out. I eased the stick back to 200 mph, at the same time trying to contact Red One on the R/T. I was then facing Dieppe and with the glycol temperature at 130 degrees I slid back the hood, opened the side cockpit door, took off my helmet, released the Sutton harness and rolled aircraft onto its side. I fell out with ease and after a few seconds pulled the ripcord. I jumped at about 4,000 feet and immediately lost sight of the aircraft. On nearing the water I was trying to blow up my Mae West using C02, but this did not function so I concentrated on the landing but could not release the 'chute till I struck the water. Once in the water there was no difficulty so I then blew up the Mae West by mouth. My dinghy came away from the pack and was still attached to the Mae West but I did not bother to blow it up as an MGB was heading my way and just visible. I was picked up six miles to the NE of Dieppe by MGB 317. I was told that my Spitfire had gone in about three miles south of that position.

Meanwhile, Johnnie had re-grouped 610 Squadron and turned inland at 20,000 feet. 'Heavy reinforcements' could be seen approaching Dieppe from the Southeast. Having informed the Wing Leader, Wing Commander Pat Jameson, Johnnie turned to outflank a 190 flying on his port beam at the same height. With only machine-gun ammunition remaining, Johnnie closed from the starboard beam and let fly. He saw strikes around the cockpit and small pieces flew off. The 190 then began streaming white smoke (not glycol, the BMW 801 being air-cooled). At just 50 yards, the Spitfire broke off and rejoined Red Three, Pilot Officer Smith. The latter had also attacked the same 190 before tagging onto four Spitfires of 411 Squadron. An Me 109F then pounced out of the sun, although Smith managed to get on his tail and fire a long shot from 500 yards. The 109 then pulled away back into the sun, too fast for the Spitfire pilot to follow.

Flight Lieutenant Crowley-Milling also reported a success:-

On climbing up into sun on the left of Colon Leader (Squadron Leader Johnson DFC), I saw an Me 109F and an FW 190 coming up behind my No Four, Pilot Officer St Remy. I turned hard to starboard over the top of Colon Leader and got on the tail of the Me 109F. I gave it a short burst of cannon and machine-gun fire, followed by three bursts of machine-gun fire only. As it turned over onto its back, I saw a small stream of glycol coming from underneath the E/A. I then had to break hard to port as an FW 190 came up on portside and behind. On doing two complete turns to evade the 190, I saw a pilot bale out of a 109 about 8,000 feet below me. I also saw two Spitfires going down pouring glycol about three minutes later.

Pilot Officer 'Hokey' Hokan:-

I saw one FW 190 go down belching white smoke and hit the sea after a short burst by Red One. I attacked an FW 190 flying at 8,000 feet, firing a two-second burst from port quarter, closing from 350-300 yards. I saw strikes on the tail and claim this aircraft as damaged. Whilst carrying out this attack, shells from another 190 hit my Spitfire, severely damaging it. Having lost sight of my Number Two and being without radio contact I returned to base alone at sea level.

Alone over Dieppe, Squadron Leader Johnson singled out a 190. As Johnnie bore down on the German, he yawed his Spitfire to check the blind spot before attacking. As he did so the enemy pilot saw him, turned and came hurtling at the Spitfire. Both pilots broke left into a tight turn, each trying to bring their guns to bear. Despite the Spitfire Mk Vs reputation at being able to out-turn the lethal 190, in this case the 190 was gaining. The two fighters had descended to virtually nought feet and it appeared to Johnnie that they were "street fighting in Dieppe itself!" The Spitfire swung out to sea, roaring over the promenade and bloody beach. Sighting a RN destroyer, despite the danger from 'friendly' flak, Johnnie pushed his throttle through the gate and, with an extra 16 pounds of boost, skimmed above the waves, hurtling towards the British ship.

Inevitably the destroyer's gunners opened fire, and tracer flashed dangerously close to Johnnie's cockpit. Hauling back on the stick to pull up over the destroyer, once clear he broke left, searching for the 190, of which he was relieved to see no sign; either the German had broken off the chase over the coast or had been hit by the destroyer.

At 0920 hours, 610 Squadron landed back at West Malling. Three pilots, including Flight Sergeant Creagh who we know was safe aboard an MGB, were posted 'Missing'.

Two hours later, 'Colon Leader' led 610 off to Dieppe once again. Little opposition was encountered on this sortie, although four 190s were chased inland beyond Dieppe. Unable to catch up, in frustration Johnnie loosed off a burst at 800 yards. Flight Lieutenant Crowley-Milling, however, was able to damage a 109 from 300 yards. At 1256 hours, 610 Squadron returned, intact, to West Malling.

At 1400 hours, 610 was off again, but again there was little incident. Johnnie again fired ineffectively at two 190s from extreme range, but both half-rolled out of sight. Four other 190s approached but were attacked by Hawker Typhoons. The Squadron was safely home at 1525 hours.

610 Squadron's last sortie of 'Dieppe Day' was flown between 1735 and 1905 hours, when the Spitfires orbited mid-Channel. Four 190s approached but were driven off and headed back towards Dieppe. Johnnie led his Spitfires in hot pursuit, but only closed within range when at nought feet over the French coast. Opening fire at 400 yards without result, Colon Leader broke off the chase. The Spitfires then gave cover to a British rescue vessel patrolling about five miles off Dieppe, before heading for home.

The ORB concluded that:-

Not the least memorable activity of the day was the take-off in rapid succession in the early afternoon of six fighter squadrons – three of Spitfires and three of Typhoons. How eagerly was news lapped up when the Squadron's first aircraft returned from the first patrol; as it happened, Squadron Leader Johnson was able to report quick successes for 610 and an altogether terrific party. What hearty congratulations there were when 'Hokey' safely landed his Spitfire with the tail almost shot away; what relief when it was learned in the evening that Flight Sergeant Creagh, who had to bale out during the first patrol, had been picked up safely from the sea.

Altogether a stirring day, but one which left among the exaltations regrets over the loss of Flight Lieutenant PD Pool and Sergeant Leech, both of whom are missing from the first patrol.

Stirring and newsworthy though August 19th, 1942, was, by the close of play the Operation had actually been a disaster for the Allies. The Germans had reacted swiftly and in consequence some 1,096 Allied soldiers were killed, 1,943 were captured, and 397 were 'Missing'. None of the objectives were achieved, and the cynical have even suggested that this was a deliberate failure intended to prove to Stalin that the Second Front was not an option at this time. If true, the point was made at a high cost of young lives, the majority of which were Canadian. It is interesting to note, however, that when the liberation of Europe was eventually mounted, no attempt was made to seize a French port. When the time came, so as to avoid another Dieppe, the Allies towed a prefabricated harbour in sections across the Channel. Disastrous though Operation JUBILLEE had been, vital lessons had nevertheless been learned.

From an aerial perspective, 11 Group believed that it had achieved considerable and success. Nearly 100 enemy aircraft were claimed destroyed, and 170 probably destroyed or damaged. Actual German losses were 48 destroyed, 24 damaged. Unpalatable though the thought may be, RAF losses of 97 to enemy action and three more to flying accidents, with 66 further aircraft damaged, made Dieppe a victory for the enemy *Jagdfliegern* and anti-aircraft gunners. To further illustrate the point, the RAF lost 47 fighter pilots, as opposed to 13 by the *Luftwaffe*. In total, the RAF had flown nearly 3,000 sorties, the enemy 945. The Operation in no way, therefore, provided the success that was intended. It must be said, however, that it was not the RAF squadron pilots and Wing Leaders at fault, but their High Commanders.

Johnnie:-

Dieppe? It was a bloody tragedy. The Canadians on the ground were slaughtered. Someone said afterwards that it was a seaborne 'Charge of the Light Brigade'; even the German gunners felt sorry for the Allied soldiers as they pounded them to pieces. Did it achieve anything? As usual we had overclaimed, so although 'LM' hailed it as a great victory, the truth has since come out. I do recall that whilst in combat that day I was rebuked for my swearing over the R/T by Pat Jameson!

August 20th

Comparative quiet after yesterday. More waiting for action than flying. The Squadron made only one patrol, late in the afternoon, covering the return on bombers, which had attacked targets at Amiens.

August 21st

The following signal was received from Air Officer Commanding, No 11 Group: 'Very many thanks for all the assistance rendered by the two 12 Group Wings during the Battle of Dieppe. Heavy calls were made upon them, which were readily carried out. Will you please convey my congratulations to them on their very fine performance in this battle' – Leigh-Mallory.

Johnnie:-

After Dieppe, I went grouse shooting with 'Cocky' Dundas, who was related to half the aristocracy of NE England, or so it seemed to me. Anyway, all of them seemed to have a bloody great house and a grouse moor! They were all his second cousins, the Halifaxes, the Allandales, and what have you. He'd write and ask whether he and I could have a walk on the outskirts, but they would always write back saying 'no, you can't walk the outskirts but you can come and join us in the butts and do it properly', and so on. So that was that. Great week, that was, shooting at Lord Allandale's. His son, now the present Lord, was already a POW.

September 4th

Flight Lieutenant Crowley-Milling DFC (78274) posted (to command) 181 Squadron.

September 22nd

Notice received that Squadron should move North to RAF Station Castletown, Caithness, on 30.09.42.

September 26th

R.93712 Sergeant Pilot Plachner, E.C., killed as a result of flying accident, at Ditchingham, Norfolk.

September 27th

Notice received that Squadron's proposed move to Castletown postponed.

October 8th

After several postponements (one of which involved a chase to recall a road party who had started out before the postponement message was received) a considerable part of the Squadron moved temporarily to Biggin Hill by air (Spitfires and transport) and road to take part in some hush-hush operation. But they were out of luck; the operation was cancelled. A sop to the Squadron's aggressive spirit was, however, provided next morning.

October 9th
A significant date in our chronicle, as it saw the most notable mission flown so far by the American Eighth Air Force.

In February 1942, the Americans had sent staff officers, under the command of Brigadier General Ira Eaker, to England where they prepared for the arrival of US combat units. These men and machines of the Eighth Air Force were to be based in England for participation in operations against Hitler's *Festung Europa* (Fortress Europe). Eaker believed in the concept of strategic bombardment as a war winning use of air power, and had already spent two years in England studying RAF operations. Although the Eighth Air Force and the RAF were to work alongside each other, there would be a major difference in their respective operations: whilst RAF Bomber Command continued to pound the Third Reich by night, the Americans intended to do so by day, thus creating 'round-the-clock' bombing.

Having already suffered heavy losses very early on in the war during daylight bombing operations, the RAF was sceptical of the Americans' intention to attack without the protective cloak provided by darkness. Nevertheless, at the Casablanca Conference on January 21st, 1943, the Combined Chiefs of Staff had agreed that a combined RAF Bomber Command – Eighth Air Force strategic bomber offensive should indeed be mounted, beginning in 1943, immediately the weather sufficiently improved. The 'Combined Bomber Offensive Directive' (CBOD) was therefore intended to be a strategic preparation for Operation OVERLORD, as the proposed invasion of enemy occupied France was code-named. The Directive to Allied air force chiefs was clear:-

Your primary objective will be the progressive destruction and dislocation of the German military, industrial and economic system, and the undermining of the morale of the German people to a point where their capacity for armed resistance is fatally weakened.

Targets were listed in order of priority:-
1. U-boat construction yards.

2. The German aircraft industry.
3. Enemy transportation networks.
4. Oil installations.
5. 'Other targets' connected with the German war industry.

On April 17th, 1942, General Eaker had flown in the lead aircraft of the second wave of B-17 Flying Fortresses to attack the railway marshalling yards at Rouen-Sotteville. Visibility was excellent, and from 23,000 feet Eaker's bombardiers dropped 36,900 pounds of general-purpose bombs. The bombing was reportedly 'reasonably accurate', with half of the bombs falling within the target area. The mission's success confirmed the Eighth Air Force's unshakeable faith in high level precision daylight bombing.

On October 9th, 1942, the 92nd, 93rd, 97th, 301st and 306th Bomb Groups of the American Eighth Air Force sent a record total of 108 B-17 Flying Fortresses and B-24 Liberators to the Fives-Lille steel works in Belgium. The 610 Squadron ORB reported:-

The Squadron helped provide cover for the withdrawal of over 100 Fortresses which bombed Lille by day – an operation that made the headlines as our biggest day bombing raid of the war and one in which sensational successes were scored by the Fortresses against enemy fighters. 610's part was comparatively quiet, however. Only Squadron Leader Johnson fired his guns and he did not make any claim.

The Americans had claimed 56 enemy fighters destroyed, 26 probably destroyed and a further 20 damaged. The more experienced British, in the main, treated these claims with scepticism, and rightly so. We now know that the more aircraft are engaged then the greater are the number of claims; actual losses are always much lower, this being because the speed of combat can often deceive the human eye. The experiences of the 12 Group Duxford 'Big Wing' during the Battle of Britain are a prime example of this phenomenon. Imagine, then, several hundred American gunners blasting away at fleeting enemy fighters. How many of them simultaneously fired at the same target and genuinely believed that they were personally responsible for the enemy's destruction? It is easy to understand, therefore, why the over-claiming on this day was so high. Nevertheless, it was a great propaganda coup and President Roosevelt himself broadcast the results to his people. Although figures were later revised to 21-12-15, it is now believed that the Germans only, in fact, lost two fighters and none were damaged. Four American bombers were lost,

however, and 46 were damaged.

This was the first mission for both the 93rd and 306th, as a result of which bombing was poor. Many bombs fell outside the target area, resulting in many civilian casualties. Nevertheless, the raid proved that heavy bombers could penetrate enemy occupied territory with but moderate losses – in daylight. The Americans therefore reasoned that with experience their results could only improve.

It is, however, important to understand that the bombers' operational radius was still dictated by that of their fighter escorts'. RAF Bomber Command's early wartime sorties in daylight, without fighter protection, had already proved how essential escorts were, all the way to the target and back. During the Battle of Britain, the *Luftwaffe's* bombers were protected by Me 109s all the way in and out when attacking targets in southern England. When German bombers attacked the north of England, however, flying from bases in Norway and escorted by the twin-engined Me 110 (which proved inadequate in this role), they were so badly mauled by Spitfires and Hurricanes that such a raid was never attempted again. The answer, of course, was to create a single-engined fighter with the range of a four-engined bomber. But how? Where does the fuel go? How can the balances be achieved between speed, power, manoeuvrability and weight? Whilst the designers struggled to overcome these problems, it fell first to the Spitfires of RAF Fighter Command, despite their limited range (even with 'long range jettisonable tanks'), to provide protection for the Americans.

Until the question of extending the fighters' range was resolved, a frustrating time lay ahead.

October 12th
Receipt of HQFC signal 0208 dated 11.10.42 authorising move of Squadron to Castletown, Caithness, Scotland, on 14.10.42. In effect, move was to be a swap of stations and aircraft with 167 Squadron; no aircraft to be taken. A 12,000 lbs air lift was to be provided – accommodation for about 60 persons – the remainder of the Squadron to travel by rail.

October 14th
Rail party started for Thurso (for Castletown) at 0630 hours from Potter Heigham.

Air party had to kick their heels in idleness. Air lift bringing 167 Squadron personnel from Castletown and which also had to be used by 610 Squadron did not make Ludham that day. By way of time-killing a number of the waiting party went into Norwich to the 'flicks' – a form of relaxation inevitably allied to the 'odd one' here and there!

October 15th

Rail party reached Castletown about 10.00 hours and rather more than two hours later the first of the transport aircraft took off from Ludham on the long flight northwards. Many stomachs 'turned out' – yes, that's the phrase – to be less stable at several thousand feet (varied by bumps) than even their owners suspected and great was the sickness thereof! The Adjutant (F/O Race), Intelligence Officer (F/O Coffin) and Engineering Officer (P/O Sanderson) were amongst those who fell by the way (figuratively). F/O Coffin gave a clear demonstration of 'delayed action'. Reserving his internal upheaval until the aircraft had actually touched down. Only one of the two transport aircraft reached Castletown this evening; the other, after an overnight stay at Leeming, Yorkshire, completed the trip the following day.

Apparently Pilot Officers Wright and Smith, in the latter's small and somewhat 'wheezy' car 'found that 720 miles seemed more like 1,720'. Pilot Officers Malton and Jones, 'battling against rough weather in a Tiger Moth, were at one time passed by a goods train!'

The logistics involved in such a move were considerable, but 610 Squadron were not, in any case, impressed with the direction of travel. Johnnie:-

We had expected to be posted back into 11 Group, Ludham being of course 12 Group, and get away from all the bloody long sea-crossings. Instead we were posted to Castletown, up in North Scotland! I went to see the AOC, Sholto Douglas, and got my arse kicked for my trouble, so to Castletown we did go! But still, we had a good time up there, plenty of game about, we were up there to protect the fleet at Scapa Flow. Not surprising, really, because from what I could make out the buggers rarely left the anchorage!

November 10th

This day the Squadron had a real excuse for a party. The CO, Squadron Leader JE Johnson DFC & Bar, having decided to take the flip (whence there is no return) into matrimony and the date of take-off (or 'prang' as you like it) being imminent. Officers and senior NCOs, with the Station Commander, Wing Commander GAW Saunders DFC, and Station Adjutant, Flight Lieutenant Reeves, as guests, chose the Dunnet Hotel as rendezvous. Much signing – and not a little 'partaking of refreshment', as the old saying has it! And so, for Squadron Leader Johnson, the beginning of farewell to batcherlordom.

November 12th
Sgt DT Jones 'pranged' on landing after convoy patrol but was unhurt.

November 14th
Squadron Leader Johnson married at the Registrar's Office, City Hall, Norwich, to Miss Paula Ingate, youngest daughter of Mr & Mrs Sidney Ingate, 73 Park Lane, Norwich. His old friend Wing Commander HSL Dundas DFC was best man. Squadron officers present, who gave the occasion something of an international flavour were Flight Lieutenant WA Laurie DFC, Pilot Officer RW Pearson, Flying Officer GS Malton (Canada) and Lieutenant A Hvinden (Norway).

November 17th
Pilot Officers PB Wright and PR Pabiot (Fighting French) sampled the hind shooting at Braemore and Langwell, arranged by Squadron Leader Johnson through the Marquess of Titchfield. Great sport, they reported. 'Bag' for the day, two hinds.

November 29th
First day of a three day visit to the Station and Squadron by the AOC No 14 Group, Air Vice-Marshal R Collishaw CB DSO OBE DSC DFC. On morning on November 30th, he addressed all pilots at 'A' Flight dispersal.
Squadron Leader Johnson was presented by the Squadron with an onyx cigarette box to commemorate his marriage.

In flying terms it was a bleak period, up in the far north. Severe weather towards the end of November 'apparently presaged a tough winter, but a few tough fellows continued their shooting expeditions and brought back the odd treat for the table'.

December 4th
Flying Officer LA Smith and Pilot Officer JT Skibinski spent the day hind-shooting; got very wet but had good sport.

December 6th
'A' Flight aircraft moved to RAF Station Tain, for Army Co-operation Exercise 'Goliath', accompanied by Harrow transport taking rather more than 20 members of ground crews for servicing purposes. In this exercise, Squadron's job was to support 'German' troops in action around northern end of Loch Ness.

December 11th

At 1600 hours began Exercise Crab II, which continued until 0800 hours on December 15th. Purpose of exercise was to test Station's security against enemy guerrillas. Strengthened night guards were maintained nightly at dispersal points and several brushes with intruders occurred.

December 14th

Highlight of Exercise Crab II from Squadron's standpoint. During afternoon enemy reported attacking in strength from west of aerodrome. 'Beat Up' of their positions by Squadron aircraft – including Tiger Moth flown by Squadron Leader Johnson! – was sharp and effective, guerrillas withdrew and were reckoned to have been largely destroyed by 610.

December 15th

Squadron Leader Johnson, having previously arranged hind shooting for various pilots, had for this evening 'organised' the gift of a hind carcass for the Squadron. Officers and Senior NCOs had a party at the Dunnet Hotel and found the hind very tasty. They also found much to admire in Squadron Leader Johnson's grand manner as he dispensed the portions with the air of a proud father administering to the needs of an outsize family! The beer flowed freely both during and after the meal, and of course there was much 'singing'.

Such are the actions of a true leader in an effort to maintain morale in poor weather and well away from any action.

Christmas Day, 1942

Despite some effects of Xmas Eve revels, a Squadron rugby team turned out smartly by about 1000 hours to give SHQ side a beating by 12 points to six. Officers and Senior NCOs served Xmas dinner to the airmen.

During the month of December, 610 Squadron flew 454 hours, 107 of which were operational. Given that flying was scrubbed on six days due to bad weather, these statistics indicate that morale and enthusiasm remained high. The credit for this must in no small part be due to Squadron Leader Johnson.

New Year's Day, 1943

Most folk were awake to see the New Year in. Not the least notable feature of the celebrations was a party in the Officers' Mess.

January 12th
News received of the award of the DFC to Flying Officer PB Wright, the 'Old Man' of the Squadron in point of service with it as pilot. There had to be a party at the Dunnet Hotel, to celebrate this honour to the Squadron and to a capable, conscientious pilot and officer. The fact that in the end several 'happy' people were a little confused as to just who had won the DFC does not really matter, but we'll record it even if only to prove that the celebration was worthy of the event!

January 13th
The CO, Squadron Leader JE Johnson DFC & Bar, left for Fighter Leader Course at Chedworth.

January 14th
Flying Officer PB Wright (119180) posted to 616 Squadron as Flight Commander. The good things have indeed arrived with a rush for 'Pappy', whom we had come to regard as unlucky where advancement and honours were concerned. All's well for him now; and its by no means the end!

Sadly, however, the end was not far off. Flight Lieutenant Peter Beresford Wright DFC, aged 22, failed to return from operations with 616 Squadron on April 5th, 1943. His body was never found and he is therefore remembered on the Runnymede Memorial, panel 122.

January 15th
Preliminary advice of a Squadron move south to No 11 Group received in HQ No 14 Group.

January 16th
Squadron's next 'home' now disclosed as Westhampnett, a satellite aerodrome of Tangmere... The Squadron is to move on January 20th, exchanging commitments with 131 Squadron; aircraft not to be taken. This move involves for 610 a throw back to 1941, when the Squadron was formerly at Westhampnett. It seems that everybody is going to like the change, especially as it means a place in the British 'Front Line' again.

January 19th
Packing up day. Some bustle and some slightly frayed tempers. Generally, however, another fairly smooth job, thanks to the considerable experience of this work brought to bear by key personnel. The loading of specially allocated railway vans at Thurso railway station completed shortly after dark.

The CO, recalled from his course at Chedworth by the AOC No 14 Group, in order to be at hand for the move, arrived back at Castletown in time for the farewell party given to Squadron Officers and Senior NCOs by the Officers' Mess. Complimentary speeches by the Station Commander, Wing Commander GAW Saunders DFC, and the PMC, Squadron Leader Caire, were acknowledged by Squadron Leader Johnson.

January 20th

Early this very dark morning the main rail party went by motor transport from Castletown to Thurso and began the long trip to Chichester (for Westhampnett) on the 0830 hours train.

On this day, 610 Squadron received a new pilot, Flying Officer Colin Hodgkinson, posted from 131 Squadron. This would have been unremarkable but for one thing: like Wing Commander Douglas Bader, 'Hoppy' Hodgkinson had no legs, having also become a double amputee as the result of a flying accident. Inspired by Bader's example, however, Colin too (now deceased but whom I had the very great pleasure of meeting in France during 1996) was determined to fly again. Like Douglas Bader, not only did he simply fly, he flew Spitfires on operations (coincidentally from Westhampnett) until he too (also coincidentally) was captured near St Omer. Such, then, was the spirit of these young fighter pilots that even incapacitating disabilities could be overcome.

By January 23rd, all elements of 610 Squadron had arrived at Westhampnett, the move having come much earlier than expected. The 'Old Timers' found Westhampnett much changed from that they had left in 1941. The station had increased in size but facilities were well dispersed, requiring service bicycles to be issued to many personnel.

Johnnie:-

Whilst at Castletown we had received a number of replacement pilots, so these chaps were keen to see action, to prove themselves. It was an exciting time for the Squadron, a challenge which 610 was ready for.

February 1st

Flying Officer N Haider (India) attached from India Office. Fourteen nationalities have now been represented in the Squadron at various times.

February 2ⁿᵈ

Captain Cuthbert Orde, the well-known artist, arrived on a five-day visit to the Squadron, during which he sketched the CO, the two Flight Commanders (Flight Lieutenants WA Laurie DFC and DO Collinge DFC), Lieutenant A Hvinden, Pilot Officer SC Creagh and Flying Officer LA Smith DFC.

February 3ʳᵈ

Squadron, along with 485 (NZ) Squadron had its first 'show' since returning to 11 Group. No excitement during sweep of French coast.

February 6ᵗʰ

First loss since Squadron returned to 11 Group. Sgt HR Parker (NZ) missing from a 'Rhubarb' operation over France and last heard of about 20 miles north of Cherbourg.

The likelihood was that the Sergeant Parker had fallen to the guns of a JG 2 FW 190. The fourth Westhampnett pilot to be lost in just three days on Rhubarbs, Sergeant Parker's body was never found, despite an extensive ASR search led by Johnnie. The 24-year old is now is now remembered on the Runnymede Memorial, panel 98. Left behind was a widow, Thelma, in Auckland, New Zealand.

Of Rhubarbs, Johnnie had this to say:-

We of 610 were called upon to fly a lot of 'Rhubarbs', from Ludham over the Dutch coast, and from Westhampnett over the Cherbourg area, you know, going over there in low cloud then popping out and shooting at whatever moved. They were very dangerous operations. The flying time, with long range tanks, being 40 minutes each way, a long, long way over the water on a single engine. Threats were numerous: mechanical failures, flak and enemy fighters. These sorties achieved virtually nothing, but we lost a lot of chaps, including some valuable leaders – just look at what happened to Paddy Finucane. Bloody murder, wasn't it?

On one occasion, we took off on a Rhubarb at 0500 hrs, with Yellow Section, that being the Group Captain and one of my chaps, turning back after the Groupie's aircraft developed tank trouble. The rest of us hit the Dutch coast and when five miles inland we broke out of 6/10ths cloud at 600 feet. Murder, wasn't it? Of course luckily the place was flat, but we didn't know what the pressure was to re-set our altimeters.

February 9ᵗʰ

A number of the pilots had a lot of fun during exercise 'King 0', organised to test both their ground navigation and camp security. They were taken in a completely closed truck to an un-named point in the countryside and, in being dropped there, were expected to make their own way back to Westhampnett and, if possible, enter the camp airfield undetected. In disguises that varied from the plumber's mate (complete with length of lead piping!) to something resembling a decrepit undertaker, all except one of the eight pilots achieved their objective unchallenged.

February 10th

A black day. On bomber escort to Caen, Squadron was jumped by FW 190s. Squadron Leader AE Robinson (supernumerary), Flying Officer LA Smith DFC and Sergeant HR Harris (NZ) all reported missing, whilst Pilot Officer KS Wright managed to stagger home with an aircraft badly shot up about the tail.

To lose three pilots on one sortie was a bitter blow indeed. All were married men.

Johnnie:-

Yes, that was a particularly bad trip. The problem was that, so as to provide as small a target as possible to the flak gunners, the Ventura leader flew just below cloud, meaning that we had no room to position ourselves above his formation. I therefore placed 610 Squadron at the bombers' rear, as other escorting Spitfires were on each flank. My intention was to sweep the target after the Venturas had bombed, but the 190s carved us up during the turn. About 30 fell on us through a gap in the cloud, so they had the advantage of height, surprise and speed.

In the ensuing combat, the tail was shot off Flying Officer Smith's tail, the pilot being seen to bale out over the sea, about three miles from the French coast. The Polish Sergeant Lisowski's Spitfire was also hit, and was smoking badly, but he ignored Squadron Leader Johnson's order to turn around and crash land in France and doggedly staggered back to England and safety. Pilot Officer Wright's Spitfire was hit by a cannon shell and flung upside down, but by some miracle his controls responded sufficiently for him to drop to sea-level and head for home, alone.

Indeed, so ferocious was the attack by I/JG 2 that diving for the deck was the only option for Johnnie and his remaining pilots. The CO of 610 Squadron knew that in the past the Germans had shown a marked reluctance to engage at sea level, so it was just above the waves that the Spitfires levelled out. If necessary they would turn tightly, just above the wave tops, enticing the

Germans to follow; only the most skilful pilot would survive. As the Spitfires streaked across the waves towards England, Johnnie was too late in shouting a warning to two Spitfires flying ahead. A pair of 190s hit them hard, both Spitfires going down. That flown by Squadron Leader Robinson suddenly became enveloped in flame. As the horrified pilots watched helplessly, the pilot screamed all the way down over the R/T. Seconds after impact, the sea had closed completely over the aircraft, of which there was no trace. Johnnie:-

That incident was awful, and will always remain pretty much etched into my memory. It was shocking, we had never experienced anything like it before. None of us spoke for the rest of the way home.

Clearly, the FW 190 was still making its presence felt on the *Kanalfront*. Not surprisingly, Fighter Command's losses were having a seriously negative impact on morale. Penetration was severely restricted, as Johnnie has previously said the 190 had pushed the Spitfires back to the French coast. Kills for the RAF pilots were now even harder to come by.

February 13th

An unlucky 13th for Pilot Officer Sibinski (Pole) missing from sweep over France. Nothing more was seen of him after the Squadron dived to assist the other Squadron in the Wing – 485 Squadron (NZ) – about 10-15 miles south of Boulogne.

The Westhampnett Spitfires had been hit by II/JG 26, led by Major Wilhelm-Ferdinand 'Wutz' Galland, brother of General Adolf Galland, and 7/JG 2. Galland's pilots shot down three Spitfires of 485 Squadron, including the younger brother of the CO, Squadron Leader Reg Grant. As with countless other casualties, Flying Officer IAC Grant was never seen again, the 27-year old New Zealander likewise being commemorated on the Runnymede Memorial. Although Squadron Leader Grant claimed to have destroyed the 190 that killed his brother, he was mistaken; the enemy pilot escaped unscathed. Johnnie, however, managed to wing a 190, which he later claimed as a 'probable'.

For the *Jagdfliegern*, the current run of success was akin to those of the previous year, when the FW 190 had first been unleashed on the *Kanalfront*. For Fighter Command's total loss of six Spitfires on this day, the *Luftwaffe* lost not one aircraft.

Johnnie:-

It seemed at the time that there was no solution to the 190 menace. As we have previously said our radius of operations was reduced to the enemy coastline for some time, and all of this because of one fucking aircraft type! We were losing a lot of chaps, far too many. It got to the stage that we had to avoid combat unless the controller gave us the perfect bounce. We needed the Spitfire Mk IX – badly. Although some squadrons were flying them, it was frustrating for the rest of us.

After this run of losses (five pilots), 610 Squadron was clearly unable to sustain such losses for much longer. Squadron Leader Grant was rested from operations, and pending the appointment of a new Tangmere Wing Leader, Johnnie, as the senior Squadron Commander, led the Wing on occasions. It would be good experience.

February 16th
Flight Lieutenant DO Collinge attended Buckingham Palace investiture and received DFC from the King.

February 20th
Flight Lieutenant PI Howard-Williams (33569) posted from 10 Group Delivery Flight.

Peter Howard-Williams, the son of an Air Commodore, was a professional airman, as was his brother, Jeremy, who became a successful night-fighter pilot. This was Peter's second tour, the first having started with 19 Squadron, in May 1940, concluding as a Flight Commander on 118 Squadron in April 1942. In November 1941, his efforts had been recognised by the award of a DFC. In between tours, he had been commanding the 10 Group Delivery Flight at Colerne, which, many years later, he described to me as having been 'a super job!'

In summary, of February 1943, the 610 Squadron ORB had this to say:-

The month saw completion of the settling-down process at Westhampnett, though this was not without shocks. Loss of five pilots on operations between February 6th and February 13th (inclusive) was grim indeed. It was but small consolation that the CO, Squadron Leader Johnson DFC & Bar, was credited with an FW 190 probably destroyed on 13th February.

March 2nd

Quite a surprise when the C-in-C, Fighter Command, Air Marshal Sir Trafford Leigh-Mallory KCD DSO 'dropped in' during the early evening, accompanied by the Wing Commander Flying, Wing Commander Brothers DFC (also acting as Station Commander in the absence of Group Captain HD McGregor DSO). Over beers in the Westhampnett Officers' Mess, the Commander-in-Chief chatted with Squadron officers, mainly about various aircraft performances. A pleasant occasion, entirely without ceremony beyond introduction of Squadron personnel to the C-in-C by Flight Lieutenant WA Laurie DFC, commanding the Squadron in the absence on leave of Squadron Leader Johnson DFC & Bar.

March 3rd

Four aircraft took off for a Rhubarb (attack on ground targets) operation, but turned back when about 10 miles off Pointe-de-la-Percee because weather was unfavourable.

March 7th

Olive Snell (artist) made dispersal her temporary studio while she continued her sketching of Squadron personalities, started a short time previously.

March 8th

Squadron, led by Wing Commander D Smith DSO DFC, together with 485 Squadron, provided withdrawal cover to Fortresses, which had bombed Rennes. Took off 1430 hours, crossed French coast at Bretteville, climbed over Valognes, turned port and came out across French coast at Pointe-de-la-Percee. Landed at 1540 hours, no combats.

March 9th

Along with 485 Squadron, 610 participated on Rodeo 177, sweeping French coastal area between Le Havre and Fecamp. No incident. Flight Lieutenant Baker (485) led the Wing, and Flight Lieutenant Laurie led 610 Squadron.

March 10th

Squadron Leader Johnson led 610 and the Wing (also including 485 Squadron) on Rodeo 180. Crossed French coast about two miles west of Dieppe, turned starboard and recrossed French coast on outward trip about five east of Fecamp. No incident.

March 11th

During ASR escort of Walrus, Flight Lieutenant Howard-Williams DFC, when about 30 miles out from Beachy Head on a course of 149°, at 1710 hours approximately, attacked two FW 190s which then dived away. Flight Lieutenant Howard-Williams broke away and being unable to locate Walrus, returned to base. At about 1730 hours, Pilot Officer Wright, still in Walrus escort and about 45/50 miles out from Beachy Head saw a FW 190 sinking in the sea. This was claimed as one attacked earlier by Flight Lieutenant Howard-Williams and therefore destroyed – a claim later allowed by Fighter Command.

March 12th
Squadron beer-and-sandwich party at the Unicorn Hotel, Chichester.

March 14th
Pilot Officer JM Cremer lost while on Shoreham-Brighton patrol – his first operational trip. While turning at a point about two miles south of Bognor his aircraft wing was seen to strike the sea and break off and the aircraft plunged straight under the water. Nothing further seen.

At the tender age of 19, Pilot Officer Cremer was amongst the youngest Spitfire pilot casualties of the Second World War. A King's Scholar of King's School, Canterbury, this teenage officer was clearly a young man of potential. Yet again, this pilot, from Brockenhurst in Hampshire, is also commemorated on the Runnymede Memorial (panel 124).

March 15th
The two Westhampnett squadrons, 610 and 485, were for the day the sole squadrons of 11 Group functioning because all other Sectors were non-operational due to bad weather.

Changes, however, were afoot. Johnnie:-

I had been getting an increasing number of calls from staff officers, asking me how many operational hours I had, how many sweeps had I done, so I told him, and he asked "When did you last have a rest?"
I said "Well, I've just had one, we've been up to Castletown, no operational flying up there whatsoever, shot lots of grouse and downed a fair bit of malt!"
He said, "Oh, so you count that as a rest, do you?"
I said "Yes I do, and the salmon fishing was pretty good too!", well, it was better than going to be an instructor at some bloody OTU, wasn't it, teaching a lot of ham fisted buggers how to fly! He said, "Oh, I'll call you back".

March 16th
Johnnie had, in fact, misread the situation. Although 'Group' was looking to promote him, there was no intention to take him off operations. Johnnie:-

The Staff Officer called me back and said "The Commander-in-Chief sends his congratulations, you are to put up your Wing Commander's stripe immediately and take over the Canadian Spitfire Wing at Kenley".

Alan Laurie took over 610 Squadron, and the Norwegian, Hvinden, replaced him as OC 'B' Flight. Both appointments were well deserved, they were good chaps who knew the score.

It would surprise no one that a party was held that evening, at the Unicorn Hotel, Chichester, to celebrate these various promotions!

On March 19th, Wing Commander JE 'Johnnie' Johnson DFC & Bar 'took his farewell of 610, which he had commanded for eight months under a promise to renew acquaintance reasonably often – a promise we all hope he will keep'.

At last the time had come for Johnnie Johnson, the policeman's son from Melton Mowbray, the young man who did not hunt but shot, to really shine.

Chapter Three

Wing Commander Flying
Kenley (Canadian) Spitfire Wing

"The dream of every fighter pilot."

By the time of Johnnie Johnson's promotion and appointment as Wing Commander Flying, his personal score of enemy aircraft destroyed was just into double figures. Being a Wing Leader, however, was not about a personal score, but that of the team. Now was the chance for Wing Commander Johnson to demonstrate the depth of his leadership qualities.

Johnnie:-

It was a quantum leap between being a Squadron Leader to becoming a Wing Commander. The dream of every fighter pilot at that time must surely to have been getting a Wing in 11 Group, which I had now achieved. To say that I welcomed and looked forward to this new challenge was an understatement!

The RAF, in my day, taking my career from Sergeant Pilot in the Volunteer Reserve to Wing Commander Flying in three-and-a half years would have been impossible in the army. No one in the Life Guards, for example, could have gone from Trooper to Lieutenant-Colonel in three years. Never. Rank and privilege, and class and breeding was very much to the fore in the army in those days, and in the Royal Navy to some extent, but it wasn't in the RAF. In the RAF if a man could do his job and hold his own in the squadron and that sort of thing, that is all we required of him. He had equal opportunities for promotion whether he had been to the local grammar school or Eton or Harrow. That was the great thing about our service, equal opportunities.

Kenley itself was situated in Surrey, south of London, was a long established fighter station which had carved its name with pride during the Battle of Britain. The personnel of the Spitfire Wing now based there were Canadian, as Johnnie remembered:-

The Canadians? They had a reputation for lacking discipline, bloody-mindedness and so on and so forth. Stan Turner, for example, a very prickly pear. Bader could handle him, Bader knew that Stan Turner, when the chips were down, would be there when lesser men had fled because he was such a fucking obstinate bastard, wouldn't give in, but he was ill-dressed and wouldn't shave occasionally, and when he was pissed he always had a six-shooter somewhere on him. When he was pissed he used to let this fucking gun off in the Mess or wherever he was! Of course on the old Bader Wing, 145 was taken out of the line and Stan was very pissed off about this, so he went up to Catterick and they'd got an old man commanding Catterick called Beisegal, who was very dyed in the wool, pre-war regular, and old Stan got his six shooter out and started loosing off, shooting pictures off the wall, and there was talk of a court martial, and Leigh-Mallory himself had to get on the blower and put the thing right. Funny thing was about Turner, later on in life he went out to the Mediterranean where he was still scruffy, ill dressed, and he finished up in 1944, beginning of 1945 as our Group Captain! He took over 127 Wing and he comes up from the desert in all his khaki, he's still got the fucking gun, and then he became the toughest disciplinarian that you ever met: "Must Court Martial the bugger, can't have that, put him under close arrest, he's not properly dressed", and this from bloody Turner! Talk about the change over from poacher to gamekeeper! What I am trying to get at is that the Canadians had a reputation, through people like Turner, of being tough and obstinate and difficult to handle. When I got the Canadian Wing, the Group Captain down at Tangmere said "Oh Christ, they'll all have six-shooters and they'll be shooting stuff off the wall, they'll never take any notice of you!". But in fact they were the finest bunch of people you ever did meet. They flew well, beautiful discipline in the air, they'd all done a lot of flying hours in Canada, many as instructors, and they could *fly*.

Wing Commander Johnson motored to Kenley in his Morris, with Sally, his Labrador, to keep him company. Many thoughts occupied his mind, but uppermost was the fact that the Kenley Wing was equipped with the new Spitfire Mk IX - the answer to the FW 190 threat:-

Really, when I had commanded 610 Squadron, flying the Spitfire Mk V, we were cut to pieces by the 190s. I remember that particular occasion when we had gone over to Cherbourg, the penetrations weren't very far because of the superiority of the 190, and they chased us out and I lost four chaps coming back across the Channel. We could see the 190s coming in, and we were breaking round and that sort of thing, but these bloody things were far superior and you couldn't turn all day in mid-Channel, you have to make a dart for it sometime. So having the Spitfire IX, which was a different aeroplane altogether, you've got a chance of getting stuck into these bastards. The IX was far more powerful, the Merlin 61 engine matched the airframe (there was no undue torque or bad flying characteristics like there was later with the Griffon marques). The IX was a very good combination of airframe and engine. The IX was the best Spitfire. When we got the IX, we had the upper hand then, which did for the 190s! We could turn inside him and hack him down, which we did. Those cannon shells were about as thick as your wrist, and when you sent them crashing through his armour, he didn't fucking like it one bit!

There were two Spit IX squadrons at Kenley in March 1943, 403 and 416, and two of Spit Vs, 411 and 421, at Redhill. I was supposed to look after the flying of the Redhill squadrons too. Kenley's squadrons were both Spitfire IXs, the Redhill squadrons still being on Spitfire Vs. This did not become a 'Big Wing' affair, however, because, because of the difference in performance, you could not operate Vs and IXs together, and also Kenley could not take any more than two Spitfire squadrons anyway.

Air Commodore HA 'Jimmy' Fenton, who had commanded 238 Squadron during the Battle of Britain, was the Station Commander:-

Kenley seemed to have everything: comfortable quarters, entertainment including a camp cinema, and an abundant source of girlfriends for the boys!

Hugh Constant Godefroy was then a Pilot Officer serving with 403 'Wolf' Squadron and remembers Johnnie's arrival:-

Charlie Magwood was made CO of 403 Squadron, and we were told that we were getting an RAF Wing Leader, Wing Commander JE Johnson DFC & bar.

Group Captain Fenton brought him in at lunchtime, and with Squadron Leader Bud Malloy's help introduced him around. He made a positive first impression. When he spoke, it was firm and decisive. He was a wiry sort of fellow who walked with almost a cocky swagger. There was none of that fishy eye aloofness about him. He looked at the person talking to him as though he was paying attention. His face broke into a smile, which emphasised the chip out of a top tooth.

He called the Wing into the Briefing Room for an introductory orientation. Using short crisp sentences and slow, almost Churchillian emphasis, he stated that he expected implicit obedience to his flying orders. Flying discipline was the only discipline he was interested in; he didn't give a tinkers damn what we did on the ground. He favoured the 'fluid four' formation to provide better cross cover. He stated that he expected it would take a little time for us to get used to each other, but that he looked forward to leading a Canadian Wing.
"Any questions?"

There was dead silence.

"OK, chaps", he said with a broad grin, his eyes twinkling, "Give me a chance for a quick squirt, and I'll see you in the bar".

There was a roar of laughter, and as the gathering broke up, it was evident that he had won the pilots' respect immediately.

On March 22nd, Johnnie flew Spitfire Mk IX, EN398, for the first time, a sortie of 50 minutes of 'Local flying'. He also made four landings and immediate take-offs, just to get used to the Mk IX. EN398 became the Wing Leader's regular mount, a Canadian maple leaf painted below the cockpit and the initials 'JEJ' painted on the fuselage. For ease of identification in the air, it had become customary for Wing Leaders to have their initials so painted, although the practice not always found favour with Intelligence Officers, as Johnnie recalled:-

To see your initials painted on a Spitfire was really something to see, you really knew then that you had made it, as it were. The 'Spy' suggested that I should not conform for fear of the enemy identifying and singling me out in the air. I told him, well, you can imagine what I told him, and 'JEJ' was duly applied!

Johnnie also had to select a radio call sign and chose 'Greycap'.

At last, Johnnie could really influence tactics himself. No longer did he have to suffer the exasperation caused by Wing Leaders such as Pat Jameson who refused to take on new and better ideas from his subordinates.

The scene really was now set for derring-do.

Chapter Four

Kenley Wing at War
March 22nd – August 7th, 1943

"Okay chaps, get into 'em!"

The weather was slowly improving, and with better flying conditions the daylight fighter war was due to increase in both tempo and ferocity. The following War Diary, researched from contemporary documents, correspondence and interviews with survivors, and existing published sources, provides a comprehensive account not only of the Kenley Wing's activities but also the developing saga of the air war over Europe.

March 22nd

Heavy morning mist cleared rapidly, the day becoming bright and sunny with a northerly wind but no cloud. One flight of six 403 Squadron Spitfires were scrambled from Kenley at 0845 to patrol Maysfield at 15,000 feet, but the sortie was uneventful. The Wing's pilots made various local sorties during the day and 403 Squadron further patrolled Beachy Head but without incident.

March 23rd

Again a cloudless sky, into which 403 Squadron soared for an uneventful patrol of Maidstone. 416 'City of Oshawa' Squadron was also called upon to patrol Maidstone, but during the afternoon practised formation flying led by Flight Lieutenant RA Buckham.

March 24th

At 1015, 403 Squadron was scrambled and once more took off into a clear sky. Having patrolled the Channel, once more without anything to report, the Spitfires all returned safely to Kenley at 1110. Pilot Officers WT Lane and HJ Dowding provided fighter cover to troops on exercise near Penshurst. As the Operations Record Book (ORB) relates, however, 'The two pilots were not too happy about it for whilst they were at the required place at the required time, the troops to be covered didn't seem to be around'. For 416 Squadron, although called to readiness in the morning, when 403 was scrambled, from noon onwards the unit's pilots were at a 30 minute state of readiness.

March 25th

Wing Commander Johnson had found that his new Wing still flew the antiquated line astern formation; he remembered:-

Yes, that it is true. We had a long talk about it early on and naturally I intended that we should fly in line abreast. Syd Ford of 403 favoured the line astern, and Foss Boulton of 416 couldn't make up his mind. We agreed that for the first few shows I would lead the Wing with 416, which would fly in finger-fours. 403 was to fly top cover, some 3,000 feet above us, in whatever formation Syd chose. I agreed to review the position after a few sorties so that a decision could be made for the whole Wing. Of course I could have insisted that we flew finger-fours from the outset, but that was not really my way. I wanted to win them round by showing them the benefits of the finger-four in action. It was more democratic that way and more likely, I thought, to motivate and encourage. In respect of one matter, however, I did follow Syd Ford. His guns were harmonised on the 'spot' principle, rather than the more usual shotgun type spread pattern. Syd's combat films showed the devastating effect of his particular choice of harmonisation, so I made it mine too.

Until this point, the winter weather had been unfavourable to offensive fighter operations, but the weather was now starting to turn. Action was not far ahead, and this particular afternoon showed promise when Rodeo 194 was ordered. At 1650, the Wing, led by 'Greycap', took off from Kenley but headed independently through cloud to RV over Dungeness. The Wing swept the are of Boulogne, St Omer, Sangatte, between 25-28,000 feet. As Johnnie led his Canadians over the French coast at Boulogne, they passed the Northolt Wing's Spitfires heading back to England. Visibility was poor and no reaction was forthcoming from the enemy. By 1830, the Kenley Wing was landing back at base.

March 26th

Due to 10/10ths cloud, there was no flying. The Kenley Wing was released for the day, most of the pilots going up to London.

March 27th

With the weather unchanged, this was another day throughout which Johnnie's Kenley Spitfires were grounded. The film 'Ziegfield Girl' was shown in the Wing Pilots' Room, thus helping to relieve the boredom on this consecutively 'duff' day.

March 28th

When dawn broke the weather had improved: bright and sunny with only scattered cloud, the wind blowing gustily from the west. Soon the teleprinter clattered away and the Form 'D' came through: the Kenley Wing would fly on Ramrod 48 and provide high cover to American bombers attacking the railway marshalling yards at Rouen.

As we have seen, the American bombers' first missions were tentative probes to targets close to the French coast, mainly those connected with the Directive's primary target: the U-boat. The Biscay submarines, however, were protected in massive concrete bunkers, built by the Germans using slave labour. Anti-aircraft units also heavily defended them, St Nazaire soon becoming 'Flak City' to the Americans. Railway marshalling yards were also important targets because through them passed supplies to the U-boat bases. Having already struck at an important marshalling yard in Germany itself, in March 1943, the 'Mighty Eighth' began attacks on such targets in France. The attack against Rouen on March 28th, in which the Kenley Wing was involved, was one of those raids.

On March 28th, 1943, Wing Commander Johnson led the Kenley Wing off at 1230, and headed for Beachy Head at 26,000 feet. There the Spitfires met the bombers, 80 B-17s and 20 B-24s, orbited right and set course for Hastings. Johnnie later wrote in his log book:-

American bombers straggled badly and the 100 covered about 20 miles.

When 20 miles off Dieppe, the bombers were instructed to 'pancake', so Johnnie hauled the Kenley Wing round and swept the Channel behind the bombers. The operation was not, therefore, a success.

March 29th

Another sunny day dawned with scattered cloud and variable wind. Wing Commander Johnson led the Kenley Wing off at 1245 on Circus 277, and attack on the marshalling yards at Abbeville. High over Beachy Head the Spitfires met 12 Ventura bombers that immediately began climbing, contrary to plan. For some unrecorded reason, five minutes later six of the bombers turned back with the Spitfire Mk V Wing. The remaining box continued on course, bombing the target from 10,000 feet. Abbeville aerodrome was a famous *Luftwaffe* fighter base, from which four FW190s were seen to scramble, but no engagements took place. The German flak gunners hammered away all the while, however, although there were no hits due to shells exploding at the wrong height. On the way out, Squadron Leader Ford reported the position of a six-inch heavy gun near Lancheras, and six E-boats were noted in the Somme Estuary as the 'beehive' passed out over Cayeux. By 1405, the Spitfires were back at Kenley, their guns again unfired. In his Pilot's Flying Log Book (PFLB), Flight Lieutenant Charlie Magwood, of 403 Squadron, wrote:-

The height of impudence! Six Venturas and 20 Spits bomb Abbeville from 10,000 feet. No enemy activity. Inaccurate flak. Lovely day!

March 30th
In the morning, Flying Officer NR Fowlow and Sergeant GR Brown of 403 Squadron flew a weather reconnaissance sortie, noting conditions in the Caen-Cherbourg area. The weather, variable cloud and sun with a 25 mph westerly wind, was found to be too good for the operation planned, so the Kenley Wing spent the day uneventfully. Wing Commander Johnson took the Station Commander, Group Captain Jimmy Fenton, on 'local flying' in a Miles Magister communications aircraft.

This day was the second anniversary of 403 Squadron, and the Operations Record Book proudly reported:-

The Squadron's anniversary party was held in the new Airmen's Mess and excellent food and ample refreshment provided the proper groundwork for an excellent evening. Flying Officer RH 'Bob' Johnson, the Adj, did a great job of getting it all organised and the rest was pretty much as reported by Flight Lieutenant Basil Dean, Press Relations Officer of the RCAF in the following despatch:-

Members of the RCAF Spitfire Squadron, which is commanded by Squadron Leader LS Ford DFC & Bar, of Liverpool, N.S., have just celebrated their second anniversary. The unit was the first RCAF squadron to be formed overseas, as distinct from the three original squadrons, which came over as complete units, and was founded in the spring of 1941. Now attached to the RCAF Fighter Wing, the Squadron celebrated its second birthday with a banquet which was attended by all squadron members as well as by Group Captain Fenton DSO DFC, RAF Station Commander, and Wing Commander Johnson DFC & Bar, who recently took over leadership of the Wing. Both these officers are members of the RAF.

Squadron Leader Ford, who has commanded the Squadron since last August, first served with it as a Pilot Officer in 1941, and is one of the original members. In his speech at the celebration, he recalled that the Squadron started off with Tomahawks but was later converted to Spitfires, on which it has carried out all its operational flying. The best days work so far was over Dieppe, he said (the Squadron destroyed five enemy aircraft that day and probably destroyed or damaged many others). "As for that day", he added, "Thank God we had ground crews, because they made the job possible. I want to say how much we appreciate the work of the people commonly known as 'erks'. Pilots come and pilots go, but erks seem to go on for ever".

Today the Squadron is flying the newest model Spitfire and has chalked up many successes since it became a part of the RCAF Fighter Wing.

March 31st
With the morning weather fair but cold, with a gusting westerly wind, the Kenley Wing was detailed to fly Ramrod 47. This time the B-17s were bound for Rotterdam, and the Kenley Spitfires rendezvoused with 70 bombers over Harwich at 1105. Ten minutes later the Wing crossed the French coast at 26,000 feet and swept the area Dunkirk-Le Touquet-St Omer. At 31,000 feet over St Omer, 20 FW190s were sighted. Later, Johnnie wrote in his log book 'Could not engage as Huns going NE and we were short of gravy'. Despite the improvements that the Spitfire Mk IX enjoyed, limited range remained a problem. The Wing returned over Dunkirk and Hawkinge, landing at 1220.

Charlie Magwood wrote with frustration in his PFLB that the Germans 'wouldn't stay and play'. Johnnie himself recognised that his Canadians needed action, and soon. He wrote, 'We wanted a full-blooded scrap with the Abbeville boys to weld the Wing together'.

Would April provide that opportunity?

April 1st
Dull and overcast with a 35-mph westerly wind, there was no operational flying of note. A morale-raising visit was made to Kenley by the Archbishop of Toronto, the Revd DT Owen, who chatted with pilots and gave a short address to the groundcrews.

April 2nd
Completely overcast with mist and rain, the weather again prevented any flying.

April 3rd

Emphasising just how changeable English weather can be at this time of year, this day dawned bright and sunny with a light northerly wind. 'Ops' were back on with Ramrod 49. The plan was for the Hawker Typhoon fighter-bombers of Squadron Leader Denis Crowley-Milling's 181 Squadron to make a low-level attack on the enemy airfield at Abbeville-Drucat. As the 'Bombphoons' turned for home, the Kenley Wing was to sweep the area between Le Touquet and St Omer, engaging any scrambled German fighters. Such a Ramrod was bound to provoke a lively reaction, and anticipation was high. Kenley was the only fighter wing involved and would be controlled by Squadron Leader Hunter, the senior controller of the new radar station at Appledore in Kent (codename 'Grass-seed'). Appledore's radar was of a higher resolution than existing appliances, which were designed for home defence, and could therefore detect bandits over France and beyond. For the first time, Wing Leaders would have the great advantage of advance information in the air regarding the presence, size and direction of enemy aircraft.

At 1445, the Kenley Wing crossed the French coast at Le Touquet, the eight Typhoons being well below and racing home having given the hornets' nest a violent stir. As the Spitfires swept over St Omer between 24-26,000 feet, Grass-seed vectored Greycap on to 15-20 FW190s of II/JG26. The bandits, having taken off from Vitry, were still climbing and flying west, towards the coast in finger-fours and at staggered heights. In a demonstration of excellent controlling and teamwork between Squadron Leader Hunter and Wing Commander Johnson, the Kenley Wing was soon positioned over Montreuil, 3,000 feet above and up sun of the enemy, in perfect position for a bounce. The only problem was that Grass-seed also reported more bandits behind the Spitfires. Although reportedly some miles away, no one knew how accurate this information was given that the radar was operating at its maximum range. What was Johnnie to do? Upon seeing the 190s below, his mind was made up: it was too good an opportunity to miss. First, remembering the fate of Wing Commander Bader, Johnnie satisfied himself that the 190s concerned were not merely bait, then led 416 down to attack on the port side whilst 403 dived on the starboard. Johnnie's combat report subsequently related that he 'attacked an FW190 from astern using cannon and MG. Opened range at 400 yards and closed to 200. I saw cannon strikes on the wing roots and fuselage of the enemy aircraft that flicked over and went down smoking and burning.' *Unteroffizier* Hans Hiess (6/JG26) baled out but his parachute failed to open.

A veritable mêlée ensued as the Canadians fell on the unsuspecting Germans. Flying Officer Fowlow and Flying Officer Cameron, both of 403, saw a 190 go down, having been attacked by Squadron Leader Ford, pouring black smoke and flames from the cockpit, later enveloping the entire machine like a 'ball of fire' (ORB). Flight Lieutenant Charlie Magwood blasted a 190 from 50 yards. There was a succession of long flashes and flames from cannon strikes all round the centre section of the fuselage and wings, chunks flew off just before the aircraft disintegrated - completely. Just a black cloud hung in the air. Flying Officer HD MacDonald fired at another 190 from 100 yards, which soon streamed white smoke, dropped an undercarriage leg and was abandoned by the pilot.

416 Squadron fared not quite so well. Squadron Leader Boulton claimed a 190 destroyed, Flight Lieutenant RA Buckham and Flying Officer NA Keene sharing a probable, and Flying Officer JA Rae one damaged. *Oberfeldwebel* 'Adi' Glunz of 6/JG26, however, shot down Flying Officer AM Watson, over Le Touquet, this being the Germans' only victory in this engagement. The pilots of the two 190s hit by the Commanding Officers of 403 and 416 Squadron, *Unteroffiziers* Heinrich Damm and Albert Mayer, were both killed, but the other three 190s claimed destroyed by the Wing all managed to struggle back to land safely at Vitry and Merville.

Now in a very hostile sky with more 190s hurrying to the scene, Grass-seed advised Greycap to withdraw. As Johnnie said:-

We didn't need telling twice! We got out as quick as we could and raced across the Channel. After the combat the Wing had naturally become fragmented, so we came home in pairs and fours. News of our success had spread rapidly and naturally the pilots were jubilant - this was what we had all been waiting for. It was a great shame that we lost Watson, however, but nevertheless we had gone over there and given the 190s a clobbering. We were all delighted and I telephoned Appledore and thanked Hunter for his excellent controlling.

Both the 'Wingco' and the Canadians had shown each other their mettle.

Richard Booth was a pilot in 416 Squadron at the time, and many years later he remembered that:-

Upon conclusion of a Wing operation we would have a re-hash of the day's activities with 'JEJ'. At the end of one of these early sessions he invited suggestions. We complained that we had difficulty understanding him on the R/T, at which point Johnnie volunteered to try and talk more like a Canadian over the ether! At the next de-brief he inquired as to whether he was clearer over the air, but to a man we advised him to go back to normal!

Eileen Steel was a young WAAF working Kenley's Pass Office, situated immediately above the Station's main entrance. From that vantage point, Eileen and her colleagues, all 'starry eyed youngsters, often watched Wing Commander Johnnie Johnson coming and going. We hero-worshipped him even then'.

April 4th

Another fine and sunny day brought with it Ramrod 51. The Kenley Wing was ordered to provide First Withdrawal cover to the leading box (of 70) B-17s returning from a raid on the Renault factory at Billancourt, Paris. Greycap led the Wing out over Beachy Head at 24,000 feet, crossing the French coast at 1432 over Quiberville. When Johnnie reached the RV, near Rouen, 'FW190s were attacking bombers heavily when we sighted them' (PFLB, JEJ). Major Oesau, *Kommodore* of JG 2, had intercepted the bombers with his I *Gruppe* and the operational squadron of a training unit, JG 105, after they had successfully hit their target. Before the Spitfires arrived, II and III/JG 26 also joined in, charging the B-17s head-on.

The 'Forts' were tightly grouped in two large boxes, providing mutual fire support, but one Fortress was seen spiralling downwards; only one parachute emerged. The backdrop was provided by way of a huge pall of smoke rising some 7,000 feet high over Paris, and flak bursts here and there. Greycap despatched Squadron Leader Ford and 403 Squadron, who were 10 miles away, to attack the 190s and 'sort them out'.

From 200 yards, Squadron Leader Ford delivered a long burst at a 190, causing a large explosion and fragments to fly off. The undercarriage soon dangled limply and the front of the aircraft became engulfed in 'solid yellow flame' (ORB). The port wing broke upward and the 190 dropped towards the ground over 20,000 feet below. Flight Lieutenant Magwood thumbed the trigger at a 190 that had hurtled vertically through the bombers, whilst Pilot Officer EL Gimbel DFC, an American, and Flying Officer WJ Cameron saw a B-17 destroy a 190 before diving themselves onto a 190 a couple of thousand feet below. Gimbel fired and Cameron watched pieces fall off the 190, which rolled and went straight down. As the two Spitfire pilots broke away they were attacked by three 190s, flying in close line astern, from 200 yards astern. Cameron shouted "Watch out, Ed!" (ORB) and broke sharply right and upwards. Gimbel did not reply but Cameron saw a Spitfire going down 'in a gentle dive streaming black smoke' (ORB).

At 1435, Flight Lieutenant Magwood fired at a 190, which dived away and crashed on the edge of a big wood near Bellencombre. Together with his Blue 2, Sergeant LJ Deschamps, Magwood climbed to 23,000 feet and got in a short burst at another 190 from 200 yards astern but without result. Deschamps gave chase and hit the 190 around the cockpit area that immediately became enveloped in flame, the stricken enemy fighter plummeting earthwards. A few minutes later Deschamps was bounced by two 190s from out of the sun. Magwood watched helplessly as Blue 2 'skidded off to starboard, streaming glycol' (ORB). Magwood himself then started a running engagement until crossing the coast about St Valery where he dived beneath a 190 that he attacked from astern. Delivering a short burst, Magwood saw 'flashes of flame from cannon strikes all around the cockpit and along the starboard wing, chunks flew back, the cockpit was enveloped in flames and he fell off, diving vertically followed by two splashes' (ORB). As the 190s pursued the B-17s across the Channel, Flying Officer MacDonald followed 20 of them, singling one out which he attacked. The 190's starboard wingtip fell off and 'bright scarlet flames' (ORB) were seen in the cockpit. This enemy fighter also crashed into the sea, witnessed by Flying Officer Aitkin who also saw both splashes.

Although Squadron Leader Boulton exchanged blows with a 190 that attacked him head-on, 416 Squadron, with which Greycap was flying, made no claims. The Wing crossed the English coast 8,000 feet above Shoreham, landing at 1525. Two Spitfires were missing. Ed Gimble had collided with a 190, safely baled out and successfully evaded; he was safely back in England by August. Although it was hoped that Leo Deschamps would make a safe forced-landing, he was, in fact, killed. The 23-year old was buried by the Germans and now lies in the Canadian War Cemetery at Dieppe). Four B-17s were lost, all before the Spitfires' arrival. Again, this emphasises the extra danger faced by the Americans when they ventured beyond the range of their fighter escort. The need for a long-range escort fighter was becoming ever more pressing.

403 Squadron claimed five FW190s destroyed and one damaged. From

available German records, we know that JG 26 lost Karl Fackler to either Magwood or MacDonald (and two other pilots to the B-17s). *Obergefrieter* Jürgen Birn, of 4/JG 54, was also killed in this battle, but by whom is not known. Five 190s, two each of II & III/JG 26 and one of 4/JG 54, returned to base with combat damage. All of the claims for 190s destroyed by 403 Squadron appear accurate, however, so it is possible that they belonged to I/JG 2 or JG 105. In return, the pilots of JG 26 claimed eight Spitfires destroyed (six of which being confirmed), and I/JG2 two. Fighter Command actually lost eight Spitfires in total that day, two of 403 and six of the Northolt (Polish) Wing.

It is worth reflecting on the sad fact that during the raid on the Renault factory, in support of which the Kenley Wing was flying, 200 Parisian civilians were killed. The death toll of civilians caused by Allied bombing in the occupied lands was high. A heavy price was therefore ultimately paid for the freedom of France, Belgium and Holland in particular.

Quite rightly, however, Johnnie and his pilots felt flushed with success. That morning, Squadron Leader Syd Ford had presented the 'Wingco' with Canadian shoulder flashes to be sewn on his battledress. This was a clear indication that Johnnie had already won the Canadians over.

Whilst the Kenley Wing was embroiled with 190s high over France, Pilot Officer JC McLeod flew several local trips in 416 Squadron's Tiger Moth 'for the benefit of the ATC boys' (ORB). What an inspiring sight Johnnie's Kenley Spitfires must have made to those air-minded youngsters. Are any of them still around today, I wonder?

April 5th
On what was another fine day, the Americans sallied forth to attack the ERLA aircraft factory at Antwerp. Ramrod 52 saw the Kenley Wing flying First Fighter Cover to the first box of a force comprising 104 B-17s and B-24s. In an effort to extend range, Johnnie had first led his Wing down to Manston, near the Kentish coast, and re-fuelled; just those few extra miles might mean life or death to a bomber crew.

Just west of Ostend and 10 minutes early, due to a strong tail wind, the Wing rendezvoused with the bombers, which were outward bound, at 25,000 feet, formating down-sun and above the leading box. The Americans had firstly feinted towards Abbeville before turning towards Antwerp, thus forcing the shadowing FW190 pilots to waste fuel. Nevertheless, Major 'Pips' Priller led 8/JG 26 and III/JG 26 straight to Antwerp and formed up for head-on attacks, the Germans' favoured method against the heavily armed American bombers. Priller charged almost immediately after Greycap and his Spitfires arrived on the scene. The 'Wingco' and 416 Squadron challenged the 190s and became engaged in a running battle on the bombers' starboard side. Johnnie subsequently claimed three 190s damaged, Squadron Leader Boulton and Flying Officer Rae one each. The 190s did not attack the port side, where 403 Squadron was positioned. Later, 403's pilots were agreed that the 190s' attacks 'were determined and persistent and were mostly from ahead, above and below in singles, fours and sixes'. Priller, of course, was an *experte* and clearly knew what he was about.

Just north of Ghent, the Spitfires were ordered to return, with fuel states very much in mind, and had to abandon the bombers to their fate. An increasing number of enemy fighter units were scrambled to attack the American 306th Bomb Group, which lost five B-17s. The 306th, based at Thurleigh, claimed the destruction of five enemy fighters, although JG 26 only actually lost one FW190: *Hauptmann* Fritz Geisshardt, *Kommandeur* of III/JG 26. This was an important loss as Geisshardt was an experienced *experte* with 102 victories (75 of which in Russia). Nevertheless the day was the most successful so far for the *Jagdwaffe*, especially considering that, for the first time, German fighter controllers had managed to co-ordinate the combined forces of three different commands (JG 1, JG 2 & JG 26) throughout the interception.

April 6th

The day dawned clear and cold with a slight wind. An interesting operation ensued, Rodeo 195, in which the Kenley Wing's Spitfire Mk IXs provided top cover to the Redhill's Mk V equipped 421 Squadron, which attacked ground targets. Close cover was provided by the other Redhill squadron, 411. This large force of angry Spitfires crossed out over Beachy Head at 'zero feet' (ORB), and what a sight and sound they must have made! Eleven minutes later, east of Le Treport, 421 Squadron crossed the French coast at 5,000 feet, 411 and 7,000, whilst the Kenley IXs held off at 11,000. Soon 421 was descending rapidly to strafe the Loudinieres - Neufchatel and Neufchatel - Dieppe railways. Near Loudinieres, four signal boxes, four small switch boxes and a goods train were attacked together with two German army lorries which happened to be travelling along a nearby road. At St Aubin-sur-Mer aerodrome 'a stone building blew up well and truly behind the Wing' (403 ORB). Although three FW 190s were seen some way off, there was no interception and the Spitfires returned to England, re-crossing the friendly coast at 1,400 feet.

During the afternoon, Greycap led 403 and 416 Squadrons off from Kenley on Rodeo 198, a sweep of the Ambleteuse-Le Touquet-Abbeville area. According to Johnnie's PFLB, the sortie passed 'Without incident'.

April 7th
A very windy and cold day, there were no offensive operations flown by the Kenley Wing. At midday the Squadron was released off the station and most of the pilots went up to London. Hugh Godefroy describes one such 'sortie' with the ever-popular 'Wingco':-

In the air, Johnnie Johnson was 'Greycap Leader', cool, commanding, and as aggressive as a bull terrier. But when the sun went down, he didn't mind being called 'Johnnie'. He was one of us. His responses seemed Canadian, pure and simple.
"What we need is a pissup! I've had my fill of liver and onions. Monty!"
"Sir!"
"Call the Red Lion at Redhill and tell them to kill the bloody fatted calf. We're on our way. Come on lads, fill up the vans and follow me. Hughie, you'd better come in mine. I may need a second pair of eyes on the way home!"
Chuckling with anticipation, everybody grabbed their caps and piled into the vans. As expected, it was a hair-raising ride. What with the masked headlights and my poor night vision, I didn't see obstructions until we were almost upon them.
"Get out of the bloody way, you stupid bastard!", Johnnie would shout, as he suddenly overtook a vehicle.
"Clear the road, the Kenleys are coming!"
"That's original, Hughie, I rather like that".
"Look out Johnnie, there's a man in the middle of the road!"
"Bloody Canadian, you obviously haven't learned to drive in England yet!"
I was greatly relieved when we pulled in the parking lot of the Red Lion.
"There we are - my kingdom for a pint of Guiness!"
To the amusement of most of the regulars we took over. There was plenty of beer, games of darts and skittles. Johnnie, with the help of Walter Conrad, led a singsong around the piano with old favourites like 'Roll out the Barrel', 'Waltzing Matilda' and the South African Zulu war dance, 'Hey zinga, zumba. Zumba, zumba'. There was food for those who wanted it: smoked salmon and excellent steak-and-kidney pie.
When the proprietor shouted:

"Time gentlemen, please!" there was a Chorus of:

"A-w-w-w-w-w-!"

"Time gentlemen, for one more for the road!"

"Right you are", said Johnnie. "OK lads, you've 'ad it. Bottoms up! There's work to do in the morning".

I offered to drive.

"What?" said Johnnie. "You drive in your present state of public drunkenness? Not bloody likely! What we need is a sober man at the wheel. Look, some stupid clot has boxed me in. I'll show the bastard!"

With a crunch, Johnnie backed the van into the car behind, shunting it a good six feet to the rear.

"That's better. All aboard, chaps!"

When the van was full, we were off in a cloud of dust. But now, with a few pints of ale and a steak-and-kidney pie under my belt, somehow it didn't seem to matter. After a while, in the dim light of our shielded headlights, I saw half-a-dozen women walking on the right side of the road. With a squeal of tyres, Johnnie slammed on the brakes.

"There they are chaps, same level, 12 o'clock, get into them and don't let any of them get away!"

Tittering with laughter, Johnnie led us in pursuit of the women who had now broken into a trot. Johnnie caught the hand of a young lady straggler and as he spun her round she butted her cigarette in his left ear.

"O-w-w-w", he said, "You nasty little bitch!"

The ladies in front stopped, and from their midst we hears a querulous voice say "Nobody calls my daughter a 'nasty little bitch'. I say, what's all this in aid of?"

"They've got us outnumbered, return to base!"

To the sound of Johnnie's giggling laughter, we all piled back in the truck again and took off. It was a happy light-hearted evening, full of harmless fun, and in the Johnson tradition punctuated with the unexpected.

There wasn't a man who didn't waken refreshed and ready to follow him in the morning.

Such was the mark of a great leader.

Johnnie:-

Personalities at Kenley? Ford I was very impressed with. He got a DFC & Bar, he had flown a lot up at Digby. We had some good flight commanders, but the rank and file had not a lot of experience. When I got there they had not done a lot of flying over France, of course you can't in the winter months because of the weather. Buck McNair had a bit of the Stan Turner in him, I remember going into the Mess one night, we hadn't done much flying then, he was promoted about May time and he had a few beers. I went into the bar after dinner and he shouts out "Hey Wingco, when are we going to do some flying? The fucking guns are rusting up!" So all eyes switched to the 'Wingco' wondering 'How's he going to handle this one?' So I said "Get me a pint, Buck, and we'll talk about it". It was the only way to deal with it, he was a bit aggressive was Buck.

Fortunately, I got there at the right time; we had the Spitfire IX, the weather was getting better all the time and these guys could fly very well, they knew how to handle their Spitfires and don't forget that Kenley was in a built up area, very difficult to find in murky weather. 'Batchy' Atcherley, who had been the Station Commander sometime before, had built a series of tents around the circuit and painted them white. If you saw the tents you just kept turning inwards and the runway appeared! It was one of the first landing aids that I ever came across.

The impressions were that the Canadians were actually a very well disciplined outfit, both in the air and on the ground, except, of course, when they got pissed. Then some pissed Pilot Officer would come and clobber a Squadron Leader or something and it all went pear shaped! Fortunately they mostly got pissed in the Mess, so it was all kept in house, and the following morning there would be an apology or whatever. There was still a leavening of peacetime guys, who had been through Kingston, the Canadian equivalent of Cranwell, 'Iron Bill' MacBrian, for example, who took over as Station Commander from Jimmy Fenton, he had been to Kingston, and he was a very nice chap.

April 8th
Sunny and cold, 8/10ths cloud heralded another 'Wing Rhubarb' (411 ORB) whereby the Kenley IXs supported the Redhill Vs whilst the latter attacked ground targets. Going out at zero feet over Shoreham, the Spitfires began climbing whilst 40 miles NW of Le Havre. At 2,000 feet, however, they were forced to turn back due to there being 10/10ths cloud covering France at 2,500 feet. During the afternoon, Johnnie led the whole Wing on an uneventful sweep of St Valery-Yvetot-Bolbeck-Fecamp. 'Without incident' was the verdict in Greycap's PFLB.

Johnnie:-

By now I had the Wing flying finger-fours. To me, the two squadron Wing was ideal, it was far more manoeuvrable than a Wing of three or more squadrons. In the air, there would be 50 yards, say, between my No 2 and me, 100 yards then the other pair, then about a quarter-of-a-mile the other four and so on. Then stepped up, down sun so that they could see, two or three thousand feet higher, would be the other squadron. We covered a lot of sky, a mile or so.

There was still no standard formation operating procedure within Fighter Command, however. The Kenley Wing became noticeable in the air, and Johnnie's formation became known as the 'Wolfpack'. Johnnie continues:-

The climb out of Kenley would depend on what the job was. If it was a fighter sweep then we would keep low level until we could see the Dutch or French coast, then climb as hard as we could to cross it at a reasonable height to get above the flak, say 12 - 14,000 feet, or 24-25,000 feet, which was our best height. If we were escorting Fortresses then we would climb high from base, because the higher you were the greater the range. The fighting height was between 24-26,000 feet. The Germans always seemed to have a little bit of height on us due to the fuel injection.

April 9th
Dull and hazy weather meant that there was no operational flying, so the pilots studied their cine-gun combat films. Johnnie took the opportunity to fly down to Westhampnett, in a Spitfire Mk V, 'DN-O', and visit 610 Squadron.

April 10th
Again, no operational flying due to unfavourable weather conditions. The pilots spent the day analysing their combat films.

April 11th
Likewise no operational flying. The RCAF padre stationed at Kenley, Flight Lieutenant Don Carlson, conducted a church service in the Ground Crews' Room.

403 Squadron ORB:-

The Squadron was quite excited by stories in the English Sunday papers about the 'Wolf' Squadron, as we have been named (and approved by HQ), 'shooting down eight FW190s in two days'. The Squadron motto of 'Stalk and Strike' seems most appropriate now!

April 12th
The weather again ensured that no offensive operations were carried out. The Wing's pilots watched a film about dinghy drill, which, though seen frequently,

still held their interest for obvious reasons. The Wing's ground crews were also given the opportunity to view some of the combat film footage.

April 13th

A change in the weather: sunny and bright with no cloud. Wing Commander Johnson led the Wing at the head of 403 'Wolf' Squadron, Squadron Leader Ford being on leave, on Circus 281. According to the 416 Squadron ORB, the Wing provided 'escort cover to Spitfire VB who covered 12 Ventura bombers'. That the Spitfire V required 'cover' by IXs is clear evidence of the 190s superiority over the former. Again controlled by Appledore, Greycap was vectored up sun of 20 190s east of Abbeville. As Johnnie led 403 down to attack, the Spitfires were sighted and the enemy formation dived away inland. There was no engagement but the Abbeville - marshalling yards were successfully 'pranged' (PFLB, JEJ).

During the afternoon, the Kenley Wing sped out over Brighton at zero feet on Ramrod 57, escorting 'Bombphoons' attacking Caen aerodrome. As the Spitfires swept the Le Havre-St Lo area at 24,000 feet, the Typhoons hit the target. Bomb bursts were seen all over the airfield and on a blister hangar. By the time that the Germans reacted, the Typhoons and Spitfires were streaking back to 'Blighty'.

April 14th

Morning haze cleared at noon and a fine afternoon ensued. At 1415, Greycap led the Wing on Rodeo 204, a fighter sweep also involving 610 and 485 from Westhampnett. The Spitfire Vs of 411, which also operated from Westhampnett for this sortie, were to attack ground targets, as the Squadron's ORB relates:-

We caused considerable damage to locomotives, transformers and various buildings, making direct hits with cannon and machine-gun fire. Two of our pilots, however, failed to return from this operation. Flight Lieutenant Johnstone's aircraft was struck by enemy aircraft fire and he was forced to bail out off Cherbourg. He was later seen floating in his dinghy. Flight Lieutenant Banford, another unfortunate pilot, was not seen after diving to attack a locomotive in a valley. Six of our pilots, led by Squadron Leader Ball, took part in an ASR sweep for Flight Lieutenant Johnstone, who was still floating about in his dinghy. The journey was an unsuccessful one for Flight Lieutenant Johnstone, and it is hoped that he is a prisoner of war. Our Squadron Commander, Squadron Leader Ball, was shot down after an attack on an enemy aircraft. There were 12 FW190s which made a swift attack on our six craft but Pilot Officer Pope, having seen the Squadron Commander's outcome, managed to destroy one enemy whilst Flight Lieutenant Semple and Flying Officer Barber shared in another destroyed.

The enemy aircraft are believed to have belonged to JG 2. This was a terrible day for 411 Squadron as all three pilots were actually lost. The 21-year old Squadron Leader Donald George Ball, and Flight Lieutenant Johnstone were never found and are remembered on the Runnymede Memorial. Flight Lieutenant Banford crashed in France and is now buried in the Bayeux War Cemetery.

Also, the first Walrus ASR aircraft was shot down during the search for 411 Squadron's pilots, although fortunately the crew was safely recovered from the Channel by another Walrus sent out to join the Spitfires as a replacement.

Before departing this day, the reference to 'both cannon and machine-gun fire' in the 411 Squadron ORB is a point worthy of further comment. The Spitfire Mk IX was armed with two 20 mm Hispano-Suiza cannons and four .303 Browning machine-guns. The 'spade grip' of such a Spitfire's control column was fitted with an oblong alloy box, offset to the left and positioned vertically, housing the trigger. The safety catch, a lever, protruded from the bottom of this box, moving from right to left and requiring a positive push. Within the box was the trigger, an oblong button with a thumb-sized depression at the top and bottom. When the pilot thumbed the top, just machine-guns fired, the middle both cannon and machine-guns, and the bottom just cannons. The original trigger was, in fact, flat, but this caused problems in making the right selection in combat. Reports submitted by the Polish Wing at Northolt led to the design and manufacture of the new trigger. Johnnie comments on the cannon:-

The Hispano was, once we had got it right, was a very effective weapon. The Browning was a peashooter by comparison and how the Battle of Britain was won with it I will never know. Don't forget that at that time the Germans already had 20mm cannons and so were ahead of us. As for selecting which weapon, I generally fired both cannons and machine-guns together.

April 15th

More clear and bright weather saw Greycap leading the Kenley Wing on Rodeo 204. The Wing crossed the French coast at 25,000 feet over Berck-sur-Mer and swept to port. Vectored by Appledore to St Omer, the Wing manoeuvred to attack various forces of enemy aircraft but without sighting any of them. As Johnnie wrote in his PFLB, 'They were under 9/10ths cloud at 20,000 feet and we were over'.

By now, American fighters were entering the arena. By the first week in April, three P-47 Republic Thunderbolt Fighter Groups, 4, 56 & 78, were ready for operations. The P-47 was a huge, radial-engined beast of an aircraft. At 15,000 lbs gross, the P-47 was twice the weight of a Spitfire and soon nicknamed the 'Juggernaut', or more commonly the 'Jug'. In comparison trials against the RAF's captured FW190, the P-47 appeared capable at 20,000 feet and above, but was found wanting below. To its advantage, the P-47 was armed with eight .05 calibre machine-guns, the standard American aircraft weapon of WW2. This packed a heavier punch than the RAF's .303 calibre 'pea-shooters' and would serve the Americans well. The P-47s made their first, uneventful, sweep, from Debden in Essex, on March 10th, 1943. Technical problems delayed the next incursion until April 8th, when the 'Jugs' sallied forth over the Pas-de-Calais. During these early trips the P-47s were escorted by Spitfires, as was the case on April 15th when all three P-47s Groups swept Ostend and clashed with II/JG 1. The soon-to-be 'ace' Don Blakeslee shot down a 190, and two other 190s were also claimed as destroyed by the P-47 pilots. One 'Jug' was shot down, however, and two more failed to return due to engine failures. Later, the 'Jug' would earn an enviable reputation as both a long-range bomber-escort fighter, as was intended, and a low-level ground-attack fighter-bomber in support of the Allied armies. To start with, however, the P-47's range was similar to that of the Spitfire, some 170 miles, so the immediate difficulty of finding a long-range offensive escort fighter remained unresolved.

The entry of another new American fighter, the P-38 Lockheed Lightning, was delayed firstly due to it being difficult and slow to build. The Lightning, featuring an unorthodox design, was, however, brilliant in concept and promising in performance. When the P-38 equipped 78th Fighter Group arrived in England during 1942, and took over Goxhill, the situation in North Africa dictated them being re-directed to that theatre. Further supplies of P-38s were subsequently sent not to England but to North Africa and the south west Pacific. It would not be until the autumn of 1943, that the Eighth Air Force would receive the Lightning for operations in the European Theatre. As things turned out, the twin-engined P-38, like the Me 110, proved no match for single-engine fighters.

American bomber losses, however, indicated that if they were to continue their task then increased protection from the German fighters was *essential*. The *Luftwaffe* had 800 fighters in the west, and the energetic *General der Jagdflieger*, Adolf Galland, was doing his level best to increase that figure. As things stood, the Germans were still able to carefully co-ordinate and time their interceptions to coincide with that point in time when the bombers' 'Little Friends' had to turn back due to the constraints of fuel.

April 16th
Sunny and bright with very little wind, the day would see the Kenley Spitfires engaged on three operations over France. At 0745, Greycap led 403 and 416 Squadrons up on Ramrod 60. Squadron Leader Crowley-Milling's 'Bombphoons' of 181 Squadron were making a low-level attack on Triqueville aerodrome, and, as usual, the Spitfires were to provide cover. Rendezvous was made over Beachy Head at zero feet, the entire formation streaking low across the Channel at sea-level until pulling up and crossing the enemy occupied coastline at 10,000 feet over Eletot. Due to 8/10ths cloud over the target, the Spitfire pilots were unable to watch the Typhoons attack the airfield. Without incident,the Spitfires were back at Kenley by 0920.

At 1445, the Wing was off again on Circus 283, flying as third fighter echelon to Venturas attacking Ostend. The Kenley Wing swept Berck-sur-Mer and St Omer, but saw just a handful of Me 109s and FW 190s over Cap Griz Nez. Unable to close range, there was no combat and the Wing was back down safely by 1540.

In the evening, 181 Squadron hit Triqueville again, escorted by Greycap and his Spitfires. The Kenley Wing was up at 1732, on Ramrod 61, sweeping D'Ailly- Fauville-Fecamp but without result.

Throughout the day, certain 403 Squadron pilots, namely Flying Officer JI MacKay, Pilot Officers FC McWilliams and HJ Dowding, and Sergeants NF Cotterill and NV Chivers, flew ASR patrols. There was no contact but 'plenty of flying to tire the boys' (ORB).

April 17th
Bright sun and no cloud suggested a busy day. Firstly, Wing Commander Johnson flew over to West Malling to examine two FW 190s that had landed there by mistake during the early hours! These aircraft belonged to

Schnellkampfgeschwader 10, a night fighter-bomber unit, which was attacking London that night. Enemy activity having been reported in the Biggin Hill Sector, a 29 Squadron Beaufighter was sent up from West Malling, and as a navigational aid a searchlight was illuminated vertically over Sittingbourne. Almost immediately an aircraft was heard orbiting the beam of light, which was directed towards West Malling. Soon a single-engine aircraft crossed over the airfield, switched on its navigation lights and landed. The unfortunate pilot was *Feldwebel* Bechthold who found himself looking down the wrong end of a rifle barrel. Several minutes later the searchlight again deflected to West Malling and another 190 entered the circuit! Having touched down, this enemy pilot, *Leutnant* Fritz Setzer, realised his mistake and tried to make off. LAC Sharlock reacted promptly, however, and gave the 190 several bursts from his Vickers machine-gun, setting fire to the enemy machine. Setzer fell from the cockpit, his clothing alight, struggled and broke free from his captors and ran around the back of a fire tender - straight into the arms of the Station Commander, Battle of Britain ace Group Captain Peter Townsend! Even then this night of excitement was not over. Realising that they had by chance imitated a *Luftwaffe* night navigation tactic, the searchlight was once more directed towards the airfield. Another 190, flown by *Oberfeldwebel* Schulz, undershot the runway, crashed and was captured by a local. Another lost SK10 pilot, *Oberleutnant* Karl Klahn, abandoned his aircraft over Staplehurst but too low for his parachute to deploy. This was SK10's first operation which had gone disastrously wrong. Four 190s had been lost, one of them intact and in the hands of the British. The station diarist at West Malling was clearly a master of the understatement when he wrote 'An intensely interesting night'!

By 1417, Greycap was back at Kenley and taking the Wing up on Circus 285 providing escort to 12 Venturas attacking the marshalling yards at Abbeville. The rendezvous took place at zero feet over Beachy Head, the bombers being four minutes late. Whilst the beehive proceeded to the French coast, a Defiant and a Mosquito were observed shadowing the raiders. Wing Commander Johnson broke radio silence and sent a section to investigate what transpired to be 'friendlies'. At 1453, the formation crossed the French coast at Cayeux with the Spitfire Mk Vs of 411 Squadron flying as close escort to the Venturas at 13,000 feet. The target was duly pranged, and Greycap would later write 'Excellent bombing' (PFLB). He had positioned his fighters to the east of the bombers, providing such an effective screen that *Hauptmann* Wilhelm Ferdinand 'Wutz' Galland was heard by the British Y-Service ordering his 190s to remain in formation as there were too many Spitfires.

Whilst 411 Squadron and the bombers re-crossed the French coast, homeward bound, between Le Treport and Cayeux, Johnnie led his Mk IX squadrons back around at 24,000 feet towards Abbeville - spoiling for a fight. As the Kenley Spitfires continued to climb inland, Greycap was informed by Appledore that the Hornchurch Wing was engaged. When the Kenley Wing was up sun and at 33,000 feet, Flight Lieutenant Godefroy, Yellow Leader, asked Greycap's permission to take his Section down to attack three 190s that he could see climbing out to sea some 10,000 feet below. The Wingco agreed, and Godefroy's finger-four peeled off to attack. Yellow Leader fired at the right-hand 190, with cannons and machine-guns, causing the port cannon magazine explode and flashes of flame along the fueslage in front of the pilot. The 190 pilot was unable to recover his aircraft from a spin and baled out; both pilot and aircraft ended up in the Channel. Meanwhile, Yellow 2, Pilot Officer PK Gray, opened fire from 200 yards astern on the port 190. The German pilot half-rolled, was hit by Gray again, and entered a spiral dive pouring white smoke. This pilot also baled out, his 190 likewise crashing into the sea. The rest of the Wing made no claims, but Johnnie recorded in his PFLB that the 'Wing was involved in a general dogfight over the French coast'.

This skirmish was probably with elements of I/JG 2, I/JG 27 and II/JG 2. The latter unit had recently returned to the *Kanalfront* from North Africa and provides clear evidence that the American daylight bomber offensive was having some effect on the distribution of German fighter forces. Although the Eastern Front remained a priority, the enemy did move fighters from the Mediterranean Theatre to bolster defences in the west. This clearly negates the popular claim that JGs 2 & 26 alone and unreinforced held the *Kanalfront*, from the North Sea to the Bay of Biscay and beyond.

Having landed back at Kenley by 1552, there was more action ahead for the 'Kenleys'. At 1745, Greycap and his Spitfires were off on Circus 286. The Spitfire pilots' task was firstly to provide Target Support for 12 Venturas bombing the marshalling yards at Caen, and then sweep the general area. The beehive crossed out at less than 500 feet above Brighton, climbing to 21,000 feet and crossing the French coast at Dives and turning south for Caen. The bombing was accurate once more but the flak was equally on target and intense over the target. The Spitfires then flew at 22-25,000 feet to 25 miles NW of Fecamp. Appledore then informed Greycap of a gaggle of bandits apparently engaged on an ASR operation near Dieppe, so Johnnie led the Wing down to

2,000 feet. Coming along the coast were four FW 190s and four Me 109s, which were attacked by the whole Wing!

Flight Lieutenant Magwood had just given lead of 403 Squadron to Flight Lieutenant Godefroy on account of his R/T suddenly becoming u/s. Godefroy, having 'Tally Ho'd', led the charge of Yellow and Red Sections, being followed by Magwood with Blue Section which engaged a single 109 from another enemy formation before also attacking the 190s. One of the 'Butcher Birds' actually pulled up vertically and went through the surprised Spitfires, breaking sharply right and racing towards France. Magwood reacted swiftly and half-rolled onto the 190 which did likewise but, being too low, crashed into the sea whilst 'trying to aileron out of it' (ORB); Magwood had not fired a shot! As Godefroy was about to fire at a 190 he suddenly had to break to avoid colliding with several Spitfires that cut across in front of him. Having recovered, he noticed two splashes in the sea, one of which being Magwood's 190, the other, smaller, probably being a pilot. Flying Officer Fowlow then fired at a 109 that pulled up in front of him, but it then dived away with no results being observed. Pilot Officer DH Dover saw a 109 climbing into the sun and fired at it, but likewise would make no claim. As the Canadian turned away from France he suddenly found himself head-to-head with a 190. Dover immediately thumbed the trigger and Sergeant Brown, flying behind, saw the 190 dive into the sea. According to the Squadron ORB, 'On the evidence available it appeared that various sections of the Squadron were all involved with the same FW 190, with no one pilot appearing to have accounted for it in clear-cut or definate style. For the reason the whole squadron shared the credit for destroying one FW 190'. Squadron Leader Foss Boulton, leading 416 Squadron, had fired a long burst of cannon at an Me 109F which was confirmed as destroyed following an analysis of his combat film. All of the 'Kenleys' returned safely to base and were all down by 1930.

By the close of play on what was a busy day, the Germans had lost a total of eight FW 190s, offset against just three Spitfires. To the great credit of their escorts, remarkably not one Ventura was lost.

April 18th
In the morning, Squadron Leader Boulton led 416 Squadron on Circus 287, close escort to Venturas, but although intense flak was experienced over the target, Dieppe harbour. The Spitfire Mk Vs of 411 Squadron also participated in this otherwise uneventful 'show'.

At 1750, Greycap led 403 and 416 Squadrons on Ramrod 63, providing support to Typhoons bombing Poix airfield. As Johnnie later wrote in his PFLB, there was 'Nothing about'.

On this day, Charlie Magwood was promoted to command 403 Squadron.

April 19th
A dull day which saw the Kenley Wing up on just one sortie, Ramrod 65. Again the Wing supported Typhoons which this time bombed Yauville. The Spitfires, again operating under Appledore, swept Doudeville-Yauville but the only enemy aircraft seen were too far away to engage. The sortie therefore passed without incident, the Wing landing at 0905. Rain stopped play for the rest of the day, although Pilot Officer RM Cook, of 416 Squadron, 'taking off on a scramble at noon failed to become airborne and crashed, seriously injuring himself and washing out the aircraft'.

News was received by 403 Squadron that their CO, Syd Ford, who was away on leave, had been promoted to Wing Commander and posted to Digby in Lincolnshire as Wing Commander Flying.

April 20th
A complete change in the weather brought clear, still and sunny skies. The day's first operation was Rodeo 209. The Wing swept the Le Touquet and Abbeville area, coming out at Dieppe. Appledore recalled the Wing, however, when '75 plus E/A were reported in the vicinity of our Wing all alone' (ORB, 403). Johnnie, as we have heard, insisted on iron discipline in the air, for obvious reasons, and this included the matter of radio silence. In his PFLB, however, he wrote regarding this sortie 'Rodeo 209 with the Polish Wing jabbering Russian over the R/T!'

Next came Ramrod 67, Target Support to eight Typhoons bombing Tricqueville aerodrome, which was successfully attacked. Afterwards the Spitfires were taken over by Appledore Control and were vectored to a formation of 21 plus bandits at 29,000 feet over Dieppe. Six 190s subsequently made a head-on attack against 416 Squadron, but Boulton and his men reacted swiftly, the CO himself destroying one, Pilot Officer RD Phillip damaging another, all for no loss. Appledore then informed Greycap that 15 FW 190s were closing from behind to attack. Low on fuel, Johnnie ordered the Wing out, this command being 'smartly obeyed' (ORB, 403).

On this day there were important personnel changes at Kenley. Wing Commander Syd Ford was replaced as Commding Officer of 403 Squadron by Charlie Magwood, who became an Acting Squadron Leader. Flying Officer HD MacDonald went up a ring to Acting Flight Lieutenant, taking over Magwood's 'B' Flight.

Whilst with 403 Squadron, Wing Commander Ford had scored all but one of his combat claims, a total of six destroyed, two probables and one shared damaged, this record being recognised by the award of a DFC and bar. Sadly whilst leading the Digby Wing on June 4th, 1943, Syd Ford was shot down and killed by flak from some E-boats off Texel. The 24-year old was buried in Vlieland General Cemetery on the Frisian Islands, lying off the north coast of Holland.

April 21st
Although a sunny day, the only operational flying were a number of scrambles and local patrols. An early 'do' had, for some reason, been cancelled (ORB, 403). 416 Squadron took the opportunity to hone its air-to-air firing skills at Friston.

April 22nd
Again emphasising England's particularly changeable weather at this time of year, this was a chilly day with persistent rain. Only one patrol was flown from Kenley, by elements of 416 Squadron. At 1300 the Wing was released.

April 23rd
Another day of the same with nothing to report.

April 24th
On this day the weather was reportedly 'crisp and sunny with 5/10ths cloud and a strong westerly wind'. Although the usual scrambles and defensive patrols took place there were no offensive operations. Sergeants NV Chevers and NF Cottrill both left 403 Squadron on this date, bound for ferrying duties in the Middle East. Wing Commander Johnson flew to Horsham St Faith, where he stayed for a couple of days.

April 25th
'Very little happening, pilots taking it easy in duff weather' (416, ORB). Flight Lieutenant Godefroy led 403 Squadron on a practice formation flight, during

which the 'Wolf' Spitfires were 'attacked' by Flying Officer KP Marshall. Six of the aircraft involved landed at Martlesham Heath, low on fuel.

April 26th
Another day of changeable and unfavourable flying weather saw no operational sorties made. A movie, 'Caught in the Draft' was shown for the pilots' amusement. Wing Commander Johnson returned to Kenley from Horsham.

April 27th
Again no operations, but cine-gun and air-to-air firing practice carried out by 416 Squadron.

April 28th
No change in the weather so the Wing's pilots took the bi-monthly aircraft recognition tests. 403 Squadron led with 97.75 %. During the afternoon, the Wing was released, most of the pilots heading for London. Wing Commnder Johnson flew first to Friston, then to Westhampnett before returning to Kenley.

April 29th
A slight improvement in the weather enabled some non-operational flying. RCAF Overseas Orders indicated that 403 Squadron's Sergeant JE Abbotts had been commissioned, despite not having been previously informed himself! 'Off to London for his outfit' (ORB).

April 30th
The last day of the month saw 10/10ths cloud and a strong wind, as a result of which there was no flying whatsoever. Another movie, 'Lady Hamilton' was shown for the pilots.

The unpredictable weather, however, still remained a key factor in influencing the pathos of the 1943 air fighting.

May 1st
On a cloudy Mayday which threatened rain, Wing Commander Johnson led the Kenley Wing down to Portreath in 10 Group, from which airfield the Spitfires were to provide Top Fighter Cover for Circus 28. Again, the movement to operate from a forward airfield was to extend the Spitfires' range. The B-17s of the 306th Bomb Group were to bomb the u-boat installations at Lorient, an important target given that the Commander-in-

Chief of the *U-bootwaffe*, Admiral Karl Dönitz, had his headquarters nearby at Kernaval. The Lorient boats were amongst the most successful operating from the Biscay coast, and therefore anything to impede or prevent their operations was vital.

Greycap's Spitfires rendezvoused with the Portreath and Exeter Spitfire Wings on time before flying first to Ushant, thence to north of Brest at 26,000 feet. The German occupied French port put up a protective screen of intense light flak as the Spitfires passed overhead and swept the area inland. Just before the Spits re-crossed the coast on the way home, five FW 190s were seen above and about two miles behind. The Kenley Wing turned about to engage but the 190s' leader sensibly chose to make off to fight another day when the odds were more favourable. The Germans half-rolled and dived away. Although this was the only incident of note so far as the Kenley Wing was concerned, sadly it was a different story for the American bomber crews. As always, *Jagdfliegerführer* (*Jafu*) Brittany waited until the Spitfires had turned back before unleashing his fighters which rapidly fell on the B-17s. Of the 78 participating in this attack, seven were destroyed and two more were damaged.

Squadron Leader Magwood recorded of this sortie in his PFLB:-

24 Liberators, 10 Spit IX squadrons, too crowded. Ushant, Brest area, accurate flak, chemical smoke camouflage. Squirt at FW 190, but out of range.

For Magwood, it was a significant day as it saw the award of his well-earned DFC.

After the operation, at 1230, Greycap took off from Portreath, the Wing following him home to Kenley.

May 2nd
According to the 416 Squadron ORB, the weather 'proved abortional'. No

operational flying was carried out, a church service taking place in the pilots' dispersal at 1000.

May 3rd
Again, the weather was 'very doubtful, cold and cloudy' (416 ORB). After a

series of aircraft and cannon tests by various Wing pilots, however, the Wing was off at 1725 on Rodeo 212, a sweep of Nieuport, Cassel, and Popperinge controlled once more by Appledore. Crossing out at Deal, the Spitfires made landfall at Nieuport, turned right and made an orbit between Cassel and Popperinge as instructed by 'Grass-seed'. At 22,000 feet over Samer, four 190s were seen approaching from the south-east. The enemy aircraft were 'properly bounced' (416 ORB) and in the ensuing engagement 190s were destroyed by two 416 Squadron pilots, Squadron Leader Boulton and Flight Lieutenant RA Buckham. The Wing came out over Hardelot and crossed the English coast at Pevensey.

May 4th

A fair but cloudy day, the Wing first flew down to Manston, again to extend range. After briefing, the Wing was up at 1725 to provide High Cover in Ramrod 68 to B-17s attacking Antwerp. The target was the Ford and General Motor Works, which was within range of the 12 escorting fighter squadrons. Six of these were P-47 units flying their first combat escort. The Thunderbolts were, in fact, an unexpected sight, so far as the Kenley Wing was concerned, and were sighted 10 miles inland flying above, ahead and behind the Wing. Once more, however, *Jafu* Brittany decided to preserve his fighters given the strong Allied escort and only superficial, ineffective, attacks by small numbers of 109s and 190s were made. No bombers were lost, and this day really was a victory for the Allied air forces. It also emphasised the desperate need to extend range so that such escorts were the norm, whatever the target. *Reichsmarschall* Göring, however, accused his *Jagdfliegern* of being 'cowardly dogs'.

Squadron Leader Magwood wrote in his PFLB:-

70 Fortresses v Ford factory – plastered the target – only about 20 e/a on way in and they were very half-hearted. Thunderbolts above.

Interestingly, in Johnnie's PFLB he later wrote 'Little fighter opposition today. Spitfire IX of 611 Squadron took a crack at me'. Such incidents of 'Friendly Fire' were not, in fact, uncommon, and it does make you wonder how many pilots, of both sides, fell victim to 'friendly' guns.

It was on this day that Flying Officer J Danforth 'Dan' Browne joined 403

Squadron. Although serving in a Canadian fighter squadron, Dan was in fact an American:-

I signed up in the RCAF in 1940, I was called up to the Commonwealth Air Training Plan in the February of 1941, and then I got my 'wings' in late August of 1941, and went home on a month's leave in New Jersey, said 'goodbye' to my mother. We were in Halifax at the time of Pearl Harbour, and we sailed a few days later. I was on a ship called the 'Letitia'. I think that Atlantic crossing was some of the most terrifying experiences of my life! We ran into 108 knot winds off Iceland, my God those waves were huge and so they decided to really hunker everything down. We had the 'Normandie' lose all its lifeboats during the storm, and several destroyers literally went straight through those huge waves, which was amazing. It was very frightening, especially when I climbed up the mast to watch proceedings. I would look down and see the green Atlantic, look the other way and just see froth! Eventually we got to Bournemouth, from where I thought that we would go to Singapore, which is why I thought we were on the High Seas. As we left Gibraltar we were attacked by FW Condors. We were picked up by the Condor two days out, and attacked by submarines on the third. We lost a couple of ships out of the convoy, although my ship, the old P&O liner 'The Viceroy of India' was safe. We went into Cape Town, picked up the Vichy French in Madagascar. Then we heard that Singapore had fallen to the Japanese, which was frustrating as I wanted to get into combat, which is why I, an American, had volunteered before my own country came into the war.

It was an exasperating time, as they then posted me to fly Gloster Gladiators in Iran, in defence of certain oil refineries. We were then shipped back, going all the way round Africa without anything exciting taking place. Back in the UK, I was then posted to the OTU at Rednal in Shropshire, near Wales. Got through the course and then had good fortune to be posted to the Canadian Spitfire Wing at Kenley in 11 Group. This was better than Gladiators, to say the least! So, with no operational combat experience I joined the Kenley Wing, which turned out to be one of the happiest events of my life. Here I am, I joined the Wing in 1943, and, at the time of this recording, Johnnie and me have been close personal friends for 54 years (December 1997). That is remarkable in itself. I later had the opportunity to transfer from Kenley to the American Air Force, but I stayed where I was. My mother was Canadian and I enjoyed their company.
One thing, we had some fine Canadians at Kenley. Some had been miners and lumberjacks, just roughnecks all their lives, so it was a weird combination. It was perhaps a stroke of genius to put Johnnie in command, although he was an Englishman.

I was delighted to find Spit IXs at Kenley, which had a two-stage, two-speed engine. When you got up to about 19,000 feet, that second stage kicked in, at which point it was *your* air, no longer the Germans' air.

Also, being 'green', it was an incredible experience to go on your first operational sortie with Wing Commander Johnnie Johnson, who was definitely headed for great things.

May 5th

A misty and dull day of 10/10ths cloud, there was no operational flying. Wing Commander Johnson was visited by his counterpart at Biggin Hill, Al Deere, whose personal Spitfire the former flew on 10 minutes of 'low flying' (PFLB, JEJ). Now that I would have loved to see!

May 6th

The weather remained unchanged, the cloud having 'no ceiling' (416 ORB).

May 7th

A fine dawn saw no time lost in the planning of operations. In the morning, 416 Squadron carried out various local flights, searchlight co-operation exercises, and convoy patrols. During the morning, Johnnie flew his usual Spitfire, EN398, on a test flight to jettison an auxiliary fuel tank. This was probably a flush fitting 'slipper' tank, fitted beneath the cockpit section and containing either 45 or 90 gallons of extra fuel, which designers had found to be the best option. The idea, however, was that, with the 90 gallon tank, the pilot would take off and for the first 1 hour 20 minutes draw fuel from the auxiliary tank. When the enemy was sighted, the 'slipper' was jettisoned, flying characteristics thus resuming normal. Using the 45 gallon tank, the Spitfire Mk IX's radii of action was 240 miles, 270 miles with the 90 gallon example.

Johnnie:-

Owing to the lack of foresight by the fucking Chief of the Air Staff, Portal, the Spitfire could have had the same range as the Mustang, but he told Churchill that it would impede its performance as a defensive fighter, which of course is quite wrong. So the Spitfire never really had the range, and we should have done, simple as that. What pissed us all off so much is that we still had the same range in a Spitfire as we had in 1940, although Churchill himself is on the record writing a minute to Portal saying 'Cannot the range of the Spitfire be improved', and Portal writes back saying 'Not without detriment to its performance as an interceptor', which was absolute rubbish. That really needs highlighting. We did have auxiliary tanks, the largest being of 90 gallons, but that meant that there was more fuel outside the aircraft than in given that the Spitfire normally carried 85 gallons. Sometimes the bloody ank wouldn't come off, so they devised a little plunger in the cockpit which, if the tank got stuck, you kicked down. The Americans also fitted tanks to their Thunderbolts and Lightnings, but although it sounds fine in theory, doubling the range and so on, in practice it was not the answer. Dolfo Galland could attack our fighters as they were on the way in, making the pilots jettison their tanks in which fuel was still plentiful, thus defeating the whole object of the exercise. No, it wasn't the answer, but the lack of range comes back to the English way of thinking, which is all about defence. Our lack of range was a big concern, and as the summer of 1943 progressed, so too did our frustration.

On May 7th, Johnnie led the Kenley Wing on Rodeo 213, a fighter sweep of the St Omer – Abbeville area under Appledore. The Biggin Hill Wing had gone in first and was engaged 30 FW 190s over Abbeville, so the Kenley Wing orbited the Somme estuary and covered their withdrawal. Although the 'Kenleys' sighted a small formation of 190s diving inland, they were enable to engage as the enemy was too far away. Returning over the Channel, there was no shipping or flak, and the English coast was re-crossed safely at Rye.

May 8th

The weather turned overnight with rain-squalls occurring throughout the day. The only operational sortie was an uneventful patrol by 416 Squadron. Wing Commander Johnson took the opportunity to get the pilots together for a 'chat' (403 ORB) in the Wing Pilots' Room.

May 9th

Again, according to the 416 Squadron ORB, the weather was 'abortional': showers and strong winds which prevented operational flying. 403 Squadron was released at 1030.

On this day, Flying Officer Bob Middlemiss joined 403 Squadron on what was his second tour of operations:-

I found the Squadron to be well led with many experienced pilots, such as Buck McNair, Wally Conrad, George Keefer, Doug Lindsay and Harry MacDonald. In fact, the Squadron could mount a full compliment of second tour pilots.

Having been rejected by the Auxiliary Air Force, James Edgar 'Johnnie' Johnson, the civil engineering graduate and police inspector's son from Melton Mowbray, joined the RAF Volunteer Reserve. Having been called up in 1939, this photograph shows Sergeant Johnson, at extreme left, with classmates from Initial Training Wing, Cambridge.

Surgery to rectify a shoulder injury prevented Johnnie from seeing action during the Battle of Britain, but by the winter of 1940/41, he was an established, although junior, member of 616 'South Yorkshire' Squadron based at Kirton. Our 'Boys Own' heroes of 616, pictured at Kirton early in 1941, are Pilot Officers Nick Hepple, Roy Marples and Johnnie Johnson.

In February 1941, 616 Squadron moved south, to Westhampnett (now Goodwood Racing Circuit & Airfield), in the Tangmere Sector. These are members of 'A' Flight. Standing, from left to right: Pilot Officer Johnson, Sergeants Mabbett, Scott and McCairns; sitting, left to right: Flying Officer Dundas, Pilot Officer Hepple and Sergeant (now Sir Alan) Smith.

A 'Finger Four' of 616 Squadron Spitfires takes off on an offensive sortie from Westhampnett, summer 1941.

At this time, the Tangmere Wing was commanded by the legendary Wing Commander Douglas Bader, who was lost over France and captured on August 9th, 1941. Back at Westhampnett, Johnnie kept 'DB's' spirit alive: 'Bader's Bus Co: Still Running'. Douglas Bader was a great influence on the impressionable young Johnnie, and the pair remained friends until Sir Douglas died suddenly in 1982.

Johnnie the movie star, Kingscliffe with 616.

Can anyone help with the who, what, where and when? Flight Lieutenant Johnnie Johnson DFC, at right, with an unknown but also decorated pilot and two civilians who appear to be the Mayor and Mayoress of an unknown town.

Squadron Leader JE Johnson DFC, Commanding Officer, 610 'County of Chester'

The 610 Squadron Spitfire Mk VB of Flight Lieutenant Denis Crowley-Milling DFC, who had flown with Johnnie during 1941, and was one of his flight commanders in 1942.

Crowley-Milling's fitter and rigger pose with BL584. Johnnie always encouraged a close relationship between pilots and ground staff.

Johnnie at Westhampnett in 1942, but this time with his own squadron, 610. The signposts, outside the pilots' hut, indicate the direction of Cherbourg, Lille, St Omer and Dunkirk, all locations above which Johnnie and his pilots saw much action.

At the time, the FW 190, however, had outclassed the Spitfire V. RAF losses were high and penetration severely restricted. This is *Oberleutnant* Arnim Faber's 190, which he landed by mistake in South Wales, thus providing the first opportunity for the Allies to examine a 'Butcher Bird' close-up.

Another view of Faber's 190, showing the cockerel's head insignia of JG 2, with which Johnnie's Spitfires had many a clash.

In March 1943, Johnnie was promoted to Acting Wing Commander and became Wing Leader at Kenley. There he found two Canadian squadrons, both equipped with the Spitfire Mk IX, a superior aircraft to the V and one which redressed the balance. This is Johnnie's regular mount, EN398, which carries both his initials and the Canadian maple leaf insignia. According to Spitfire historian Dr Alfred Price, in combat this was the most successful Spitfire of all.

At Kenley, Wing Commander Johnson found the Canadians to be 'a keen bunch'!
421 Squadron 'scramble' for the press, 1943.

Amongst the early sorties led by Wing Commander Johnson were escorts to Hawker Typhoons attacking German airfields in Northern France.

The 'Tiffies' were commanded by none other than Squadron Leader Denis Crowley-Milling DFC (181 Squadron), pictured here. The artwork is commendable!

The Kenley Spitfires sometimes flew together with the Hornchurch Wing, commanded by the New Zealander Wing Commander Bill Crawford Compton DFC. These sorties were not a great success, however, owing to the large number of fighters operating together (something which does not, conversely, appeared to have caused the Germans any problems). Compton is pictured here at Hornchurch with Spitfire Mk IX 'The Magic Carpet'.

The Station Commander at Kenley was Group Captain Jimmy Fenton a Battle of Britain veteran. Here Fenton is pictured at left with Wing Commander Johnson, and Squadron Leaders Foss Boulton and Syd Ford.

Squadron Leader Bud Malloy DFC, CO 401 Squadron.

J Danforth Browne was an American who volunteered to fly with the RCAF before his country came into the war. Dan won his spurs with the Kenley Wing in 1943.

Squadron Leader Birtwhistle, the Kenley Wing Intelligence Officer.

Squadron Leader Syd Ford and Flight Lieutenant Charlie Magwood.

'One of our Spitfires is Missing': Flight Lieutenants Norman Fowlow (left) and Dagwood Phillips await the return of an overdue pilot together with their Wing Leader. Note that Johnnie is wearing the 'Canada' shoulder flashes presented to him by his pilots soon after his arrival at Kenley.

Dean MacDonald, 'Trapper' Bowen, Hugh Godefroy, Walter Conrad and Johnnie.

Flight Lieutenant Dean MacDonald DFC, 403 Squadron.

Squadron Leader Foss Boulton, 416 Squadron.

'With Sally at Kenley, 1943'.

Squadron Leader Hugh Godefroy DFC, his Spitfire showing three victory symbols.

Hugh Godefroy and groundcrew. A successful and popular fighter pilot, Godefroy would succeed Johnnie as Wing Leader.

Flying Officer Jackie Rae of 416 Squadron, who was later a well-known TV presenter.

Pilots of 421 Squadron before a sortie. Note the Red Indian chief's head painted beneath the Spitfire's exhausts.

The 'Flat Hats': Jackie Rae, 'Ping' Pow, Doug Booth.

3019 Servicing Echelon, RCAF, Kenley, May 1943.

Johnnie and groundcrew, Kenley.

Canadian pilots (including Flight Lieutenant Hugh Godefroy at second left) with visiting Canadian government delegation at Kenley, May 1943.

The visiting delegation included the AOC, 'LM' (fourth from left). Note the Red Indian chief's head insignia, this time painted beneath the Spitfire's windscreen.

The Spitfire shown to the visitors was LZ996. Squadron Leader PLI Archer DFC was shot down and killed in this aircraft on June 17th, 1943.

53 years later, Dilip Sarkar led an expedition to recover LZ996 from its crash site near St Omer. Although not W3185, the mount of Wing Commander Douglas Bader, as had been hoped for, it was quite a coincidence that the Spitfire concerned should be that of one of Johnnie's squadron commanders, and

more so that a picture of that particular aircraft appeared in the great man's photo album!

A large quantity of LZ996 was recovered, including the Merlin engine and these interesting items: the pilot's head, seat and instrument armour, both compressed air bottles and the pilot's oxygen supply cylinder.

During the research for this book, Dilip Sarkar was able to show some of the LZ996 items to Johnnie and Dan Browne, the latter pictured here, in Johnnie's office, holding a shrapnel holed compressed air cylinder.

Squadron Leader Archer DFC was buried by the Germans at St Omer cemetery, but Dilip Sarkar and Bernard-Marie Dupont found that his gravestone incorrectly recorded him as an 'Air Gunner Instructor'. Following evidence supplied by the author, the Commonwealth War Graves Commission has since rectified this inaccuracy.

Three days after Squadron Leader Archer was killed, the Kenley Wing lost Pilot Officer FC McWilliams in combat over the French coast. This is the 21-year old's grave in Etaples Cemetery (which contains some 11,000 casualties from both World Wars), pictured in 2001 by Bernard-Marie Dupont.

Those in peril: Canadian pilots of the Kenley Wing pictured before a sweep. The group also includes the padre (centre).

Johnnie with pilots of the 'Wolf' Squadron, probably at Headcorn, in September 1943 (note the temporary runway surface). Front row, from left: F/O JP Lecoq, F/L CP Thornton, P/O JA Wilson, Sgt S Barnes (reported MIA shortly afterwards), WO1 CE Rae & Sgt JR MacKinnon. Second row: F/O L Foster, F/O RG Middlemiss, F/O JF Lambert, F/L D Dover, S/L FE Grant, JEJ, F/L NJ Ogilvie, F/O H Dowding, F/O JD Browne, P/O PK Gray. Back row: F/O TA Brannagan, F/O J Hodgson, F/L AC Coles, F/L HJ Southwood (also MIA), Sgt NV Chevers, F/O J Preston, F/L D Goldberg, F/O MJ Gordon & F/L HA Pattinson. Most of these men hailed from Hamilton.

127 Wing, JEJ leading, takes off from Lashenden, Spitfire LF Mk IXs.

After the war, Johnnie always maintained strong links with his wartime friends. Here the Air Vice-Marshal is pictured in 1994, with Dr Hugh Godefroy (extreme left), Wing Commander Rod Smith and Squadron Leader Dan Browne.

In retirement, Johnnie was in his element attending enthusiast events all over the world, and is pictured here with Dilip Sarkar at the launch of *Bader's Tangmere Spitfires*, Worcester Guildhall, October 1996. The event was a huge success.

Photo courtesy Worcester Evening News

In September 1943, Johnnie destroyed the Canadian Wing's 99th Hun. Together with the pilots responsible for the 98th and 100th, Johnnie received this engraved silver tankard from the Station Commander.

Typically, Johnnie was still using the tankard as an everyday drinking vessel when photographed at The Stables by Andrew Long in August 1998. Visitors to The Stables would not be surprised, however, given that the great man's commission was actually displayed on the downstairs toilet wall!

Dilip Sarkar, inspired by Johnnie's story since childhood, became close friends with 'Greycap' in adult life. During the preparation for *Johnnie Johnson: Spitfire Top Gun, Parts One & Two,* the pair spent many hours either face-to-face, corresponding or on the telephone, recording this important chronicle.

This is an interesting point, as in the *Luftwaffe* there was no such thing as a 'tour'. German fighter pilots served on the front line, without respite, until killed, incapacitated by wounds, or until capitulation. In this way, the *Jagdwaffe* maintained experience on the front line and, it could be argued, German fighter pilots never lost the 'edge' (but arguably could become exhausted). This protracted period on active operations also goes part way towards explaining why the Germans' scores were so great when compared to Allied fighter pilots.

Bob Middlemiss continues:-

From soon after my arrival, whenever Johnnie Johnson led the Kenley Wing it was often with me flying as his No 2. He was a great leader and had the knack of knowing where the Huns were, and was always there, personally, leading the squadron in for kills. Flying with him was great and of course as No 2 your job was to ensure that the Wing Leader was not attacked by the 'dreaded Hun'.

Bob is also able to share with us his memories of service life at Kenley:-

The food at Kenley was generally very good, teatime we had toast and jam mostly, dinner was often mutton, with three types of potatoes: boiled, mashed, or roasted, and brussel sprouts and often cabbage. The main course was followed by a sweet, generally some type of cake and custard, this being followed by a savoury consisting of a piece of toast with either cheese or a sardine.

Dances were held in the Mess at Kenley every so often. The local belles and nurses from nearby hospitals were invited. On a part night the bar opened around 6.30 pm, and there were always about four bottles of rum available. The early birds would soon consume the rum and Coca-Cola and then branch out to rye, Scotch, gin, and eventualy beer. On one occasion I remember about 0400, with all the above drinks gone, we were down to drinking liquers like cherry brandy etc. Of course being young and virile, I guess our stomachs could stand anything!

The weather in the Kenley area was not always the best and on many occasions we relied on the railway line, known to us pilots as the 'Iron Compass', just south of the aerodrome that ran from the coast. We used it to navigate our way back to base.

Dan Browne elaborates on navigation:-

You find that navigating over England is very difficult. Because of the weather it can be easy for an inexperienced pilot to get lost. We had primitive aids, a gyro which had to be set constantly, and VHF. We used to come home along the long, straight railway line that goes up to Redhill. The Controller used to drop us down, we'd break out of cloud onto that rail track, follow it on up and when it disappeared we'd do a right turn and find Kenley; very scientific it was too! We had this D/F system so you could just transmit for a fix, those gals in the Ops Room were marvellous, no telling how many guys they saved.

Bob continues:-

Squadron Leader 'Cam' MacArthur was our Senior Medical Officer, a great chap who not only looked after our medical requirements but also kept a sharp look out for any sign of fatigue and 'twitch' in the pilots. He always attended our operational briefings and afterwards would be at the runways to wave and give us the thumbs up before take-off. He was always there if you had a problem or just wanted a chat. He had a great personality and I always felt that he was a tremendous inspiration to all. Don Carlson, our Protestant padre, was another always in the thick of it with the pilots, always available for a drink or game of cards with the boys. Many a day that the Group Captain, 'Iron Bill' MacBrien, would gather up Cam MacArthur, Don Carlson and myself for a game of 'knock rummy' right after lunch.

May 10th
No change in the weather, no flying whatsoever. 'Interrogation of Prisoner of War' seen by 70 men of ground crew from all sections of 403 Squadron and 3076 Echelon. Flying Officer RG Middlemiss reported to 403 Squadron for flying duties.

May 11th
Sunny and warm with a light southerly wind, it was no surprise that Merlins soon roared.

First thing, Wing Commander Johnson flew another tank jettisoning test, a sortie of 40 minutes in his usual Spitfire, EN398, and 416 Squadron practised deck landings at Dunsfold. Then came the briefing for the day's operation: Circus 295, in which the Kenley Wing would provide 'second fighter echelon' (ORB, 403) to a formation of B-25 Mitchells bombing the port of Boulogne. At 1210, Greycap led the Wing to North Foreland at 500 feet before making a wide orbit off Dunkirk at 14-16,000 feet. The Spitfires, however, were recalled by 'Wytex' (Codename for Kenley, ORB, 416) and then vectored under Appledore to cross the enemy occupied coast at Mardyck, there being 'Huns about' (PCR, JEJ) inland. Having orbitted St Omer, code-named the

'Big Wood', by which time the other aircraft involved in the Circus had wthdrawn, as Greycap prepared to leave France via Gravelines a gaggle of bandits was 'Tally Ho'd', as Johnnie's combat report relates:-

FW 190s were sighted above when the Wing was over Gravelines, so we turned to engage in order to avoid an enemy bounce. Eight 190s flying in fours line abreast passed under my section, followed by a further three 190s in line astern. I turned after these three E/A and attacked No 3 from 10 degrees starboard astern, with cannon and m/g – range 300 yards. I saw a piece of E/A fall off near the perspex hood, and E/A climbed steeply for 200-300 feet and then fell over and dived vertically. I broke away and immediately afterwards searched below in order to locate this a/c. I saw an a/c go into the sea about two miles off Gravelines.

Greycap's No 2, Flying Officer R Wozniak, confirmed the victory, adding that 'I saw a splash in the sea in the area of W/Cdr Johnson's combat immediately after he had fired'.

Red Section of 403 Squadron was also engaged, attacking 11 190s which were sighted beneath the Canadian Spitfires. As a high-speed running fight developed, Squadron Leader 'Foss' Boulton of 416 Squadron managed a long burst at a 190, but made no subsequent claim. As quickly as it had began the engagement was over, and the Wing returned safely to Kenley at 1335. During the de-brief, pilots reported that red tracer flak had been seen over Gravelines, which was believed to have been a marker for the German fighters. There had also been some heavy and accurate flak near Dunkirk, thus emphasising the various threats experienced by fighter pilots during this early summer of 1943; Bob Middlemiss:-

Flak was not one of our main worries when flying over enemy territory, but the 'flak boys of St Omer' seemed to be the most accurate in tracking and firing at the fighters. On one of our sweeps when I was flying No 2 to Johnnie, above cloud and in the vicinity of St Omer, I had turned my head to the right when suddenly a large black explosion to my left erupted. I thought that the Wingco had been hit but fortunately the 88mm shell had expoloded between us and we got away scot-free.

For Johnnie, the day's flying was not over. In his PFLB he recorded a local familiarisation flight of 20 minutes in a Spitfire Mk XII (serial number not given). This is interesting, given that this flight was his first in a Griffon powered Spitfire. Although the Rolls-Royce Merlin was extremely successful, having proved capable of development, there were nevertheless limits to the power that could be obtained from a 27 litre engine. This had, in fact, been recognised very early on in the Spitfire's development programme and work had begun on a new engine shortly after the outbreak of war. The new engine was another of 12 cylinders, called the Griffon, but the capacity was more: 36.7 litres. The resulting output was a potent 1,700 horsepower. Pilots would find the main handling difference from the Merlin being that the Griffon rotated in the opposite direction, so instead of swinging to the left on take-off, therefore, the Griffon variants swung to the right.

May 12th

Due to adverse weather, there was no flying and the Wing was released at 1030.

May 13th

Again another change in the weather, sunny and warm with a light southerly wind, meant that operations were back on. The Kenley Wing's first task of the day was to provide 'second fighter echelon' (ORB, 403) on Circus 296. Greycap led the Spitfires out over North Foreland at 5,000 feet, crossing the French coastline over Dunkirk's historic beaches at 22,000 feet. Heading east towards Cassel, control passed to Appledore and the Spitfires climbed towards St Omer, which was reached at 27,000 feet. Given that in total 15 Spitfire squadrons were active over France, escorting just six B-25s to Boulogne, the Germans wisely refused to engage *en masse*. Nevertheless, the Kenley Wing was attacked by some 20 FW 190s from both above and below. Another running battle ensued.

403 Squadron's CO, Squadron Leader Charlie Magwood DFC, leading Yellow Section, was attacked by a *schwarm* of 190s from 4,000 feet below. The Canadian half-rolled out of the sun, forcing all but one of the one-time 'Butcher Birds' to take evasive action. With Magwood 350 yards astern and closing, that 190 broke to port, but it was too late: Yellow 1 opened fire with cannon and machine-guns. The 190's hood and bits of wing flew off as the missiles found their mark; it then rolled over and spun down with 'smoke and flames billowing from the cockpit' (ORB, 403). The outcome was in no doubt, and Magwood later claimed this 190 as destroyed. On the way out, Yellow 1 engaged another FW 190, which he hit and claimed as damaged.

416 Squadron also enjoyed success, 190s being claimed destroyed by Squadron

Leader Boulton, Flying Officer RH Walker and Flying Officer JA Rae; Boulton also claimed another as damaged. Although there were no personnel casualties, three 416 Squadron Spitfires landed back at Kenley having sustained varying degrees of damage.

The next offensive sortie for the Kenley Spitfires was Ramrod 71, the AOC Fighter Command, Air Vice-Marshal Sir Trafford Leigh-Mallory KCB DSO, sitting in on the pilots' briefing. He gave a short address, complimenting the Canadians on their good morning's work and explained a little of the current strategy of aerial warfare as it affected all fronts.

In this afternoon sortie, Johnnie's Kenley Spitfires were to meet B-17s of the Eighth Air Force's 1st Bomb Wing attacking the Potez repair facility at Meulte. Covered by three P-47 Fighter Groups, the B-17s of the 4th Bomb Wing made a diversionary attack on the already pockmarked airfield at St Omer. The *Luftwaffe* did not react, however, watching closely the progress of the larger 1st Bomb Wing force which, after zig-zagging northwards up the English Channel, finally turned for France. Over Berck, the Kenley Wing joined the last boxes of Fortresses, watching 'nibbling' (ORB, 403) attacks by enemy fighters on the lead bombers before the force reached Amiens. On the way in, one B-17 was seen to go down 15 miles inland of Berck.

Between the target and the approaching Fortresses was now a strong force of JG 26 190s led by Major 'Pips' Priller. The 91st Bomb Group soon lost two Flying Fortresses to Major Priller and *Leutnant* Hoppe, whilst another went to flak. Amongst 11 B-17s damaged during these attacks, was one hit by a bomb dropped by 190, so determined were the Germans to defeat the Americans by whatever means available. Nonetheless, the B-17s' target was soon wreathed in brown smoke and completely hidden to the aircrew fighting for their lives high above. For one American crew, violent death came suddenly when their B-17 exploded and disintegrated over Meulte.

By now, the Kenley Wing was heavily engaged, fighting off attacks as best the Spitfire pilots were able. Many fighters, of both sides, now whirled their death dance between burning Meulte and the Channel at Le Touquet. Red Section of 403 Squadron was bounced by a *schwarm* of 190s, one of the assailants attempted a head-on attack against Red 2, Flying Officer RD Bowen, but Red 4, Pilot Officer HJ Dowding, responded in like fashion, opening fire at 200 yards and closing *rapidly*. Hits were seen around the 190's cockpit, and it was soon going down.

As Fortresses approached the French coast on their homeward journey, Greycap saw a *schwarm* of 190s approaching and clearly bent on attacking the bombers from the starboard side:-

I closed in on the leader and gave him several short bursts from the starboard beam, closing to starboard quarter, strikes being seen near his wing root. The enemy aircraft turned left and flicked right over. He dived and I followed for three or four thousand feet. E/A flicked over twice more and I gave him a short burst although at this stage I was almost out of range. I then broke away and rejoined the bombers but my No 3 (F/O Foster of 416) followed the aircraft down and saw the pilot bale out.

As ever with Wing Commander Johnson's combat reports, there was no question regarding the accuracy of this claim.

After their respective combats, Flying Officer Bowen and Pilot Officer Dowding, of 403, then formed up with Greycap and Flying Officer Foster, who were heading home. Minutes later, the four Spitfires were attacked by two 190s when half way back across the Channel. One of these the three Spitfires isolated and 'chased into the sea' (ORB, 403). Red 3, Pilot Officer WT Lane, dived on two other 190s, giving several bursts of cannons and machine-guns, strikes being witnessed by Greycap. Flight Lieutenant HD MacDonald, Blue 3, attacked the last of two Me 109s at 23,000 feet, striking the target with his second burst of cannon and machine-gun fire. A lone Me 109 flew below Yellow Section, positioning himself down sun, attacking above and to port. Flight Lieutenant HC Godefroy, Yellow 1, fired at the 109 and saw hits on the tail and rear fuselage.

Back at Kenley, the pilots of 403 Squadron excitedly made out their combat reports, but three Spitfires were missing: Sergeant WG Uttley of 403, who had last been seen over Doullen (and was possibly the Spitfire reportedly seen going down over that location {ORB, 403}), and both Squadron Leader Foss Boulton and Sergeant CW McKim of 416. The latter had been heard to shout over the R/T that he had been badly hit and was seen to ditch his Spitfire in the Channel, 20 miles west of Le Touquet, but of Boulton nothing had been heard or seen. Immediately their Spitfires could be turned around, Greycap led a number of his pilots to sweep back over the Channel, searching for their missing comrades. An 'oil patch, pieces of aircraft wreckage and a barrel or unexploded torpedo with red and white circle at one end' were seen, but no trace of the three missing Kenley pilots. Sadly, Uttley and McKim, both 21, were both dead; the former's grave can be found at Grivillers British War Cemetery (near Bapaume), whilst McKim's name is amongst those 'Missing' aircrew remembered at Runnymede. The 416 Squadron CO, however, was more fortunate: having baled out at 26,000 feet in spite of head, back and arm wounds. Squadron Leader Boulton was captured, and whilst later a prisoner at the infamous *Stalag Luft* III his much-deserved DFC award was gazetted. So serious were Boulton's wounds, however, that the Red Cross would arrange his early repatriation a few months later. The liklihood is that all these three Kenley Spitfire pilots were those victories claimed by Major Priller, *Hauptmann* Naumann, the *Staffelkapitän* of 6/JG 26, and *Leutnant* Leuschal, *Staffelkapitän* of 10/JG 26.

That day, Fighter Command lost a total of seven Spitfires, the enemy six fighters. The heat was on for both sides. Bob Middlemiss:-

On many of the sweeps and escort missions with Bostons, Marauders, Flying Fortresses and Liberators, many of these aircrat would be shot up and badly damaged, so we did our best to escort them safely back to England. At times this would be difficult because if you flew too close, the bombers' gunners took no chances and opened fire at friend or foe. We learned to close carefully, keeping a safe distance but still providing the required protection.

May 14th

The Kenley Wing were not to be amongst those able to afford the luxury of enjoying this 'hot and very lovely day ' (ORB, 403), the morning's Form 'D' having provided all necessary details for Ramrod 73. The Canadian Spitfires were to escort 40 B-17s of the 4th Bomb Wing attacking the base of III/JG 26, the airfield at Wevelgem, just across the French border into Belgium, near Courtrai. Greycap's Spitfires rendezvoused with the bombers at 8,000 feet over South Foreland, and course set for France. Another beehive could be seen, this being the 1st Bomb Wing and a B-24 group bound for the shipyards at Kiel.

Some enemy aircraft were sighted shortly after the Courtrai force crossed the French coast over Dunkirk, and when 15 miles inland a B-17 turned back, although not due to enemy action. As the bombers approached the target, Me 109s and FW 190s began harassing the formation but, in the main, were driven off by the Spitfires. Flight Lieutenant Buckham of 416 Squadron shot down a 190 which became a fireball, and Greycap nailed another.

Some 10 miles west of Courtrai on the homeward run, Flight Lieutenant Godefroy of 403 Squadron pressed home an attack on a 190, and watched with satisfaction 'the cannon mounting and perspex hood come off and then a big ball of black smoke eneveloped the E/A, as though it were disintegrating'(ORB, 403). Flight Lieutenant MacDonald, also of 403, dived onto an Me 109 that was flying with two FW 190s, fired and noted strikes on the cockpit and wing roots as chunks of debris span into the air. Flying Officer Bowen saw this 190 spin into the sea.

In spite of the Spitfire pilots' best efforts, two Fortresses were shot down. *Oberleutnant* Hans Naumann, *Staffelkapitän* of 6/JG 26 claimed one of these, having fired at a 351st Bomb Group B-17 near Wevelgem with his last 20 rounds. The crew baled out, however, and these may have been the American parachutes later reported by 403 Squadron.

Wevelgem had nonetheless been hit hard. Enemy aircraft had been destroyed and damaged, and a number of personnel, including both pilots and ground staff, were killed or wounded. The airfield was also badly cratered. A newcomer to the western front, *Oberleutnant* Erwin Leykauf, *Staffelkapitän* of 12/JG 54, actually tried to get up in his 109 during the attack, but the aircraft's undercarriage legs were sheered off by a bomb crater. So badly damaged was Wevelgem, in fact, that III/JG 26 was forced to move temporarily to the smaller field at Lille-Nord. It was the first, but not the last, time that a JG 26 airfield was rendered unserviceable by Allied bombing.

The Americans had also made another first this day by putting a total of 200 bombers in the air. After their earlier losses, an ever-increasing quantity of replacement aircrew and aircraft, including fighters and both heavy and medium-bombers, had been arriving in England from America, despite the u-boats' best efforts. The process was even afoot to convert certain B-17s and B-24s into heavily armoured and armed 'destroyer escorts'. At the time, given the limited range of the single-engined fighters available and considering that auxiliary fuel tank tests had yet to be finalised, this was really the only realistic short-term option to afford the bombers greater protection all the way to the target and back. All of this indicates the resolve of the Eighth Air Force to succeed and see the job through. As Johnnie said to me many years

later, 'You couldn't help but admire them, could you?'

The B-17, more commonly the Flying Fortress, was aptly named, given that it carried more defensive armament than any other Allied bomber throughout the Second World War: 13 0.50in machine-guns. To put that into perspective, a formation of 100 B-17s therefore possessed a total of 1,300 heavy calibre machine-guns, each with an effective range of 2,000 yards. One experienced *Jagdflieger*, Hans Philipp, the Kommodore of JG 1, once wrote of engaging B-17s: 'The curve into 70 Fortresses lets all the sins of one's life pass before one' eyes. And when one has convinced oneself, it is still more painful to force to it every pilot in the Wing, down to the last newcomer'. There was a weak spot, however, which the enemy was quick to exploit: head-on, less guns could be brought to bear than at another other angle on the B-17. Indeed, RAF fighter pilots had already used the same tactics during the Battle of Britain when attacking German bomber formations. Given the mighty Boeing's extensive armour plating, the enemy found itself needing to increase the calibre of its firepower. The Fortress also enjoyed the benefits of self-sealing fuel tanks, and, as Johnnie says, great accuracy could be achieved with the Norden bombsight, certainly from 20,000 feet or below and in clear weather. The downside for the Eighth Air Force was that each B-17 lost represented the deaths of capture of nine American airmen.

Returning to May 14th, 1943, after the morning's maximum effort, the Kenley Wing flew no more operational sorties of any significance that day. The pilots of 403 Squadron, however, carried out 'practice sails in dinghys at WAAF Officers' Mess Swimming Pool' (ORB, 403).

May 15th

In the morning, Greycap flew a Spitfire V, 'DN-O', across to Horsham St Faiths where he liased with the P-47 Thunderbolt-equipped 56 Fighter Group. At this stage of the game it was vital for the Americans to listen to the experiences of RAF pilots like Wing Commander Johnson who had been 'at it' for a long time before Pearl Harbour. These liaisons were also important to morale and developing a spirit of mutual co-operation. Johnnie remained with the 56th Fighter Group for two days, leaving on the morning of May 17th for Bassingbourne, where he lectured fighter tactics to the 91st Bomb Group, a B-17 unit.

Back at Kenley, in Greycap's absence, Squadron Leader Magwood of 403 Squadron led the Wing on May 15th, on Circus 297, a raid on Poix, the home of I/JG 27, by 12 Bostons. As the Spitfires took off from Kenley, Gordon Lane of the RCE, visiting the station, waved off his brother, Pilot Officer Willie Lane, Yellow 4 of 403 Squadron. Rendezvous was made at zero feet over Bexhill, the French coast crossed at Le Touquet. Again the bombers hit the target accurately, bombs being seen to explode on various buildings and alongside one runway. The Bostons were seen in and out safely by the Spitfires, which remained to see off any intercepting German fighters. A small group of bandits had first been seen immediately after the bombing, followed by 30-40, mostly Me 109s, several thousand feet beneath the Kenley Wing. 416 Squadron provided cover whilst 403 went down to attack. Flight Lieutenant MacDonald, leading Blue Section, climbed and protected Red Section, which had turned to port to engage two 109s. MacDonald then saw two more 109s below and to starboard. He dived onto the rearmost and closing from 200 yards blew it to bits with his cannon before firing at and damaging the first 109, this being witnessed by Flying Officer JE McKay. Flight Lieutenant LB Madden, Blue 2 dived after the damaged enemy aircraft but made no reply when recalled by his Section Leader; following an enemy aircraft down was a cardinal sin, Madden's action later being described by Squadron Leader Magwood as 'a Clot's trick on first sweep'.

Flying Officer GD Aitkin and Pilot Officer WT Lane, Yellow 3 and 4 respectively, were then isolated from the rest of their Section when attacking a *schwarm* of 109s, which split into two *rotten*. Another 12 109s had penetrated the Spitfire formation and these fell on Aitkin and Lane, both of whom immediately took violent evasive action. Then a single 109 and a *schwarm* of 190s, all flying in a 'star formation' (ORB, 403), attacked the Spitfire pair from port astern. Unfortunately Lane broke to port and flew into their combined fire. It was the last time he was ever seen or heard of by his comrades.

Back at Kenley, the headcount indicated two pilots missing offset against one Me 109 destroyed and another damaged. The Wing had probably clashed with I/JG 2, which, in the air battles around Caen (the target of a Circus) and Poix, claimed a total of six victories and lost four pilots. Sadly, the two missing 403 Squadron pilots were both dead. Flight Lieutenant Lyn Bertram Madden's grave can now be found in the churchyard at Poix-de-Picardie, and Pilot Officer William Thompson Lane lies in the Dieppe Canadian War Cemetery. Telling Gordon Lane, who had awaited the Wing's return at Kenley, that his 21-year old brother was 'Missing' was 'rather hard' (ORB, 403).

May 16th

The weather sunny and warm with only a light northerly wind, in the morning 12 Spitfires of 416 Squadron carried out a test flight to measure petrol consumption, whilst other aircraft of the Squadron practised deck landings at Dunsfold. In the afternoon, Squadron Leader Magwood led the Wing again, this time on Circus 298, during which the Spitfires were to provide high cover to B-25s bombing the airfield at Tricqueville. Due to the Spitfires being up at 30,000 feet, the result of the Mitchells' attack was not seen, but 15 Me 109s reported south of the target and at 17,000 feet turned away without engaging. 416 Squadron, which had become seperated from 403 by a thin layer of cloud, briefly clashed with 12 FW 190s, one of them being damaged by Flight Lieutenant Buckham. A section of 403 Squadron returned home early due to 'one pilot being in trouble' (ORB, 403), and Flying Officer RD Bowen, Blue 3, saw Blue 1, Flight Lieutenant MacDonald DFC, suddenly dive out of formation before climbing vertically, his Spitfire apparently out of control. Squadron Leader Magwood called up Blue 1 to check his oxygen supply, but there was no response. 'Everyone thought he had had it' (ORB, 403), but MacDonald fortunately recovered at a lower altitude and returned safely to Manston. His oxygen supply had indeed failed him, with potentially fatal result, but he recovered high enough to regain control and return home with the bombers.

On this day, 403 Squadron's Flight Lieutenant Buck McNair DFC was promoted to Squadron Leader and posted to command 416, which was still in need of a replacement following the loss of Foss Boulton. Flying Officer JD Browne, Warrant Officer AV Hargreaves and Flight Sergeant GM Shouldice went..... sailing!

May 17th

Another fine day, Squadron Leader Magwood led the Wing on Circus 299. Whilst the Eighth Air Force bombed the U-boat pens at Lorient again, the Kenley Wing was amongst those Allied fighter units sweeping northern France in the hope of keeping German fighters well away from the American bombers. Although III/JG 2 hacked their way through the close escort and downed five B-17s, the RAF held the rest of JG 2 at bay.

Crosing into France over Port-en-Bassin, thence on to Caen at 27,000 feet, heavy flak greeted Magwood and his Spitfires above Cobourg. The Canadians then saw 'six small balloons or parachutes … at 26-27,000 feet, two of which exploded, one of them was seen to have a small red sack underneath it. No cables were seen, no enemy aircraft or shipping were seen'.

Back at Kenley, at mid-day, one section of 416 Squadron Spitfires carried out an uneventful patrol of Winchester, thus marking the Squadron's last operational flight of this tour. Having been subsequently declared non-operational, 416 took over the Spitfire Mk Vs that 421 'Red Indian' Squadron had flown to Kenley from Redhill, the latter, in turn, taking charge of 416's Mk IXs. Whilst 416's pilots practised deck landings at Dunsfold, the ground crew began the unenviable task of moving to the other side of the aerodrome whilst 421 took over the Squadron's former dispersal. A few days later, 416 exchanged aircraft again, this time with 411 'Grizzly Bear' Squadron, and moved to Digby in 12 Group. There it would remain, receiving replacements and working up for its next tour on operations.

The 'Red Indians' of 421 Squadron, commanded by Squadron Leader JD Hall, were delighted at the prospect of being a part of the Spitfire Mk IX Wing at Kenley, as the ORB remarked, the Squadron was now in the 'Major League'!

After having led the morning sweep, Squadron Leader Magwood flew to Bassingbourne where he met Wing Commander Johnson and contributed to the liason with the Americans. The Spitfire pair returned to Kenley that afternoon, Johnnie then taking up 10 Spitfires of 421 Squadron on a practice formation flight and giving them a 'good work out' (ORB, 421).

May 18th
Early in the morning, Sergeants GR Brown and KD Windsor of 403 Squadron were scrambled and chased two FW 190s towards the Cherbourg peninsula. The fleeting 190s had the edge, however, so the Canadian pair returned to Kenley, their guns unfired. At this time the 190s, particularly those of SKG 10, were mounting an increasing number of successful 'tip'n run' raids on targets in southern England.

On what was another warm and sunny day, 421 Squadron was busy familiarising itself with their new Spitfires. The Squadron also received four pilots from 416 Squadron, Flying Officer Sidnall, Pilot Officer Terrie, and Sergeants Packard and Linton, all of whom had operational experience but were considered fresh enough to remain active. Although their experience was limited, it was nevertheless important to 421's pilots to have amongst their ranks some who had already flown the Spitfire Mk IX.

On this day, 421 Squadron flew its first operation with the Kenley Wing, Rodeo 218, a fighter sweep. At 24,000 feet above Le Touquet, control of the Spitfires was passed to Appledore, which vectored Greycap to Hucqueliers – Hesdin – Desvres – Cap-Griz-Nez, then back out at Le Touquet. There were no enemy aircraft seen but 421 Squadron considered the experience 'beneficial' (ORB).

May 19th

At 1405, Greycap led the Kenley Wing up on Rodeo 220, a fighter sweep of the Pas-de-Calais under Appledore. Crossing out at 10,000 feet over Bexhill, the Wing climbed over the Channel to 25,000 feet, entering France above Le Crotoy. Sweeping inland, four FW 190s were seen at the same height but 'would not engage' (ORB, 403), and two Me 109s were chased from 30,000 to 15,000 feet between Berck and Hucqueliers, but could not be caught. The Wing then turned for home and made landfall at 3,000 feet over Dungeness.

Flying Officer McLachlan of 421 Squadron had recently returned to his unit from leave and took up a Spitfire Mk IX on a familiarisation flight. Unfortunately his oxygen system failed, causing the pilot to lose consciousness. Suddenly he regained his senses and found himself plunging to earth, his aircraft uncontrollable. He baled out and floated safely to earth, the Spitfire breaking up in the air before impacting.
During the afternoon, two sections of 403 Squadron patrolled Maidstone whilst another Section escorted a convoy off Beachy Head. Both sorties were uneventful.

May 20th

A warm and sunny day, the Kenley Wing took off at 1220 on Rodeo 222, but due to unfavourable weather conditions over France the Spitfires were recalled when over North Foreland. 421 Squadron spent the rest of the day flying training sorties, including air-to-air firing, and two convoy patrols. Likewise, 403 Squadron used the cancellation of operations as an opportunity for new pilots to gain experience on the Spitfire Mk IX.

May 21ˢᵗ

A similar day, Greycap led the Wing on Circus 301 but was again recalled due to poor weather developing over France.

May 22ⁿᵈ

Although sunny and bright, there were no operational sorties and again the Wing undertook numerous non-operational flights of various natures.

May 23ʳᵈ

Another sunny day but with 5/10ths cloud and a westerly wind. At 1145, the Kenley Wing was up on Circus 302, a raid by Venturas on Zeebrugge. The bombers were three minutes later at the agreed rendezvous over Bradwell Bay, but soon the beehive was heading for France at 'sea level' (ORB, 403). The bombers ultimately attacked from 12,000 feet, the Spitfires stationed 3,000 feet above. The bombing was reportedly good, but although the Spitfires orbitted Knocke there were no enemy aircraft seen. Heavy flak was fired from Ostend, and three German minesweepers were seen in the harbour there. After the Wing re-crossed the British coast at Deal, in the Detling area Greycap was vectored to some bandits that had bombed Hastings. The Spitfires raced along the coast to Dungeness and Rye, trying to cut the enemy aircraft off over the Channel, at zero feet, but none were Tally Ho'd. Abandoming the fruitless search, the Wing came in over Hastings, observing the result of the enemy attack. The raiders were once more the FW 190s of SKG 10, which had also attacked the coastal town of Bournemouth. Four 190s were lost.

Back at Kenley, a treat was in store for two 421 Squadron pilots, Pilot Officers Cook and Packard, who 'took advantage of a standing invitation from a yacht club near London and did a spot of sailing' (ORB, 421).

In his PFLB, Johnnie wrote simply 'Awarded DSO'. The citation for this Distinguished Service Order was more descriptive, and in part read:-

Acting Wing Commander Johnson has led a Wing on a large number of occasions and has displayed outstanding skill and gallantry. During an operation one morning in May 1943, his formation was heavily engaged by a large force of enemy fighters. In the ensuing combats four enemy aircraft were destroyed without loss. The same afternoon he took part in a similar sortie and three enemy fighters were destroyed, one of them by Wing Commander Johnson. The next day, this officer took part in another successful sortie. By his skilfull and courageous leadership, Wing Commander Johnson contrbuted materially to the success achieved. He has personally destroyed at least 13 enemy aircraft.

In addition to being a superb fighter pilot, Johnnie was now receiving recognition for the one thing that I personally think marked him as a genius: leadership. His charisma was engaging, his presence enormous, and his leadership skills came naturally. As he once said to me:-

Leadership can be taught, you know, how to be straightforward with your subordinates and so on, but the last 10% is an indefinable quality, a gift which you either have or haven't got, just like the gift of a great painter or writer, for example. Bader had it, and when my time to lead came I modelled myself on him.

With the latter part of that statement I disagreed then and still do today. I said:-

You say that, Johnnie, but in fact you did everything differently. Douglas based himself at Westhampnett and always flew at the head of 616 Squadron. This, we know now, frustrated Billy Burton (CO of 616) and alienated the squadrons at Merston. You, on the other hand, flew with all of your squadrons and therefore forged a real team spirit. Also, you came from different backgrounds, Douglas being a Cranwell graduate and public school boy, whereas you were the son of a policeman, a grammar school boy, albeit with a university degree, who had started out as a Sergeant in the VR. That must have made you more able to relate to a wider spectrum of serviceman than just the commissioned elite?

As the winter sun went down that afternoon over the Derbyshire Peaks, which lay beyond our immediate environment in Johnnie's conservatory-like office, in response the great man just shrugged his shoulders and just said 'Dunno'. He would not be drawn, so we left it at that!

Dan Browne, however, added his view regarding the successful combination of Johnnie and the Canadians:-

We had some fine Canadians at Kenley. Some had been miners and lumberjacks, just roughnecks all their lives, so it was a weird combination. It was a stroke of genius in itself to put Johnnie in command, although he was an Englishman, and they gave us these Spit IXBs, and I suspect that there was some politics behind that to keep us colonials quiet. Johnnie got along with them beautifully, he'd go out and shoot crap with them. Johnnie has the most extraordinary vocabulary of evil songs, drinking all night long you know, we'd draw off that oxygen bottle in the morning, it just revived you!

Johnnie's leadership was not about iron discipline, it was just that everybody wanted to do things the way that he wanted them done, because they were so proud of being in that Wing. All Johnnie had to do was ring London and say "I want this pilot off my Wing". No questions would be asked and when the guy landed he would just be ordered top report to some obscure duty in the middle of no where! Johnnie would shoot crap with us on the ground, and everybody would call him 'Wingco'.

Hugh Godefroy:-

As a leader, Johnnie Johnson was like the Pied Piper. We found ourselves bounding out of bed repeating his catchy phrases like 'OK chaps, get into 'em!'

Johnnie:-

Yes, it was quite something to get the DSO, especially on the same day as a chap like Al Deere, who I admired and respected enormously because he had been at it for such a very long time.

Air Vice-Marshal Sir Trafford Leigh-Mallory, Commander-in-Chief of Fighter Command, wrote a letter of congratulation to Johnnie on the occasion of his first DSO:-

Dear Johnson

It gives me great pleasure to congratulate you most heartily on being awarded the DSO.

I was very much impressed by what I saw of your work during my short visit to Kenley the other day, and I am satisfied that the high standard of the Kenley Wing is very largely due to your high qualities of leadership.

Wishing you the best of luck,

Yours truly,

Trafford Leigh-Mallory

Another letter arrived from Air Vice-Marshal 'Dingbat' Saunders, the Air Officer Commanding No 11 Group:-

My Dear Johnson

My heartiest congratulations on your well-earned DSO. The Kenley Wing has done marvellous work recently under your leadership, and I am quite sure will continue its good work.

Good luck and good hunting!

Yours sincerely

Saunders

On the night of May 23rd, 1943, the 'Kenleys' headed for London to celebrate their Wing Leader's DSO. The Biggin Hill Wing Commander Flying, the New Zealander Wing Commander Al Deere, had also been awarded the DSO and arrangements were made for a joint celebration at the Kimmul Club in Burleigh Street. A popular venue with aircrews, the Club was run a former RFC Captain, Bobbie Page, and the DSO party was soon in full swing. Also present that night, with a crowd of 'Bomber Boys', was Wing Commander Guy Gibson DSO & bar, DFC & bar, who had led the highly publicised 'Dambusters' raid only the previous week. Five days after that night in the Kimmul Club, when he bought Johnnie a pint on account of his DSO, Guy Gibson's Victoria Cross was gazetted.

May 24th
Apalling weather, heavy rain and high winds, saw no operational flying, which a few pilots with hangovers probably appreciated! In the afternoon, the Wing's pilots watched a movie, 'My Favourite Wife', starring Cary Grant and Irene Dunne.

May 25th
In complete contrast to the previous day, the weather was sunny and bright. At 1016 the Kenley Wing was up on Circus 304, escorting Mitchells bombing the airfield at Abbeville. Greycap led the Wing out over Bexhill at zero feet, climbing to 21,000 feet and making landfall at Le Treport. Although a few small formations of Me 109s and FW 190s were seen over France, only Yellow Section of 403 Squadron managed to get in a squirt, albeit ineffective. Approaching the

target, moderate flak was fired at the bombers, and an aircraft was seen ablaze on the south bank of the Somme estuary. Squadron Leader Magwood saw both a B-25 and a Close Escort Spitfire 'destroyed by flak' (PFLB).

May 26th

Although sunny and bright there were no operational sorties. At noon there was a 403 Squadron formation practice flight, during which Squadron Leader Magwood and Pilot Officer McGarrigle 'bounced' the other Spitfires. 421 Squadron also used the day for training, practising the line abreast formation so favoured by Greycap.

The august achievements of 403 Squadron's flight commanders, Flight Lieutenants Godefroy and MacDonald, were today recognised by the awards of DFCs.

May 27th

A dull day, at 1715 Wing Commander Johnson led the Kenley Wing out over Hythe at 12,000 feet on Rodeo 224, a sweep of Sangatte, Cassel and Cap-Gris-Nez. To the east of the 'Grand Old Duke of York's' fabled hill at Cassel, four FW 190s were seen flying 7-8,000 feet beneath the Wing and were engaged by Greycap and a Section of 403 Squadron, but no results were seen. Due to the extreme range involved, Johnnie only fired cannon. Pilot Officer Kelley of 421 Squadron returned home alone due to engine trouble, and left France at zero feet. On the Wing's return journey, a pilot of 403 noted the position of 'a fairly large ship'.

Back at Kenley, several bags of mail were received from Canada, just about all Canadian personnel on the Station receiving several letters each from home. This came after a long spell of 'mail-less days' (ORB, 421), so must have been morale boosting.

May 28th

A hazy day of intermittent cloud and sun, Circus 305 went ahead as planned, a fighter sweep in conjunction with another bombing raid on Zeebrugge in Belgium. Once more, all the Canadians had to report upon return were the sightings of several German ships.

May 29th

Sunny and warm, Circus 306 saw the Kenley Wing sweeping Eletot, Tricqueville and Dieppe, once again without result except for the sighting of a number of enemy ships off Octeville, Le Havre and Fecamp.

During the evening, several officers of 421 Squadron 'attended a dance at Redhill and had a very enjoyable time, as many friends from other squadrons were also there' (ORB, 421).

May 30th

A dull morning gave way to a pleasant and sunny afternoon. Shortly after 1500, Squadron Leader Magwood of 403 Squadron led the Wing on Ramrod 81, supporting 'Bombphoons' attacking Hondeville power station, situated in a suburb of Caen. The Kenley Wing went in ahead of the 'Tiffies'. Sweeping behind Caen and out over Port-en-Bassin at 1548, the sortie was again uneventful for the Canadians, although other Wings were engaged. Some 35-40 miles south of Newhaven, 403 Squadron reported having seen two Spitfires orbiting two aircraft in the sea. Two splashes were seen in the sea, one believed to be a Spitfire, 20 and 35 miles NW of Le Havre respectively. A small amount of accurate heavy flak was reported over Caen and Bayeux, 'directed at 403 Squadron' (ORB).

Interestingly, the JG 26 *Geschwadergruppe* escorted the 190s of SKG 10, which were returning from another raid on England. This time the fighter-bomber unit had lost another seven pilots, making a total of 21 for the month. Not surprisingly, the unit switched over to nocturnal operations.

May 31st

On this sunny day, Circus 308 was planned for the morning, an attack by Bostons on a power station at Grand Quiville, a suburb of Rouen. Diversionary raids were also mounted against the German airfields on Caen and Abbeville aerodromes. When Greycap was just five miles north of Shoreham, the Wing was recalled due to deteriorating weather over France and consequently pancaked at Kenley.

421 Squadron was then ordered to Manston, to escort 'Whirlibombers' (ORB, 421, referring to Westland Whirlwind fighter-bombers) attacking 'E' boats, but was recalled shortly after take-off from Kenley.

Then came Circus 309, at 1655. The Kenley Wing was to mount the second wave of a fighter sweep whilst 12 Venturas bombed Zeebrugge from 12,000 feet. The Spitfires crossed out over Deal at 100 feet, climbing to 18,000 feet and crossing the French coast at Nieuport. Sweeping towards Bruges and Ostend, at 21,000 feet, 25 FW 190s of II/JG26 were seen by Greycap, some 500 feet below and diving on the port side. Followed by two 403 Squadron Spitfires, Johnnie headed for the 190s. 421 Squadron came down to cover 403 but also became engaged. Five of the Squadron's pilots fired their guns, damaging two 190s. One minute after the combat began, Greycap saw a 190 dive vertically past him, its pilot apparently trapped in the cockpit, and watched it crash into the sea. Flying Officer NR Fowlow then shouted at Sergeant GR Brown, of 403 Squadron, to 'break hard port' on account of their Section being attacked by two 190s. The first overshot, but the second, *Oberleutnant* Sternberg, *Staffelkapitän* of 5/JG 26, hit Brown who skidded to port, his Spitfire pouring black smoke. With relief, Fowlow saw a white parachute blossom at 8,000 feet, off Nieuport. According to the 403 Squadron report, 'Three other pilots of the Squadron heard someone say "Goodbye" in a debonair manner', which was presumed to be Sergeant Brown.

Three splashes were seen in the sea, all so large that crashing aircraft could be the only possible cause. One was Brown's Spitfire, the other two 190s, one of which had been seen by Greycap. The latter was later credited to Flying Officer Fowlow, who had seen a 190 'go straight down' after he had hit it from 200 yards. The second 190 was associated with a brown parachute seen later in the combat and was shared by Pilot Officer Isbister and Horten of 421 and Sergeant Small of 403. These claims were perfectly accurate given that II/JG 26 lost two 190s, both of which went into the sea, their pilots being killed (*Leutnant* Georg Mondry, 5 *Staffel*, and *Feldwebel* Hans Danneburg, 4 *Staffel*). Squadron Leader Hall and Flight Lieutenant Quint, both of 421, also claimed one damaged 190 each.

The Spitfire pilots experienced heavy flak over Ostend, with moderate heavy flak at Bruges and Nieuport. This was 'exceptionally accurate', and one shell exploded between Johnnie and his No 2, Flying Officer RD Bowen. Hugh Godefroy remembers:-

A shell went off behind and to port of Greycap, blowing him almost over on his back. There was a pregnant silence as we all watched him come back straight and level. For a second his aircraft dodged around a little bit like a bird that had experienced a near miss. Finally he came on the R/T: "Makes you bloody think, dun it!"

Flying Officer McNamara of 421 believed flak to be responsible for putting a hole in his engine cowling, but he may, in fact, have been hit by *Oberleutnant* Sternberg, who claimed a Spitfire destroyed just off Ostend.

In his PFLB, Squadron Leader Magwood wrote:-

Flak from Ostend extremely accurate. Bob Bowen collected a piece in his intercooler from a near miss.

Magwood describes the ensuing dogfight as 'Terrific'. This was just the kind of action that the Kenley Wing needed after a few days inactivity; as the 421 Squadron diarist recorded, Circus 309 had certainly turned out to be a 'real show'.

June 1st

The weather was 7/10s cloud, perfect for the search and destroy mission, Rodeo 225, that the Kenley Wing found itself flying at 1130. The Wing was the second wave of a fighter sweep of Hardelot-Doullens-St Pol, controlled by Appledore. *Jafü* 2 scrambled I/JG 27 from Poix, and all available JG 26 fighters, to intercept, and attempted to sandwich the Spitfires between the two German formations. Greycap's pilots, however, saw some 30 plus bandits climbing from a direction of Albert, so 421 Squadron provided cover whilst 403 went down to attack. The enemy broke right, and a huge dogfight began involving some 80 aircraft. Warrant Officer AV Hargreaves, of 403, damaged one of a pair of 190s flying in close line astern at 10,000 feet. Flight Lieutenant Harry MacDonald saw 'a FW firing at an Me 109 from close range astern. This was seen by Blue 1 to go into a moderate steep dive and explode between St Pol – Hesdin. It was claimed as destroyed by the Squadron because the Squadron's attack led to the FW mistaking the 109 for a Spitfire and attacking it' (ORB, 403). In fairness the Me 109G, of I/JG 27, which this would have been, looked remarkably similar to the Spitfire, given that the design had lost the angular features of the 'Emil'. Such incidents, given the speed of combat were far more frequent than we perhaps appreciate, I am positive. That having been said, the 190 pilots of JG 26 made no claims – perhaps the 190 pilot realised his mistake!

On the way back, Greycap scored again:-

After engaging 30 plus enemy aircraft in the Doullens – St Pol area, the Wing reformed and we headed towards the French coast on the outward journey flying at 23,000 feet. When 4-5 miles inland of Berck-sur-Mer I saw about eight Me 109s behind 403 Squadron. We turned to engage and all enemy aircraft dived away except two 109s which went into a shallow dive towards Le Crotoy. Enemy aircraft were flying line abreast and I opened fire with cannon and machine-gun on the starboard aircraft from 500 closing to 300 yards. I saw several cannon strikes on the rear portion of the fuselage and on the tail plane. At 9,000 feet I broke off the attack as e/a was now diving vertically; he did not recover and I saw him crash on to the north bank of the Somme. My No 2, Flying Officer Bowen DFC also fired at this enemy aircraft and I claim it as destroyed, shared with him.

During this combat, Johnnie had fired 250 rounds of cannon, and 580 rounds of .303.

In total, I/JG 27 lost three Me 109s, including the *Kommandeur*, *Hauptmann* Erich Hohagen, who baled out wounded. Interestingly, although the Kenley Wing suffered no losses, and were the only Allied formation engaged, I/JG 27 claimed a Spitfire destroyed. This poses an interesting question. Could, perhaps, the 'Friendly Fire' 109 have been shot down not by a 190, but by another 109? Could Flight Lieutenant MacDonald himself have wrongly identifying the 109's assailant? We will never now, but an interesting moot point nonetheless.

The Kenley Wing's next offensive operation on June 1st, 1943, was Ramrod 82, in which the Spitfires were to fly third fighter sweep in support of 'Whirlibombers'. Unfortunately, France was found to be covered by cloud at 10,000 feet, so the sortie was aborted.

June 2nd
Due to showers, there was no flying and the Wing was released for 24 hours, from 1300 onwards. According to the 421 Squadron ORB, 'Majority of the pilots took advantage of the rest and went up to the big town to see the sights'.

June 3rd
The weather had improved by evening, and at 2030 the Kenley Wing was up and *en route* to Warmwell airfield, near the seaside town of Weymouth in Dorset, and remained there overnight for an operation the following day. As ever, the

requirement for operating near the coast was to increase range.

403 Squadron reported that Flying Officer R Wozniak had been posted to 55 OTU, Aston Down, for a rest. This was one of the Spitfire training schools, near Stroud in Gloucestershire, where a great many young Canadian pilots were introduced to the Spitfire. It is perhaps worth reflecting on the fact that a number of them died during that process, before ever they met the enemy. According to the 403 Squadron ORB, ' 'Wozzie had been with the Squadron for a long time and had seen many a "shakey do"'.

June 4th
Due to adverse weather, the proposed operation from Warmwell was cancelled, so the Kenley Wing returned home. Wing Commander Johnson used the time to talk to 421 Squadron about tactical formations, after which Squadron Leader Hall led his pilots on a practice flight of 45 minutes duration.

June 5th
Again the only flying was non-operational. Flight Lieutenant Quint of 421 Squadron left Kenley for a Combined Operations Course, and Warrant Officer Barnett received notification of posting on a Special Low Level Attack Course.

June 6th
Although the weather was fair over England, conditions over Northern France led once again to a 'show' being cancelled.

Sergeant NF Houghton landed with wheels-up at Shoreham, but he was fortunately unscathed. Flight Lieutenant Cadham, 421's Medical Officer, was posted from the Squadron. His replacement arrived and was none other than Flight Lieutenant GR Hall, a brother of the CO.

June 7th
Although the weather had improved, the day's first show was aborted. At 1100, however, the Kenley Wing was up and bound for France on Rodeo 227, a sweep of Gravelines, Aire and Sangatte under Appledore. No enemy aircraft were seen but heavy flak was fired from Calais, bursting below and behind 403 Squadron.

June 8th
Due to the weather being 'duff' (ORB, 421), the only sorties carried out were

three non-operational flights by 403. The pilots were given lectures on aircraft recognition and dinghy drill, followed by a movie, 'Next of Kin'.

New filtered through to 403 Squadron that Pilot Officer Willie Lane had been killed on May 15th, and that Pilot Officer Charles Cumming, missing since an engagement on March 13th, had been buried by the Germans at Le Touquet.

June 9th

As the weather was still 'duff', all available pilots first watched a technicolour film on camouflage. 421 Squadron then practised formation flying, led by Flight Lieutenant Blades, whilst Squadron Leader Hall led a section of four as 'jumpers'. Whilst practising a crossover turn, however, Flying Officers Sherlock and McFarlane collided at 10,000 feet. The latter was trapped in his spinning machine, but managed to extricate himself and bale out safely at 3,000 feet. The young Canadian landed safely in some treetops just east of Crowborough. Although Sherlock's port wing was badly damaged, he managed to jettison his auxiliary fuel tank in the Channel before making a safe wheels-up landing back at base.

403 Squadron recorded that Flying Officer GD Aitkin had been posted away on rest, commenting that 'Georgie has been on a good many shakey "dos" since he came to England, having baled out near the English coast returning from a sweep, and he certainly deserves a rest. Everyone was sorry to see him go'.

Greycap flew a performance test on a 'modified Spitfire V' (PFLB).

June 10th

Only non-operational flights were carried out. Pilot Officer Johnson of 421 Squadron, engaged on a tail-chasing exercise with Flight Lieutenant Blades, developed a glycol leak and had to make a wheels-up landing at Biggin Hill.

The Wing was released at 1300 for 24 hours.

June 11th

An early ground haze cleared and the sun came out. At 1605, Wing Commander Johnson took off with his Wing on Rodeo 229, this time leading at the head of 421 Squadron. In this operation the Kenley Wing was to be the second wave of a fighter sweep between Abbeville and Poix. At 25,000 feet over the latter, 15 plus bandits, mainly Me 109s, were seen flying from a direction of

Abbeville and 1,000 feet below. Greycap turned his Spitfires to starboard and engaged with 421 Squadron, the fighters whirling around between 26,000 down to 7,000 feet. Squadron Leader Hall shot the tail unit completely off a 109, and damaged another, but although other pilots of 421 Squadron fired their guns there were no other claims. As the Squadron's ORB states, it was a 'good show'.

June 12th

7/10ths cloud early on cleared throughout the day, and orders were received for Ramrod 91. The Kenley Wing was again to provide the second wave of a fighter sweep, this time in support of Bostons attacking the Grand Quevilly power station at Rouen. The Spitfires went out over Shoreham at 10,000 feet, climbing and crossing the French coast above Etretat at 16,000 feet. Over Tricqueville, at 22,000 feet, the Wing turned to port, flying due east, when six FW 190s were seen to the north, following the coast. Soon after turning to follow these bandits, however, the Spitfire pilots lost sight of their quarry and so turned about to investigate another formation. North of Rouen, 15 Me 109s were seen below the Spitfires, but these were just bait. Above the 109s were another 20 enemy fighters, up sun. The Wing immediately set off in pursuit when three more 109s were seen, flying in a 'vic' formation, well spread out and to starboard of the main gaggle, and 1,000 feet below. Greycap despatched Flying Officer NR Fowlow with his Blue Section to intercept. Blue 1 blasted the starboard 109 with cannon and machine gun. Strikes appeared on the cockpit, engine and port wing. Suddenly the port wing exploded and broke off. The 109 was last seen by Fowlow and his Blue 2, Pilot Officer JC Elliott, going down out of control and pouring black smoke. Blue 4, Flying Officer Bob Middlemiss, attacked the centremost 109, as the German rolled onto his back, and saw strikes on the 109's belly before having to break upwards. Wing Commander Johnson, leading Red Section, also fired at the vic of 109s but without result.

Having 'lost sight of the main gaggle by now' (ORB, 403), the Wing reformed and headed home, landing at 2025.

Back at Kenley there was an important change of personnel, as the 403 Squadron ORB relates:-

Squadron Leader CM Magwood DFC was taken away from 403 Squadron today and posted to RAF Station Kenley as Gunnery Officer for the Wing, with effect from 13.06.43. He has done well for himself in 403 Squadron, having been promoted from a Pilot Oficer through the ranks to Squadron Leader of our Squadron and then winning the DFC. Squadron Leader Magwood has always shown a great interest in the Squadron and its personnel, and everyone was sorry to see him leave but he has earned a well-deserved rest. Flight Lieutenant HC Godefroy DFC now promoted to the rank of Squadron Leader and CO of 403 Squadron. He has also done very well, having won his DFC as a Flight Commander in our Squadron. He succeeds Squadron Leader Magwood and has taken over command of the Squadron as of today.

June 13th
The weather having improved, it would be a busy day.

First, the Kenley Wing was detailed to fly Ramrod 93, the second wave of a fighter sweep in support of Bostons attacking Gosnay power station, near Bethune. At 0945, Greycap led the Spitfires off. At 24,000 feet over Fruges, two formations each of 15 bandits were sighted. Before the Wing could attack one of these, however, the Germans awoke to the danger and rapidly made off. By 1125 the Wing was safely back at Kenley and preparing for Ramrod 94.

At 1345, Wing Commander Johnson led the Wing to Abbeville, sweeping over Doullens, Hoinoy and Montreuil at 26,000 feet. No enemy aircraft were seen, so the Spitfires returned home.

Before the day was over, the pilots were given a talk about the new 'Tactical Air Force in Great Britain' by an Army officer. The pilots concluded that this was 'very interesting' (ORB, 421). It is certainly worthy of further explanation.

Fighter Command had originally been created as a defensive force, but when the long awaited invasion of enemy occupied France eventually came, there would clearly be a change of role. Then, RAF fighter pilots would not be defending their homeland, as in 1940, but on the contrary providing tactical support to the advancing British and Canadian armies (the American Ninth Air Force would similarly support American troops). The Allied fighters would also have to ensure aerial supremacy over the battlefield, and become mobile units able to keep up with the advancing armies. The idea was, therefore, to create composite, tactical, force of fighters, bombers, fighter-bombers and army co-operation aircraft, independent of existing Commands. This tactical air force would exist exclusively for deployment in support of the Allied Expeditionary

Force, which was being formed to undertake the proposed invasion. On June 1st, 1943, this new aerial entity officially became the 2nd Tactical Air Force (TAF), comprising largely units formerly of No 2 Group Bomber Command (the RAF's light bomber force) and various from Fighter Command. Soon, Fighter Command itself would, in fact, cease to exist altogether, the responsibility for home defence becoming that of 'Air Defence Great Britain'.

June 14th

There were no operational sorties, and the pilots received another talk regarding the 'new mobile air force' by Captain Feenborough.

On this day, Wing Commander Johnson analysed his operational flying on this tour, which had started on July 13th, 1942, and wrote the result in his PFLB:-

Operational Flying Times this Tour	120.30
Nos of Circuses	37
Nos of Ramrods	16
Nos of Rodeos	20
Nos of Roadsteads	NIL
Nos of Rhubarbs	2

An impressive account, by any standards.

At the other end of the spectrum, at this time, was Flying Officer J Danforth Brown, who had only recently started flying on operations with 403 Squadron. Of that early period he remembered:-

Getting into the combat experience, you were first treated like a mother treats a chick, get your feet under you and then start to think up there in the air. I remember telling Johnnie, the first time that I flew in combat, which was with him, that if someone had asked me what my name was I was not sure that I could have remembered it! He bounced a 109, and my job was to stay with him and cover him. I saw this plane right in front of us, right close, and all of a sudden I saw little tiny puffs of something, all the while thinking in nano-seconds, all the while thinking 'Well, I wonder what in the world that is?', when I realised, idiot, that he was shooting a plane down! We watched it take on fire and smoke and watched it crash into the Somme delta. With that, you steadily gained more experience, but when you first start, you just don't get the opportunities. Remember that the German Air Force was not to be sneezed at.

One of the great things about war is that you have to learn to get along with and be trusted by your fellow pilots. If you're not accepted then you might as well go home.

June 15ᵗʰ

Although a showery day with a good deal of low cloud, the Kenley Wing was briefed regarding Ramrod 95, providing the second wave of high cover to elements of a force comprising 40 B-17s bombing Bernay aerodrome. Due to adverse weather, however, the bombers aborted before reaching the rendezvous over Fecamp, so Greycap was given permission to proceed inland at his own discretion. Climbing towards Rouen, Appledore informed Johnnie of bandits nearby. Going down to 24,000 feet, the Spitfire pilots saw 15 FW 190s of I/ JG 2 flying in line abreast. Ordering 421 Squadron to remain as top cover, Greycap led 403 Squadron down to attack the bandits, which were 2,000 feet below and ahead. Johnnie attacked and destroyed the starboard 190. Another 15 FW 190s were then seen up sun and to port, apparently top cover to the first enemy formation. Greycap immediately ordered 421 Squadron to engage, wheeling 403 Squadron back round and after them, and shot down the rearmost 190. Squadron Leader Godefroy, fired at a 190 which crashed NW of Rouen. Flight Lieutenant MacDonald hit another, which he later claimed as probably destroyed, and Flying Officer Bowen, again flying wingman to Greycap, damaged another. By 0910 hours the Wing was safely down, the press later making much of the fact that Wing Commander Johnnie Johnson, the fighter 'ace' from Melton Mowbray, had got 'two Huns before breakfast'. The probability, however, is that only one of those was definitely destroyed, as I/JG 2, the only enemy unit engaged, is known to have lost two 190s in this combat, and clearly Squadron Leader Godefroy's was a certainty. The newspapers were right about one thing, however, describing Johnnie's Canadian Wing as 'one of the busiest in Fighter Command'.

Back at Kenley, Squadron Leader PLI Archer DFC reported to 421 Squadron as 'supernumerary for operational flying' (ORB, 421).

June 16ᵗʰ

A completely overcast day, there were no operational sorties and very few of a non-operational nature. At 1300, the Wing was released for 24 hours.

June 17ᵗʰ

From dawn until 0830, 421 Squadron was at Readiness, although there was no scramble. The Squadron's CO, Squadron Leader Hall, was posted on rest to

58 OTU, the ORB recording that 'All sorry to lose our chief who was a good fellow and well liked by all personnel'. His place was taken by Squadron Leader Philip Leslie Irving Archer DFC, who had reported as 'supernumerary' just two days previously. Archer had flown with the highly successful 92 Squadron from Biggin Hill during 1941, thence 416 Squadron the following year. He had now returned to operations following, it is believed, a spell as an instructor, with five enemy aircraft destroyed and one damaged to his credit. Interestingly, his last claim was a Do 217 on July 18th, 1942, and all those previous were Me 109s. He had not yet met the FW 190.

The weather was reportedly 5/10ths cloud and very windy, but nevertheless the Kenley Wing received orders to fly Rodeo 231. In this operation, the Wing was to provide the third wave of a fighter sweep of the Pas-de-Calais. Greycap led the Spitfires out over Dover at 15,000 feet, crossing into France at 24,000 feet over Gravelines. 'Sector Operations' (PCR, JEJ) informed Greycap of the presence of some 30 plus 190s climbing from Ypres towards Dunkirk.

Earlier in the day, a dozen Bostons had attacked Vlissingen, and elements of JG 26 had engaged the Spitfires providing rear cover off Zeebrugge. When the first wave of the afternoon Rodeo swept in, *Jafü* 2 expected bombers to follow, but when this did not happen two *Gruppen* of JG 26 were vectored towards the last wave of Spitfires, the Kenley Wing.

The Spitfires slowly orbitted until the bandits were sighted climbing towards the French coast, strung out in line abreast, and some 10,000 feet below. This was the *Geschwadergruppe*, acting as bait, whilst *Hauptmann* 'Wutz' Galland, *Kommandeur* of II/JG 26 and brother of the legendary 'Dolfo', climbed his 190s with the intention of bouncing the Spitfires as the latter took the bait. As predicted, the Spitfires pounced. Wing Commander Johnson led 421 Squadron down and attacked the last *schwarm* of 190s, as his PCR relates:-

I attacked No 2 on the starboard side, and as I commenced fire with cannon and m/g he turned slowly to starboard. I closed in to 150 yards range and saw cannon strikes on the cockpit and wing roots. As I was overshooting, I gave him a final burst and pulled steeply upwards, the enemy aircraft caught fire and started to burn, spiralling slowly down.

Johnnie had hit *Unteroffizier* Günther Freitag, of 8/JG 26, who crashed and was killed at Steenvorde in Flanders. A confused fight followed which involved 80-100 FW 190s and some 24 Spitfires.

By this time, Galland was diving into the Spitfires' rear, so the two Kenley squadrons turned to face the attack. Flying Officer KP Marshall, Yellow 3 of 403 Squadron, saw Squadron Leader Archer of 421 Squadron flying alongside him at about 21,000 feet. Marshall saw two 190s closing in on Archer, and was about to yell 'Break!' when his own aircraft was hit. He broke upwards and to port but did not see the 421 Squadron CO again. Flight Sergeant GM Shouldice, Yellow 4, fired a long burst of cannon and machine-gun at Yellow 3's assailant, but then had to break due to being attacked himself. Although Shouldice himself so no result, his kill was confirmed by Pilot Officer Bullick of 421, who saw a '190 with bits flying off and streaming black smoke, going straight down' (ORB, 403).

Having disengaged, Blue Section of 403 Squadron came out over France at 16,000 feet, whilst Red and Yellow Sections turned back inland over France to allow Marshall and Shouldice time to catch up. The former's aircraft was damaged, but the young Canadian managed to land safely at Redhill.

Squadron Leader Archer of 421 was credited with having destroyed a 190, but sadly the new CO failed to return himself. Flying Officer McNamara of the same Squadron was awarded a 190 'damaged', but he too was 'Missing'. According to the ORB, he was a 'grand little guy', and both casualties were a 'sad loss' to the Squadron. Although it was hoped that both pilots had baled out and were safe, although prisoners, sadly both were killed. The 27-year old Squadron Leader Archer was buried at Longuenesse Souvenir Cemetery, St Omer, but Flying Officer James Emmett McNamara was not found; he is remembered on panel 174 of the Runnymede Memorial.

Oberleutnant Horst Sternberg, *Staffelkapitän* of 5/JG 26, was awarded a Spitfire destroyed, 5km SW of Hazebrouck, and *Unteroffizier* Paul Schwarz, of 6/JG 26, made his first 'kill' 10km SW of St Omer. Both German kills were made in roughly the same area, therefore, which makes sense given that both of the Kenley Wing's casualties were from the same squadron. It is therefore impossible to say which German shot down which Spitfire pilot. Sternberg's kill was timed at 1545, and at the same time he later reported having collided with a Spitfire, forcing him to bale out, wounded. As none of the Kenley pilots reported having witnessed such a collision, the probability is that

Sternberg collided with the crashing Spitfire of either Archer or McNamara.

Back at Kenley, the Wing claimed three FW 190s destroyed and one damaged. The Germans had, in fact, lost two, Freitag to Johnnie and Sternberg to an alleged collision. Given that Sternberg was only wounded, however, and both of the missing Kenley pilots dead, in human terms JG 26 were the winners of this combat.

The following day, the British press reported:-

A Canadian Spitfire Wing added three more FW 190s to its score during a sweep over Belgium yesterday afternoon, bringing the day's score of our fighters up to a total of nine enemy aircraft destroyed.

The Canadians' three victims were destroyed in a series of combats between Ypres and the coast at heights varying rom 22,000 feet to 26,000 feet. The Wing was led by Wing Commander JE Johnson DSO DFC & bar, who himself shot down a FW 190, bringing his score to 17.

The Spitfires first encountered a formation of about 30 enemy aircraft. Shortly after a dogfight with them about 20 more enemy fighters were seen. The Spitfires immediately dived in amongst the FW 190s and scattered the formation.

Two of our Spitfires are missing.

On the evening of June 17th, a farewell dinner was held in the Officers' Mess at Kenley for the Station Commander, the popular Group Captain Jimmy Fenton, and 421's former CO, Squadron Leader Hall. The tenure of office of the latter's successor, Squadron Leader Archer, must have been one of the shortest on record as he was CO of 421 Squadron for just a few hours. This emphasises how quickly fortunes and emotions could change in this exciting but deadly business.

Many years later there was an unexpected sequel to this sad story.

In 1995, I started working on a book concerning the period March – August 1941, when Wing Commander Bader led his famous Tangmere Wing. Amongst matters under investigation was the confused events of August 9th, 1941, when 'Dogsbody' was brought down over France and captured in circumstances yet to be fully explained, to my satisfaction anyway. It was hoped that if the crash site of his Spitfire, a Mk VA, W3185, could be found, the resulting artefacts might yield certain clues. Furthermore, if the remains of this Spitfire could be recovered, certain items might be conserved and included in a travelling exhibition aimed at increasing the profile of The Douglas Bader Foundation (the registered charity founded as a living memorial by 'DB's' family and friends after his death in 1982). Accordingly, I engaged the assistance of my close French friend, Dr Bernard-Marie Dupont, a fellow author and historian, who had lived in the Pas-de-Calais all his life.

To cut a long story short (but as recounted in my *Bader's Tangmere Spitfires*, see Bibliography), all we had to go on was the fact that the combat concerned had taken place in the 'area of St Omer', that being the only location given in the claims of both sides. From Paul Brickhill's best-selling Bader biography *Reach for the Sky*, we knew that Wing Commander Bader had been taken to a hospital in St Omer, from which he later escaped, being recaptured whilst hiding at the home of an elderly local lady. Bernard was soon at work, tracking down the descendants of that brave patriot, Madame Hiècque, who now lived in the house next door to where those dramatic events of 1941 had taken place. From there the trail led to Madame Petit, widow of Gilbert who had escorted 'Le Colonel' through St Omer's curfewed streets after the legless fugitive had knotted bedsheets together and climbed down this makeshift rope from his ward on the Clinique Sterin's first floor. Next to provie information was one Georges Goblet, a child during the Second World War, now an amateur local historian. According to Georges, he knew where 'Le Colonel Bader' had crashed, and could introduce us to an eyewitness, Arthur Dubreu. Soon I too was in France and interviewed Dubreu who told us that as a 13-year old boy he had seen an apparently one-legged RAF pilot land by parachute in a field near Steenbecque. That afternoon he visited the Spitfire's crash site at nearby Blaringhem. Only years later, when Brickhill's book was published in French, did Arthur realise that he had seen the great 'Colonel Bader'.

Soon we were standing in a Flanders field where, George and Artur claimed, the Spitfire had crashed. Searching the ploughed surface, we found several fragments of what was undoubtedly aircraft. My concern was that, given the quantity of aircraft brought down in this area between 1940-44, and considering the human memory's fallibility, it could be any type from a Hurricane to a Mustang. Then we happened across an oval piece of sheet aluminium bearing a serial number starting '300', which, as any Spitfire 'buff' knows, indicates the Spitfire part numeric prefix. So, it was a Spitfire! Furthermore, the piece also bore the stamp '6S', confirming that this item had been manufactured at Southampton. This appeared significant as Bader's Spitfire was one of only 124 Mk VAs, all of which were built at Southampton (as opposed to the Castle Bromwich Aircraft Factory which was producing most Spitfires from thereon).

Again cutting a long story short, our excavation, 'Operation Dogsbody', took place in May 1996, attracting a huge amount of media interest all over the world. As usual, the press had jumped the gun, proclaiming that we had 'Found Bader's Plane in French Field' (Sunday Telegraph). In reality, and as correctly reported by The Independent, although the circumstantial evidence was certainly strong, we knew that until we had excavated the site we could not be sure. Even then, due to problems associated with locating serial numbers, we also knew that it might never actually be possible to identify the aircraft involved beyond doubt.

The excavation, however, was awesome, although we knew very early on that this was not Wing Commander Bader's eight Browning machine-gun armed Mk VA. Close to the surface was the remains of a single, exploded, 20mm Hispano shell, immediately indicating that this was not a VA. Then a broad, metal, propeller making us suspect that this was a Mk IX. As the mechanical digger worked away, a huge amount of crumpled, oily, Spitfire emerged from the hole. At 17 feet deep we found the Merlin engine, the rocker covers of which still proudly bore the name 'Rolls Royce', and a boss allowing for four propeller blades. We knew then that this was definitely a Mk IX, but which one?

During the excavation we were approached by a Monsieur Queurleu, who was living locally at the time of the crash and told us that the victorious German pilot had visited the crash site and removed a souvenir. He was also able to confirm that the Allied pilot had been killed, and that the Germans had dug out his remains, which they took away compacted into the cockpit, the wreckage of which was also removed. That explained two things. Firstly, again shortly after the excavation had started, Larry McHale had found the metal remains of a privately purchased wristwatch, and a section of Mae West lifejacket. We suspected then that this was a fatality, and became concerned that the pilot's remains may not have been recovered. Fortunately this fear was unfounded, as no human remains were either disturbed or found.

Secondly, although we had recovered masses of Spitfire, no cockpit items were amongst the haul. We now knew why.

Eventually, my friend, colleague and 'Dogsbody' team-member, John Foreman, the 'oracle' on the subject of losses and claims, was able to provide just one potential candidate from a shortlist of a staggering 69 possibilities: LZ996 of 421 Squadron, flown by Squadron Leader Phillip Leslie Archer DFC of 421 Squadron. Records indicated that LZ996 had been lost on June 17th, 1943, nearly two years after Wing Commander Bader. Monsieur Dubreu had no reason to lie, and I am sure that he really did see 'Le Colonel' land by parachute. Over the years since, however, my belief is that his mind had confused the two separate incidents into one and the same.

The Commonwealth War Graves Commission confirmed that Squadron Leader Archer's grave could be found at Longuenesse Souvenir Cemetery, just across the road from the old German airfield at St Omer. Soon Bernard and I were there, paying our respects, but found that Squadron Leader Archer's headstone indicated that he had been a 'Air Gunner/Instructor'. Back home, I provided the Commission with the necessary evidence to prove that Archer, who hailed from the British West Indies, was actually a *pilot*, and the correction was eventually made accordingly. It was a moving moment for both Bernard and myself.

The bulk of LZ996 remains in France with Bernard, pending a decision over where it will eventually be displayed. Here I have the propeller blade, instrument, seat and head armour, both compressed air bottles and the oxygen bottle, which will be displayed at various locations upon publication of this book.

So, although not 'Le Colonel's' Spitfire, what a coincidence that this should transpire to be a Spitfire of the Kenley Wing, lost on a sweep led by none other than Johnnie Johnson himself who, by further coincidence, was a keen supporter of both 'Operation Dogsbody' and my Tangmere related research! It gave me great pleasure, during the research for this book, to show the Spitfire's remains to Johnnie and his great friend Dan Browne, who name appears throughout this book. What both men were thinking as they ran their hands over the twisted metal I could only imagine. Dan provided their departed comrade's epitaph:-

Sure, I remember Phil, he used to go with the 'Queen Bee', the chief WAAF!

June 18th

A day of 10/10ths cloud, there was no operational flying for the Kenley Wing. During the afternoon, the pilots of 403 Squadron watched an educational film on 'Sex Hygiene', followed by a movie, 'Talk of the Town'. 421 Squadron flew a number of training sorties, a Spitfire Mk V being flown by Sergeant Ball crashing on landing back on Kenley. The aircraft was damaged but the pilot was fortunately unhurt. At 1300, the Squadron was released, at which time most of the pilots 'migrated to London, attending the wedding of P/O PD Smith who left the Squadron on June 5th (ORB).

The outgoing Station Commander, Group Captain Jimmy Fenton, sums up his time at Kenley:-

For the first time I had enjoyed a comfortable office with staff, and I kept wondering if it was another incarnation! The whole Sector comprised some 2,000 people, nearly half of them WAAF working in or associated with the Ops Room. 1,000 or so Canadians and 800 WAAF was a deadly combination!

As Wing Leader, Johnnie Johnson was undoubtedly type-cast for the role, being outstandingly successful both as a fighter pilot and leader. As we were the most successful Sector in the Group, some reflected glory came my way, of which I was always happy to be the recipient! We were in a well organised and well-led Group with Air Vice-Marshal 'Dingbat' Saunders as AOC. Morale was at its highest. It was the lead up to the invasion, still a year ahead, and the phase was vitally important in providing the disciplined and experienced fighter force that we were, in the event, lucky to have.

Kenley seemed to have everything, and sometimes I was able to entertain in style. I remember particularly a lunch for Wing Commander 'Billy' Burton and Squadron Leader 'Pedro' Hanbury, both back from North Africa for a fighter leaders' conference. Our catering officer had excelled himself with food and drink, and, as it happened, Johnnie's first DSO had just come through. Billy and Johnnie had, of course, flown together in 616 Squadron, which Billy then commanded. A Cranwell Sword of Honour man, Billy Burton was apparently destined for great things, but it was sadly not to be. During the return flight to North Africa, the Hudson in which he and Hanbury were passengers was shot down over the Bay of Biscay. Between them, the officers lost in that Hudson had three DSOs, three DFCs and an MC. It was a great loss to the Desert Air Force and was kept secret for a while. None of the men were ever found. The first that I heard of it was when Billy's wife, Jean, called me saying that she had heard that Billy was missing and could I get details. What a tragedy.

Group Captain Fenton's successor as Station Commander at Kenley was 28-year old Group Captain PG Wykeham-Barnes DSO DFC & Bar, who for two years had been in the thick of fighting out in the Western Desert and over Malta. Reporting on the appointment, newspapers published that 'A Mosquito intruder pilot whose favourite 'sport' when, based on Malta, was train-busting in Italy and Sicily, now commands a front-line fighter station in SE England'.

June 19th

Again due to the weather there was no operational flying. The pilots watched their practice and operational cine films in the Wing Pilots' Room. One Section of 403 Squadron was scrambled to Horsham at 20,000 feet, but saw nothing. Apparently 'some Huns playing on the other side but did not attempt to cross the Channel' (ORB). Squadron Leader RW Buck McNair DFC reported from 416 Squadron to take command of 421 Squadron, whilst Flight Sergeant Decourcy, of the same Squadron, received notice of his commission and moved into the Officers' Mess. Just like earlier in the war, although Sections were of mixed rank in the air, on the ground, whilst off duty, officers and non-commissioned ranks remained largely segregated.

June 20th

The weather significantly improved, being sunny and bright with only 3/10ths cloud and a light south-westerly wind. Circus 313 was scheduled for mid-day, and the Kenley Wing was to be led by the CO of 403 Squadron, Squadron Leader Hugh Godefroy. During this sortie, the Canadians were to sweep over the Abbeville, Amiens and Poix area ahead of 12 Bostons which were to bomb Poix aerodrome.

At 1230, the Kenley Wing was up, crossing out over Rye and joining up with the Hornchurch Wing. Climbing across the Channel, the Spitfires crossed the French coast above Quend-Plage at 12,000 feet, flying thence to Abbeville and Amiens at 22,000 feet, reaching Poix at 23,000. Appledore Control then gave a vector of 010°, the Wing reaching Aux-le-Chateaux at 24,000 feet. Again, these were the FW 190s of the *Geschwadergruppe* and II/JG 26, with which the Kenley Wing had clashed just three days before. The former engaged the Hornchurch Spitfires, whilst *Hauptmann* Galland split the latter into two formations.

Yellow Section of 403 Squadron went down to intercept three FW 190s flying 1,000 feet below and in the opposite direction, but were unable to engage. Six more 190s were then sighted, with 12 more cutting round behind the Wing at 24,000 feet. Godefroy turned his Spitfires to face the attack, and 421 Squadron was the first to engage. Squadron Leader McNair was the first to fire, shooting down *Unteroffizier* Erwin Hancke of 4/JG 26, who was wounded and subsequently crash-landed at Douai. Pilot Officer Sherlock, also of 421, claimed a 190 'probable'.

After the initial charge, the Wing had split up and this Squadron Leader Godefroy tried to address whilst the Spitfires approached Abbeville. A further 50 plus FW 190s were then seen bearing down on the Kenley Wing, this preventing the heavily outnumbered Spitfires from re-forming. 403 Squadron dived towards the Somme Estuary, but Blue Section became cut off from the Squadron. Near Aux-Le-Chateaux, Flight Lieutenant MacDonald, Blue 1, spotted a 190 making for Sergeant KD Windsor, Blue 4, and immediately shouted "Blue Section, break!" The warning came too late, however, and Blue 4 went down trailing black smoke. Afterwards, Blue Section tried to re-form, but Blue 2, Pilot Officer JC Elliott, dived, apparently due to oxygen failure. Blue 1 & 3, Pilot Officer FC McWilliams, followed but lost sight of 2 in cloud. Now completely isolated, the two surviving pilots of Blue Section made for the coast. Almost immediately the Spitfire pair ran into a gaggle of 20 190s, and one actually formated on the Canadians! Blue 1 again shouted "Break!", but instead of hauling sharply round, Blue 3 described a gentle turn – and was hit hard by a 190. The last Blue 1 saw of McWilliams was him in a spin, still pursued by eight 190s. Blue 1 himself was still in the woods, however, and south of Le Touquet was engaged by more 190s, which he managed to skilfully out-turn before landing at Friston, on the south coast. 421 Squadron, meanwhile, had climbed to 32,000 feet, and crossed out safely over Cap-Gris-Nez.

The three Kenley pilots had fallen victim to *Hauptmann* Galland, *Kommodore* of II/JG 26, *Oberfeldwebel* Glunz and *Unteroffizier* Crump, of 4 & 5/JG 26 respectively. Blue 2, Pilot Officer JC Elliott, was never found and is now remembered on panel 173 at Runnymede, and Blue 3, Pilot Officer FC McWilliams, now rests in the British Military Cemetery at Etaples, near Le Touquet. Blue 4, Sergeant KD Windsor, was more fortunate in that he survived this traumatic engagement to become a prisoner.

June 21st

Despite fine and sunny weather, apart from a few uneventful scrambles, the Kenley Wing flew no operational sorties of any significance. Both 403 and 421 Squadrons, however, flew co-operation sorties with two P-47 Thunderbolts 'now attached to Kenley' (ORB, 421).

June 22nd

At 0500, the 'Wingco' briefed his pilots regarding Ramrod 99, in which the Kenley Spitfires were to meet and escort a formation of B-17s returning from attacking industrial targets in Germany's Ruhr Valley. By now, the Americans had accepted that if the daylight offensive was to continue, especially in the absence of a long-range offensive escort fighter, priority must be given to targets connected with the *Luftwaffe*. These included not only enemy airfields but also targets connected with the German aviation industry, such as aircraft factories and other associated depots. The target today, for 235 Flying Fortresses of the 381st and 384th Bomb Groups, was the synthetic rubber plant at Hüls. As Germany was cut off from supplies of natural rubber, this *Chemische Werke* was of vital importance to the aircraft manufacturing industry given that it produced 30% of the nation's total output of synthetic rubber. This trip to the Ruhr was the deepest penetration so far attempted by the Americans, and amongst the formation were the B-24 YB-40 'escorts'. The Ruhr flak belt, as RAF Bomber Command knew only too well, was lethal, however, and this time the bombers also had to run the gauntlet of *Jafü* Holland-Ruhr.

At 0540, the Kenley Wing took off, pancaking, at Manston, at 0615. At 0930, the Spitfires were up again, bound for the Dutch coast. Greycap set course for Schouwen Island, which was reached at 20,000 feet, and from there inland to Sleidrecht, over which the Spitfires arrived at 24,000 feet. Six boxes of B-17s were seen coming out over the Dutch coast, escorted by 'Little Friends', crossing out over Schouwen between 24-27,000 feet. The Kenley Wing remained over the exit point until the last box of bombers had left. Although some 20 Me 109s and FW 190s were seen, no substantial attacks were made and the Canadian Spitfires were not engaged.

The bombers had, in fact, hit the target accurately and hard. Just under a quarter of the total tonnage of bombs dropped had fallen within the factory itself, the damage arising rendering the factory completely useless for a month, and normal production was not resumed for a further six. Sixteen bombers were lost, including a YB-40 which was destroyed by flak, and 170 more B-17s were damaged. Over the North Sea, about 40 miles west of Schouwen, the Kenley pilots saw a Fortress at 5,000 feet, covered by eight Spitfires. Later, a large flash was seen mid-Channel, and when the Spitfires arrived over the area shortly afterwards, large patches of oil marked the last resting place of more brave American airmen.

At 1130, Wing Commander Johnson and two pilots of 403 Squadron landed back at base, whilst the others pancaked at coastal aerodromes, short of fuel.

Another show was planned for the afternoon, the Wing being led off by Greycap at 1554 on Circus 341. Together with the Hornchurch Wing, the Canadians were to support 12 Venturas withdrawing after bombing Abbeville aerodrome. Whilst the Spitfires were in the Abbeville area, an aircraft was seen going down in flames, and a large fire was seen near Dieppe. Seven enemy aircraft were seen, but these were too far east and could not, therefore, be engaged. The sortie was otherwise without incident and Johnnie's Spitfires were back at Kenley by 1728. As the 421 Squadron ORB commented, it had been a 'long day'.

Of interest is that the Kenley Wing operated in conjunction with the Hornchurch Spitfires, led by the New Zealand 'ace', Wing Commander WV Crawford-Compton DFC & Bar. The Spitfires, as we have seen, always seemed to be outnumbered over France, so Johnnie thought it worth trying to meet the Germans on equal terms. Air Vice-Marshal 'Dingbat' Saunders agreed to an experiment, and arranged that the Kenley and Hornchurch Wings would operate together. This represented a four-squadron force of Spitfire Mk IXs, some 48 aircraft in total.

During the Battle of Britain, and as we now know, the Duxford 'Big Wing' clearly did not work in a defensive role. In 1941, Wings comprising three Spitfire squadrons frequently over claimed and rapidly became fragmented once enemy fighters were engaged. When large numbers of fighters were engaged, the greatest danger seemed to be a collision, as on August 9th, 1941, when the Tangmere Wing and JG 26 clashed over St Omer, and Wing Commander Bader was lost. Given Wing Commander Johnson's experience, it surprised me that he proposed this tactic. Johnnie:-

It was just that the Huns always had greater numbers, which didn't seem to cause them problems from a defensive viewpoint, which is perhaps worth studying, so we just thought that it was worth a go.

June 23rd

First thing in the morning, Johnnie flew up to Hornchurch and worked out the finer points with Wing Commander Crawford-Compton, then returned to Kenley, all ready for Ramrod 100. Over Beachy Head, the Kenley and Hornchurch Wings met and rendezvoused with 17 Flying Fortresses bound for Bernay aerodrome. After a penetration of 10 miles into hostile airspace, the bombers turned back due to unfavourable weather conditions. The Allied force returned without incident via St Valery.

June 24th

A clear, warm and still day, this would be the Kenley Wing's busiest day so far in 1943, and would set the scene for high summer.

After an early briefing, Greycap led his Spitfires up from Kenley at 0705, on Ramrod 102, a sortie that did not include the Hornchurch Wing. The Spitfires roared over Deal at zero feet, climbing to 18,000 feet en route to Flushing docks, which was being bombed by 12 No 2 Group Bostons. The Spitfires swept over the target, which was smoking, at 25,000 feet, and experienced some accurate and heavy flak. After sweeping Nieuport and Ostend, the Kenley Wing returned via Deal, having seen not one enemy aircraft.

The next sortie was Ramrod 103, in which the Kenley Wing was to fly the second wave of a fighter sweep over the Le Touquet, Fruges and St Omer areas, in support of 2 Group Bostons attacking railway facilities at St Omer. Greycap climbed the Spitfires hard immediately after take-off, at 1125, crossing out over Rye. When 10 miles off Hardelot, Appledore informed Johnnie that there were bandits off Cap-Gris-Nez at 25,000 feet. After several orbits, during which the Spitfires clawed for more height, the French coast was crossed at 24,000 feet over Le Touquet. Appledore then vectored Greycap north-east of Hazebrouck, where Flight Lieutenant HD MacDonald, Red 3 of 403 Squadron, sighted what appeared to be three Me 109s below at 14,000 feet. Together with Red 4, Sergeant D Small, Red 3 was despatched to engage the enemy, but the Germans dived away and escaped. Red 3 and 4 then re-joined Red Section, Red 1 being Greycap, and Red 2 Flying Officer NJ Ogilvie, and the Wing proceeded to St Omer.

Whilst the Spitfires cruised at 25,000 feet, 15 FW 190s, in several small formations, were reported at 18,000 feet, so Greycap, leaving 421 Squadron as top cover, ordered Yellow Section of 403 Squadron down to engage whilst he led Red Section towards some other bandits. Again, however, the Germans half-rolled away and refused to engage. Whilst Red 3 followed Red 1 and 2 down, however, a Spitfire suddenly cut between him and the leading pair. To avoid a collision, MacDonald immediately broke to starboard, and upon straightening out at 20,000 feet he saw two formations of enemy aircraft being chased by Spitfires, and a third gaggle which broke starboard and went into a defensive circle. These six FW 190s soon straightened out, in pairs. Red 3 dived out of a steep turn onto the port aircraft of the last pair and delivered a short burst of cannon and machine-gun fire from 150 yards. The Canadian noted strikes on his target's port wing, then, upon breaking away, saw the 190 doing a series of lazy downward rolls. At 6,000 feet a parachute opened adjacent to this 190, making MacDonald believe that he had destroyed it. What had, in fact, happened, however, was that Red 4, Sergeant Small, had been attacked and shot down by *Unteroffizier* Gomann, of 5/JG 26, and it was he who MacDonald had seen bale out. The latter had hit and wounded *Oberfeldwebel* Alfred Günther, also of 5th *Staffel*, but the German managed to land his damaged 190 safely at Vitry.

After Yellow Section's unsuccessful attack, the Spitfires were shadowed to the coast by some 10 FW 190s, but no interception took place. Having left France over Cap-Gris-Nez at 27,000 feet, heavy flak had tracked the Wing from St Omer to the coast. Throughout the entire proceedings, 421 Squadron had maintained top cover, but four pilots came home very short of fuel: Pilot Officer Linton forced landed at Dungeness, and three others landed at Redhill. By 1315, the Wing was all accounted for, excepting Sergeant Small who had been captured by the enemy.

Ramrod 106 was the next show, Greycap leading the Wing from Kenley at 1645. The Spitfires were to be Forward Target Support Wing, sweeping the Rouen area, whilst 12 Venturas bombed Yainville power station. The English coast was crossed at zero feet over Newhaven, the Wing then climbing until offshore at St Valery-en-Caux, where an orbit was made. Heading inland at 14,000 feet, Greycap received reports of 40 enemy aircraft climbing up from Rouen towards Le Havre. Although the Germans had the tactical advantage, the Kenley Wing engaged in an effort to prevent them from molesting the bombers. The brief clash was inconclusive, so the Spitfires re-formed and attempted to engage three FW 190s, flying from Rouen towards Fecamp, again unsuccessfully. Two more 190s were then sighted shadowing the Wing and apparently intending to catch the odd straggler, as Johnnie's PCR relates:-

They were about two miles behind the Wing and I climbed both squadrons steeply into sun and carried out one orbit to port. The FW 190s, which were then down sun of us, appeared to lose sight of the Wing and flew beneath us, repreenting an excellent target. They were seen 1,000 feet below my Section and a mile ahead. I ordered my No 2, Squadron Leader McNair, to engage these aircraft with me. The remainder of the Squadron (421) were told to kep high in order not to scare the Huns.

I closed in on No 2 E/A from line astern and opened fire from 300, closing to 150 yards. Cannon strikes were seen on the fuselage and tail plane of this E/A and a large piece fell away from the starboard half of his tail unit. The E/A spun down and was seen to crash at Valmont.

Squadron Leader McNair destroyed the leading 190, these two enemy fighters probably being from *Jafü* 3's I/JG 2.

The two successful Spitfire pilots then re-joined the Wing, returning home via Eletot and Beachy Head. Two pilots of 421 Squadron had to put down at the coastal airfield of Friston, out of fuel. By close of play, it had been another long, hot, day.

June 25th

Another fine day over England, the Kenley Wing first flew to Martlesham Heath, to operate therefrom in conjunction with the North Weald Wing on Ramrod 19. The Kenley Wing was to provide Target Support for Venturas attacking Amersterdam. Unfortunately, 10/10ths cloud was encountered at 10,000 feet, obscuring the target. The Wing turned to port at Eta, at 29,000 feet, crossing the Dutch coast south of Ijmuiden at 9,000 feet, then heading back to England. An aircraft, believed to be a Spitfire, was seen to plunge into the sea some 40 miles off Orfordness, but otherwise there was nothing to report. For Greycap, however, the sortie had only lasted 30 minutes, as his Spitfire, EN398, developed a technical fault.

Due to the poor continental weather, Ramrod 19 was the only operational sortie of the day. Two pilots of 421 Squadron flew to Eastchurch where they watched a tank-busting demonstration by some Hurricanes. The Canadians found the exercise 'very interesting and instructive' (ORB).

June 26th

After the morning's ground haze cleared, the rest of the day was sunny with a slight northerly wind. It was not until 1707, however, that Grecap led the Kenley Wing off on Ramrod 108, during which the Canadians were to provide escort to 40 B-17s bombing Tricqueville aerodrome. For some reason, the Wing Commander was not flying his usual Spitfire, EN398, but 'KH-V'. Unfortunately this aircraft's wireless went unserviceable before the English coast was reached, so Greycap had no choice but to hand over leadership to Squadron Leader McNair, of 421 Squadron, and return to base.

The sortie's second mishap befell 403 Squadron. Whilst climbing through cloud, Squadron Leader Godefroy, Red 1, and Flying Officer Bowen, Blue 1, collided. Red 1's propeller chewed up Blue 1's tail, forcing Bowen to bail out with a broken arm. Squadron Leader Godefroy's Spitfire was also damaged, although he returned to base and landed safely. Three other Wing pilots were forced to abort due to technical failures before the enemy coast was reached, leaving six of 403 and eight of 421 providing top cover to the B-17s, which were met at 25,000 feet over St Valery. Later, the B-17s crossed out over Coburg, but the result of their attack was obscured by cloud. Various formations of enemy fighters attempted to attack the bombers, but were driven off by the Spitfires. Responding to a request from the Americans to protect stragglers, Squadron Leader McNair led his Spitfires to sweep the rear of the beehive, but no Fortresses were in trouble and not was any flak forthcoming (probably due to the 7/10ths cloud covering at 17,000 feet). By 1840, the Kenley Spitfires were safely back home without anything of particular incident to report.

June 27th

Again cloud was 7/10ths, but the day was otherwise bright. At 1015, Greycap, back in EN398, led the Wing on Rodeo 235, a free-lance sweep of the St Omer area in conjunction with the Hornchurch Wing, controlled by Appledore. The Hornchurch Spitfires were positioned to the port-side of the Canadians.

Johnnie (PCR):-

…after making rendezvous at Dungeness, I set course for Berck. When half way across the Channel, Appledore gave me a vector of 090° but I had to swing to starboard to avoid Boulogne. Appledore then warned me of bandits approaching and instructed me to steer 070°. Shortly afterwards in the St Omer area I saw approximately 30 FW 190s approaching from the port bow at 25,000 feet with a high cover of 20 Me 109s to port and above them. Kenley bottom Squadron was then at 23,000 feet. I asked Hornchurch to engage and 403 also turned into the high cover. I climbed 421 steeply under the 190s, which split up and carried out a moderate turn to port. Six 190s, however, straightened out and flew in line abreast heading in the Nieuport/Ostend direction. I instructed my Section to engage these six enemy aircraft but just as I was within range they all dived steeply. I followed my aircraft and opened fire from 250 yards with cannon and M/G. Several strikes were seen on his fueslage, wing roots and tail unit and he commenced to emit thick black smoke, as I broke away I saw at least one half of a wing break off.

The combat had taken place 'West of St Omer' at 1053 (PCR, JEJ). The *Geschwadergruppe* of JG 26 (FW 190s) had been scrambled from Vendeville at 1030, and the Me 109s of 11/JG 26 engaged the high-flying Hornchurch Spitfires. Although the latter claimed two 109s destroyed, JG 26 actually lost no machines during this engagement. There would appear to be no doubt, however, regarding the fate of Wing Commander Johnson's victim, although which unit this 190 belonged to is unknown.

After the brief combat, the Spitfires re-formed over Gravelines before going home independently. When mid-Channel, the Kenley Wing was informed of bandits in the Dover area, so Greycap took the Spitfires down to sea level, sweeping towards Boulogne, but no enemy aircraft were seen. By 1145, the Spitfires were safely back at base.

June 28th

A morning show was scrubbed due to poor weather conditions over France, but later Ramrod 114 was able to go ahead. The Kenley Wing was up at 1900, soon afterwards passing out over Beachy Head at 10,000 feet where the B-17s were met and escorted in over Fecamp. The target for today was the JG 2 aerodrome at Beaumont-le-Roger. Bombs were seen to drop west of Beaumont and on the target, from which dust and smoke soon rose to a height of 10,000 feet. Nevertheless, no flak was experienced, no enemy aircraft were seen and by 1829, the Kenley Wing was safely down.

A De Havilland Mosquito, flown by Wing Commander Davoud, visited Kenley and gave that station 'a fine display of how the Mosquito will perform' (ORB,

403).

June 29th

After a dull morning and early afternoon, the evening was about 5/10ths and sunny. At 1900, the Hornchurch and Kenley Wings flew Ramrod 114, a sweep of Fecamp, Bolbec and Dieppe, in support of B-17s heading for targets around Le Mans. Once more, however, there was no opposition and the Spitfires were safely home by 2030.

On this day, Flight Lieutenant Walter AG Conrad of 403 Squadron travelled to London to receive his DFC at an investiture held at Buckingham Palace. Conrad was not only a popular personality but also a first class fighter pilot. In 1939, he had graduated with Honours in Political Science, from McGill University, Quebec, and joined the RCAF in August 1940. Having served in the Middle East, Conrad had joined 403 Squadron at Kenley in May 1943. By the time he received his DFC, his tally of enemy aircraft was at least four destroyed, with a number of anothers probably destroyed or damaged. Interestingly, on May 31st, 1942, whilst flying a 274 Squadron Hurricane IIB north of Bir Harchem, Conrad had damaged an Me 109. Many years later it was confirmed that the German pilot involved was none other than *Leutnant* Hans-Joachim Marseille of I/JG 27, the fabled 'Star of Africa'.

June 30th

Duff weather prevented operations and the Wing was released for 24 hours as from 1300.

In Wing Commander Johnson's PFLB, he recorded that his total number of enemy aircraft destroyed to date was 18 and two-thirds. So having been a Wing Commander Flying for several months now, what were Johnnie's impressions?

My life as a Wing Leader was fantastic. It just revolved around fighter pilots, Spitfires, flying and fighting. The Wing Commander Flying appointment was excellent, not least because previously the senior squadron commander would lead, but then there was always argy-bargy about who was the senior!

Being a Wing Leader was the best job in Fighter Command. You had no administrative duties whatsoever, apart to recommend chaps for a gong. I don't think I put pen to paper at Kenley for any other reason. All you had to do was look after your pilots and

aeroplanes with a very simple chain of command. It was a marvellous job. The Station Commander was usually a Group Captain, who had to do the food and the clothing, the general well-being of the Station with perhaps 2,000 personnel. Occasionally, like Jimmy Fenton, he would fly with us, just to keep his hand in, but he had to fly a desk most of the time! So the whole command structure was simply Fighter Command C-in-C, the Group AOC, the Station Commander, then the Wing Commander Flying. Very short, sharp chain of command, a very good one and a very nice relationship between the guys at the top. I remember on one occasion we had come back from escorting some Fortresses and we had got into some rather stiff fighting, although we had done well, and I got back in my office about 5 'o' clock in the evening and some Staff Officer from Fighter Command HQ rang up and said "Hello, is that Wing Commander Johnson?"
I said "It is".
He said "Well just a moment, the Commander-in-Chief would like a word".
All the Boss said was "I thought that I would call you up Johnnie and say how very well you have done today, thank you very much, goodnight".
Marvellous, wasn't it? *Leadership, real leadership.*

We held conferences at Uxbridge when the AOC 11 Group, Air Vice-Marshal 'Dingbat' Saunders called a conference, or we'd go up to Bentley Priory when Leigh-Mallory called one. Mind you, these chaps, Leigh-Mallory and so on, were all the while coming down to see us. 'LM' was very good at keeping a good liaison, he didn't fly much himself but he'd get flown down in some old Proctor or something about once a month. He'd always come down if you got a 'gong', he was very much a father figure, he wanted to help all the time.

What did used to happen was that if there was a good show, the chaps at Fighter Command would produce a document containing extracts of the relevant reports and circulate this amongst the Wings. They were very good at disseminating information this way and had really got it together by 1943. By mid-1943, Al Deere and I were the 'Old Boys', so they had to listen to what we had to say. Old 'LM' would say "So tell me, Johnnie, what did you do then", and so on, "Can we improve that, is there anything I can do? Do you want another squadron, perhaps, do you want to lead more squadrons?" So we always had this backing. I held Leigh-Mallory in high regard. He could be a little bit pompous but he had a heart of gold, super chap, and we were all very sad when he was later killed.

Also, due to his increasing number of aerial victories, Johnnie was starting to attract significant publicity:-

It wasn't until early May time, when we started to escort the Fortresses and hack a few Huns down, that I got a bit of publicity. They used to produce a Fighter Command score sheet, of which 'Sailor' Malan was at the top, and it also showed you who was deceased! The PR chaps used to push the score sheet out to the newspapers. Of course there wasn't much good news at the time, lots of disasters in the Middle and Far East, so the air fighters became a bit of news, 'glamour boys'!

Clearly it was a time for heroes, and Wing Commander Johnnie Johnson was now amongst the foremost 'knights of the air'.

July 1st

As the 421 Squadron ORB commented, it was 'Dominion Day in Canada, July 1st over here', and a sunny, warm, start to a new month it was. Fighter Command had planned a large-scale operation, Ramrod 117, for the afternoon. Two formations of paired Spitfire Wings were to sweep the area between Courtrai and Abbeville, whilst Typhoons attacked the airfields at those locations. The Kenley and Hornchurch Wings were to fly together as usual, and sweep the area of Abbeville, St Pol and Fruges.

For some reason, although the 'Bombphoons' did not ultimately proceed to Abbeville as planned, the Kenley and Hornchurch Spitfires nevertheless did. The Wings rendezvoused on time, less than 500 feet over Hastings, before climbing almost immediately to arrive over Berck at 20,000 feet. The grey and green camouflaged Spitfires struck inland over France, over Merville turning back for St Omer. On the latter south westerly course, five Me 109s of 11/JG 26 were sighted by 403 Squadron. The enemy aircraft were flying south, climbing, and passed behind and below 403. When the 109s were ahead and also at 28,000 feet, Squadron Leader Godefroy attacked with Red and Blue Sections, leaving Yellow as top cover. One of the enemy pilots obviously saw the approaching danger, and immediately dived away. Squadron Leader Godefroy, Red 1, attacked the leader of the remainder, which were flying as a *schwarm* in line abreast. The 109 took evasive action, first turning right, thence left. Godefroy's opening 3 second burst, however, resulted in strikes around the fuselage and cockpit. The 109 went into a turn, started spinning, and was seen by Greycap to crash near Abbeville. Red 2, Flight Sergeant GM Shouldice, fired at the 109 third from left, as it was about to open fire on Red 1. After Red 2's second burst, there were explosions on the enemy aircraft, pieces of which dropped off. Red 1 watched proceedings, noting that the engine of Shouldice's victim exploded as the port undercariage leg dropped. It then went into a spin. Blue 3, Flying Officer Fowlow, had hit another 109, hard, with cannon and machine-gun fire. Strikes were seen all along the 109's fuselage and cockpit before the engine 'disintegrated' (ORB, 403). Blue 1, Flight Lieutenant MacDonald, fired at the remaining 109, but this half rolled away and made good its escape.

11/JG 26 lost two pilots killed during this engagement, *Leutnant* Hans-Joachim Heinemeyer and *Unteroffizier* Albert Westhauser, these probably being the 109s claimed by Squadron Leader Godefroy and Flying Officer Fowlow. The third Kenley claim, that by Flight Sergeant Shouldice, managed to crash land back at the *Staffel's* Vendeville base.

The Kenley Spitfires all returned safely. As the 421 Squadron ORB noted, it had been a 'good show'. Dan Browne:-

We did these missions called the 'Milk Run' and the 'Mail Run', one of which was to Abbeville. We'd all cross over on the deck, with propellers no higher than an office desk above the water, to avoid radar detection. Of course there was rigid radio silence. The bombers would then climb up, and we'd climb up and get above them. As you know, Abbeville was a very active fighter field so pretty soon the bombers would drop their bombs, the target being just 18 miles from the coast. The bombers would then turn, dive back out and go home. We would be still climbing up, going inland towards Germany, and soon start getting reports: 'There are 200+ coming up over Cambrai', 'There's 200 plus coming up over Lille' and so on. There were only 24 of us! We would keep climbing until we got to a safe altitude, then we'd turn around and head back. Of course we had superior altitude in the Spit IX, so as the 190s couldn't reach us they'd pull up vertical and fire at us from some way below. The trick was to stall and spin out. One day they caught Johnnie out on the side, on his own, and really gave it to him! When he got out of his Spitfire at Kenley we all had a good laugh about it, I bet he crapped in his pants that day!

This particular operation, Ramrod 117, was the last sweep led by Wing Commander Johnson for two weeks, as he was sent off on a fortnight's well-earned leave.

July 2nd

In Johnnie's absence, Squadron Leader Godefroy of 403 Squadron was the most senior of the two squadron commanders, and so deputised for the Wing Leader.

On this day, Squadron Leader Godefroy led the Kenley Wing down to Tangmere, landing there at 1135. It had originally been intended that the Wing would participate in an operation involving B-17s, but for some reason this was scrubbed. Instead, the Kenley and Hornchurch Wings swept the Fecamp, Bernay and Le Treport areas. The Canadians flew as top cover to Hornchurch, the latter Wing being led by the more senior Wing Commander Crawford-Compton. Over Bernay, Appledore vectored the Spitfires towards Doullens, where 20 enemy aircraft were reported at 20,000 feet. These bandits were engaged by Hornchurch, whilst Kenley remained as top cover. As soon as it had begun the clash was over, and the Spitfires were all safely back at Tangmere at 1545. After a debrief, Godefroy and his pilots were back at Kenley by 1715.

July 3rd
Due to the ever changeable weather, the day's first offensive operation was scrubbed. Instead, the Kenley Wing, again led by Squadron Leader Godefroy, flew Rodeo 238, an uneventful sweep of Abbeville, Poix and Le Touquet.

During the afternoon, the pilots of 421 Squadron took an aircraft recognition test in the Intelligence Building. The results were good: with a potential maximum score of 40, eight achieved full marks, six got 38, one 37 and two 36.

In the evening there was a party and dance hosted by the Officers' Mess, this being, according to the 421 Squadron ORB, 'a howling success, especially the plumbing act put on by seven members of the Squadron'.

July 4th
For the Americans, this was not only Independence Day but also the first anniversary of Eighth Air Force bomber operations from bases in the UK. Both events were marked by three major raids, one to the Gnome-Rhone aero-engine works at Le Mans, another to the SNCA aircraft factory at Nantes, and the third to the U-boat pens at La Pallice. The Kenley Wing was detailed to fly Ramrod 122, fighter cover to the 192 B-17s of the 1st Bomb Wing returning from Le Mans. Squadron Leader Godefroy led the Spitfires off at 1205, meeting the Fortresses as planned over Argentan. 403 Squadron formated to the bomber's starboard side whilst 421 positioned itself above and behind. Incredibly, the bombers were 'unmolested' (ORB, 403), and no enemy aircraft were seen. *Jafü* 2's fighters were not scrambled until the B-17s bound for Nantes and Le Mans had reached Laval, the idea being that the fighters should await the bombers return in the Le Havre area. Due to the presence of so

many Spitfires, however, the German fighters were unable to find an opening through which to attack the Americans. Eventually the enemy pilots had to break off and return to base, low on fuel. By 1355, the Kenley Wing was safely home, making this one of the longest trips so far over enemy occupied France.

In the evening, Squadron Leader Godefroy led the Wing on Ramrod 124, in which operation the Canadian Spitfires were to be the second wave of a fighter sweep in support of Mitchell bombers attacking Amiens. Over France, the Kenley Wing was vectored towards what was supposedly a large force of enemy aircraft, but only two FW 190s were sighted. These were not engaged, just in case they were merely bait for a larger force which was known to be about. The latter, however, turned out to be another Spitfire Wing. Other small formations of aircraft were investigated between Amiens and the Somme Estuary, but they too proved to be friendly. Although the Kenley Wing was home without event by 1820, four Spitfires belonging to other Wings had been shot down, as was a 109. It was simply a case of not having been in the right place at the right time.

July 5th
A clear and bright day, as there were no offensive operations both Kenley squadrons spent the day flying air-to-air firing, cannon tests and routine local flying. Pilot Officer Hicks and Sergeant Joyce of 421 Squadron were scrambled to intercept a high-flying bandit, but the German turned about smartish and disappeared into the far distance.

July 6th
In the morning, cloud was 5/10ths and visibility was good. At 0945, Squadron Leader Godefroy led the Kenley Wing, operating in conjunction with the Polish Northolt Wing, on a fighter sweep, Rodeo 240. Having crossed out over Beachy Head at zero feet, the Spitfires entered France some 17,000 feet over Dieppe. Over Poix, enemy aircraft were reported, the Wing swinging to port with 403 Squadron at 22,000 feet, 421 3,000 feet higher. The Spitfires had, however, attracted the attention of a large force of Me 109s, made up from both 3/JG 27 and II/JG 2. The Canadians soon saw 12 of these 109s, flying south-west at 18,000 feet. The Germans realised their danger, however, and all but one dived away. That remaining 109 was rapidly pounced on by Flight Lieutenant MacDonald, Blue 1 of 403 Squadron, who gave it a short burst from 200 yards. Hits were seen on the fuselage and white smoke poured out; the enemy

aircraft was seen to crash 10 miles south of Abbeville.

Having re-formed, the Spitfires flew towards Amiens. Approaching from the north-east, at 24,000 feet, were two more *schwarms* of Me 109s. As 421 Squadron climbed to 28,000 feet, one *schwarm* dived away. The remaining four 109s made a turn to starboard and were bounced by 421, which was covered by 403. Squadron Leader McNair, CO of 421, destroyed one of these 109s, and Flight Lieutenant Sager, commander of 'B' Flight, damaged another. Again the Wing re-formed, proceeding first to Abbeville, thence up the French coast to Boulogne, where the Spitfires crossed out at 26,000 feet, returning home via Dover and Folkestone.

Over France, the Northolt Wing had also been successful, shooting down three enemy aircraft. Amongst these was *Leutnant* Paul Fritsch of II/JG 26, whose FW 190 crashed into the Somme Estuary. Despite extensive search operations, Fritsch was never found, his name joining countless other German servicemen who remain officially *Vermisst*.

During the afternoon, the weather closed in with rain and thunderstorms lasting until 1600. At 1905, the Kenley Wing was up again, however, this time on Rodeo 241, Squadron Leader Godefroy and his pilots being the third wave of a fighter sweep of the Le Treport, Amiens, Abbeville and Le Touquet areas. Over Amiens, 15 FW 190s were seen flying from east to west at 26,000 feet. The Spitfires climbed to 29,000 feet. Whilst 421 Squadron fell on the unsuspecting Germans, out of the sun, 403 remained high as top cover. Flight Lieutenant Conrad attacked a 190, this being the last of a group of three. After firing, Conrad found his opponent 'turn violently towards and pass underneath him. However, Red 3, Pilot Officer HJ Dowding, saw the e/a being attacked and noticed strikes along the wing root and cockpit, and then saw it wallow a bit, roll over and go down in flames with a large amount of black smoke. This aircraft was last seen going down in flames and is claimed as destroyed' (ORB, 403).

After the combat, the Wing re-formed and returned home via Le Touquet, landing at 2035.

Back at Kenley there had only been three non-operational sorties during the day, two of which were co-operation flights with the American Thunderbolts.

July 7th
Sunny and warm with a 20 mph strong wind, the Form 'D' showed the Kenley Wing on Rodeo 242. Squadron Leader Godefroy led the Wing off at 1248, sweeping St Valery, Rouen and Le Havre. The sortie was uneventful, however, and the Spitfires were all back safely by 1415.

The remainder of the day was spent flying cine-gun practise and 'Thunderbolt co-operation' (ORB, 403).

July 8ᵗʰ
No sweeps were carried out, but a number of routine, non-operational, flights were made.

July 9ᵗʰ
Having taken off with the Wing at 1130, on Rodeo 243, Squadron Leader Godefroy was forced to return early due to technical problems. The lead was taken by Flight Leutenant HD MacDonald DFC, also of 403 Squadron. The Wing was the first wave of a fighter sweep of the Gravelines – Thielt area. In fact, the Canadians went as far as Ghent on this occasion, over which Belgian city the Spitfires arrived at 33,000 feet. A couple of *schwarms* of bandits were reported in that area, and nine plus over Thielt. The latter, a formation of Me 109s, was engaged by Squadron Leader McNair at 35,000 feet. Due to the extreme height, his windscreen iced over during the attack, so no results were observed. There were no other combats and the Wing left France via Dunkirk at 25,000 feet. A large ship, thought to be a gunboat, was seen in that port, and another similar but smaller vessel was reported travelling north-east. The Spitfires re-crossed the English coast over Sandwich and were safely down at base by 1315.

According to the 421 Squadron ORB, 'two or three enemy bombers flew over our airfield at tea time and Flight Lieutenant Sager was scrambled but was unable to locate them as there was 10/10ths cloud. One Do 217 crashed about five miles south of the drome'. This aircraft of 5/KG 2 had been hit by AA fire from Kenley and crashed at Bletchingly. The crew of four were all killed.

On this afternoon, a total of 10 enemy aircraft, taking advantage of the low cloud and generally poor weather conditions over southern England, penetrated as far as London, attacking Croydon. A factory there was seriously damaged

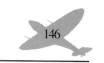

and nine people were killed, and at East Grinstead 108 people were killed when the Whitehall Cinema was hit. Although these raids were pointless from a strategic perspective, it still showed what havoc just a few bombers could wreak, operating in the right conditions.

July 10th

Again a day of scattered cloud, the Kenley Spitfires were detailed to fly on Ramrod 128, providing cover to B-17s attacking Villacoublay. Whereas the German 'hit and run' raiders favoured the current conditions, such cloud prevented the Eighth Air Force from using the Norden bombsight. Unlike today's laser devices that do not require the pilot to see the target, the American bombardiers' equipment required just that. A few inconsiderately positioned banks of cloud could, therefore, scupper an entire operation. This is exactly what happened on this operation, the bombers turning back over Evreux. In total, the B-17s were protected on this occasion by no less than 18 Spitfire squadrons and eight of P-47s. Nevertheless the Germans put up strong fighter opposition. As the bombers turned around, 12 plus bandits were seen approaching the beehive from the west, and another 12 plus hung off to the west. 403 Squadron chased the latter formation but the Germans made off. The former gaggle of bandits then came between 403 and 421 Squadrons, with another eight Me 109s dropping out of cloud onto 403. Squadron Leader McNair sent a Section of 421 Squadron down to help, and himself destroyed a 109 whilst Flight Lieutenant Sager and Flying Officer Zary each damaged another. After the skirmish, the Spitfires re-formed and went home, being short of fuel. At this point the enemy attacked the bombers, and the Candians watched helplessly as one B-17 blew up and went down near Rouen, another west of Bernay. Indeed, so short of fuel were the Kenley Spitfires that the majority first landed at forward bases due to fuel shortage. The sortie had lasted nearly two hours.

Back at Kenley, 421 Squadron's Flying Officer de Nancrede found a bullet lodged in the tail of his Spitfire, but fortunately no serious damage had been done. 421 Squadron said farewell to Flight Lieutenant Phil Blades, who had completed his tour, and his 'A' Flight was taken over by Flight Lieutenant Fowlow who had been posted from 403.

July 11th

Due to duff weather there was no operational flying. A church service held at Dispersal by the Padre, Flight Lieutenant Carlson, was well attended by both pilots and support staff.

July 12th
No operational flying again, due to bad weather. On this day, the 403 SquadronORB makes a significant comment '82 of the ground personnel of this Squadron posted w.e.f. today to No 127 Airfield HQ'.

For the RAF fighter squadrons earmarked for operations with 2nd TAF, the change in role placed the emphasis on mobility. As the Allied ground forces advanced, so too would the fighter units. No longer for them, therefore, comfortable and well-appointed stations such as Kenley, but, by way of complete contrast, bell tents and field kitchens. Workshops and other equipment were housed in specially designed lorries, the whole concept was that the Wing could break camp at short notice, moving rapidly to operate from another temporary field. Naturally, fighter squadrons had to practise and adapt to these new operating conditions, and so a number moved to 'Advanced Landing Grounds' (ALG) in southern England. Temporary runways were made from a variety of materials including 'Pierced Steel Planking' (PSP). The experience gained by the RAF's Airfield Construction Branch in the building of these temporary runways would also be put to good use on the Continent the following year.

Each ALG was numbered, 127 being, for example, Lashenden, near Maidstone, in Kent. Since the 1920s, a local landowner and his friends had operated their civilian aircraft from this field, but all pleasure flying ceased, however, upon the outbreak of war. In 1942, the Lashenden site was requisitioned by the Airfield Board and was now at the 2nd TAF's disposal. The Kenley Wing was, therefore, allocated 127 Airfield. It was in preparation for that significant move that certain of 403 Squadron's support staff had moved to Lashenden on July 12th, 1943.

Flying Officer Bob Middlemiss received a new Spitfire on July 12th, MA585, 'KH-Z'. The young pilot's ground crew were Bob Tronnes (fitter) and Walt Bell (rigger), who were, as Bob himself says, 'Two great lads'.

July 13th
On what was a bright and clear day with very little cloud, at 0835, Squadron Leader Godefroy led the Kenley Wing up on Rodeo 244, a fighter sweep over Poix, Amiens and Doullens. There was, however, a disaster on take-off: Pilot

Officer JI MacKay, Blue 3 of 403 Squadron, suffered an engine failure and crashed on the edge of the aerodrome. He was taken to hospital, his condition 'serious' (ORB, 403).

Over Kenley, Godefroy's remaining Spitfires met the Hornchurch Wing, and set course for France. Although visibility over the Continent was excellent, no enemy aircraft were sighted and by 1010 the Kenley Wing was safely back home.

July 14th

A bright and clear morning saw the Kenley Wing detailed to fly Ramrod 133, an escort sortie to 240 B-17s attacking the FW 190 repair facility at Villacoublay, and the airfields at Le Bourget and Amiens. So far, July had seen good weather over England but Continental targets had frustratingly been shrouded by intermittent cloud. On this day, however, conditions over France were good.

Squadron Leader Godefroy led the Wing up at 0700, crossing out at 15,000 feet over Newhaven. The Spitfires then climbed to 25,000 feet and met a box of 60 Fortresses. The Wing took up station to port and ahead of the bombers, the beehive crossing into France over Fecamp. The Spitfires then swept ahead, between Rouen and Evreux. Over Louviers, nine Me 109s were seen flying at 20,000 feet, coming from the east in line abreast. As 403 Squadron turned to engage, nine more 109s turned behind Godefroy's Spitfires, and another nine enemy fighters struck at the B-17s. Soon, one Fortress was in flames, and two others crashed. Also, an Me 109 was seen to explode, the victim of the B-17 gunners. The Kenley Wing was unable to engage, however, and had to turn about over Evreux due to fuel constraints. By 0838, the Spitfires were safely back at Kenley.

On this day, Wing Commander Johnson's leave ended and he flew from Rearsby (in Leicestershire) to Kenley in an Auster, his co-pilot being a Squadron Leader Edwards. Bob Middlemiss, of 403 Squadron, had spent some of that leave with Johnnie in Melton Mowbray:-

Johnnie organised a trip in the latest Auster IV at Rearsby, with the Chief Test Pilot, a Mr Waite. The latter was taking up a new Auster, MT454, and went along on the test flight. He taxied out to the runway in use and said that he would demonstrate a short field take-off. He applied the brakes, opened full throttle, got tail up into flying position, then let go of the brakes and after a very short run indeed we were up and flying. On completion of the air test he said "I will now demonstrate the very short field landing capabilities of this aircraft." After touchdown he applied full brakes – needless to say we stopped after a very short run, and no doubt was left in my mind of the aircraft's short take-off and landing capabilities!

At Kenley, 'Wingco' then re-familiarised himself with EN398, in which he undertook an hour of local flying.

July 15th
Greycap's first flight was a cannon test in EN398, lasting 15 minutes. On this day of scattered cloud and good visibility, the Kenley Wing was not up on operations until 1613. The sortie was Rodeo 245, a sweep of Hardelot, Abbeville and Poix, controlled by Appledore. The Wing began climbing soon after take-off, crossing out over Rye at 5,000 feet before making landfall over Hardelot at 20,000. From Boulogne, accurate and intense flak was sent up, after which Greycap was vectored to the Poix area, just south of Abbeville. Bostons of No 2 Group's 107 Squadron had just bombed Poix airfield, escorted by Typhoons and Spitfires. Combat had been joined with losses resulting for both sides, the fight having just finished when the Canadians arrived on the scene. Appledore warned Greycap of bandits ahead, however, and he immediately saw two *schwarms* of Me 109s directly ahead and at the same height. Johnnie's PCR describes what happened next:-

I turned slightly starboard to get advantage of the Hun but all E/A except two Me 109s climbed and were not seen again. These two Me 109s flew head-on towards the Wing and when not more than 1,000 yards away turned to port and away from the Wing. I lead my Section to attack and when almost within range E/A started to climb steeply. We had the advantage of speed, after one dive, and so experienced no difficulty in overtaking the E/A. I instructed my No 2 to take the highest Me 109, and I opened fire on the lowest with cannon and M/G from dead astern, range 300 yards. I gave him a four second-burst, strikes being seen on the port Wing root, engine cowling and fuselage. E/A at once started to pour thick glycol vapour and went down in a wide spiral. His course was easy to follow as he left a strong trail of white glycol in the air. He was seen to crash in the Bangy-Senarpont area and continued to burn and smoke for some minutes. This E/A is claimed as destroyed.

As usual there was no doubt regarding the accuracy of Johnnie's claim.

The other Me 109 was attacked three times by Flight Lieutenant MacDonald, Red

3 of 403 Squadron, with which Section Greycap was leading the Wing. On Red 3's second pass, the 109 half-rolled to port and dived, and on the third attack strikes were seen on its port wingtip, fuselage and cockpit. From 12,000 feet, the 109 dived straight in.

Three FW 190s were then sighted near Le Treport, but these quickly dived away and escaped when a section of 403 Squadron Spitfires gave chase. The Wing then re-formed and left France via Berck, crosing back in at 5,000 feet over Dungeness. By 1750, the Wing was safely down with two more confirmed victories to add to a growing tally.

At 1945, the Kenley Wing was up again, on Rodeo 246, sweeping Hardelot and Poix, again under Appledore. When offshore at Hardelot, Greycap was vectored south and found six FW 190s flying south at 12,000 feet over Le Touquet. 421 Squadron dived after them but were unable to close the gap, the 190s having half-rolled and dived inland. After the unsuccessful chase, Greycap re-formed his Spitfires and headed home, landing at 2015. He wrote in his PFLB:-

Six FW 190s intercepted but E/A ducked as we were just opening fire!

July 16th

A dull and wet morning cleared by noon, the weather improving steadily throughout the afternoon. The Wing was up at 1915, Greycap leading on Ramrod 144, a sweep with Hornchurch of Dieppe, Grandvilliers, Abbeville and the Somme Estuary, in support of Marauders bombing Abbeville marshalling yards. The Spitfires crossed out over Beachy Head, then climbed steadily, making landfall just west of Dieppe at 22,000 feet. The Wings then flew to Grandvilliers and given a vector: bandits below at Angels 12. The Spitfire Mk IXs dived and intercepted the 'enemy', which proved to be the Tangmere Wing's Spitfire Mk XIIs! The IXs then re-formed and climbed to 23,000 feet, the Hornchurch Wing slightly above and up sun of Abbeville. At this point, 20 FW 190s were seen coming head on, so Greycap manoeuvred to give Hornchurch the advantage. Although the Germans were bounced by Wing Commander Crawford-Compton and his men, no claims were subsequently made. The Kenley Spitfires then left France over the Somme Estuary at 20,000 feet, flying north to Berck before setting course for Rye. By 2050 the Wing was safely down, although Sergeant Campbell of 421 Squadron, on his first offensive sortie, had returned early with flap trouble, landing at Redhill. In his PFB, Johnnie wrote:-

Hornchurch rather missed a good opportunity.

July 17th
In the morning, the Eighth Air Force sent 332 B-17s to attack targets in north-west Germany and Holland. Greycap led his Spitfires across to Coltishall, in Norfolk, and took off on Ramrod 145 at 1057. Unfortunately, deteriorating weather conditions saw the Spitfires soon recalled, when 30 miles out over the North Sea off Yarmouth, and the mission postponed. Later, the Wing took off again, only for the mission to be cancelled. After returning to Kenley, the Wing was released for the rest of the day.

July 18th
Although a number of non-operational sorties were carried out, duff weather prevented any sweeps. Flying Officers Ogilvie and Browne, of 403 Squadron, flew a weather recce in the afternoon, prowling up the French coast from Dieppe to Gris Nez. No enemy aircraft were sighted but the weather was reported as 'unserviceable' (ORB, 403).

Johnnie flew EN398 to Sutton Bridge, to see Group Captain PR 'Johnnie' Walker DSO DFC, the Commanding Officer of the Central Gunnery School based there. The reason for the meeting is unknown.

July 19th
Another day of poor weather, the Wing was recalled when half way across the Channel on Rodeo 249.

July 20th
A warm day with scattered cloud, Rodeo 249 was again laid on but postponed before take-off. The only flying undertaken was of a non-operational description.

According to the 421 Squadron ORB:-

Everybody preparing for move to 127 Airfield in 83 Group. Practically all Squadron personnel, except pilots, are already posted to 127 Airfield, which is forming here at Kenley.

For some reason, 2nd TAF fighter wings were at first called 'Airfields', but this was later changed to the more appropriate and hitherto commonly used 'Wing'.

July 21st
So bad was the weather today that there was no flying whatsoever. Air Vice-Marshal Saunders CBE MC DFC MM, AOC 11 Group, visited 421 Squadron, after which the Wing was released until 1100 the following day.

July 22nd
Poor weather again prevented any offensive operations, and the period of release was extended to 1300.

July 23rd
Again the weather was so bad that 403 Squadron only managed one local, non-operational, sortie. Flying Officer Love and Pilot Officer Isbister of 421 Squadron were scrambled but patrolled without incident. The Wing's pilots then watched Fighter Command combat films and watched the movie 'International Lady' in the Intelligence Building.

Wing Commander Johnson flew to Northolt in the morning for a Wing Leaders' conference with the AOC.

RAF meteorologists reported that the frequent low pressure spells that had disrupted flying over the past three months would soon give way to a 'high'. With the welcome prospect of clear skies ahead, the Eighth Air Force prepared to launch a sustained period of operations in accordance with the Combined Bomber Offensive objectives.

July 24th
Another dull day, the planned evening sweep was scrubbed. The only action was when 'A' Flight and 'B' Flight of 421 Squadron played softball, the game being won by the former.

On this day, the Eighth Air Force started 'Blitz Week'. The objective was to weaken and further extend the German fighter defences by flying seven major bombing missions in as many days. This opening attack was made against Heroya in Norway, where nitrate production was halted for three-and-a-half months, and adjacent aluminium and magnesium plants were abandoned. The harbour at Trondheim was also hit, but that at Bergen was covered in cloud, preventing

bombing. The Germans had been caught off guard by this unexpected northerly thrust, and no bombers were lost to enemy action. It was a good start.

That night, RAF Bomber Command attacked Hamburg. The concentration of bombs in the city centre led to an unprecedented firestorm with catastrophic consequences for the inhabitants. The events of this day, therefore, indicated the level of destruction that the Combined Bomber Offensive could achieve.

July 25th
According to the 421 Squadron ORB, there was a 'big improvement in the weather', which perfectly suited the Allied air forces' purposes. In the morning, 100 B-17s bombed Hamburg, following up the RAF's nocturnal raid. To prevent the enemy fighters of *Jafü* Holland-Ruhr engaging the Americans, the RAF's No 2 Group despatched a dozen B-25 Mitchells to bomb the Fokker aircraft factory at Amsterdam, and Eighth Air Force B-26 Marauders bombed the coke ovens at Ghent.

First off, the Kenley Wing flew across to Coltishall, to operate therefrom on another escort sortie, Ramrod 158, this time providing Target Support to the Bostons attacking Amsterdam. At the Norfolk aerodrome, the pilots were briefed whilst their Spitfires were re-fuelled before take off at 1415. The Spitfires crossed the Dutch coast at 24,000 feet over the target area and sighted the bombers. The Wing then skirted north of Amsterdam and followed the Bostons out over the Dutch coast. Greycap then led his pilots on a sweep along the Dutch coast to Noordwijk but no enemy aircraft were encountered. By 1555, the Spitfires were back at Coltishall, being 'turned around'.

At 1915, the Kenley Wing was up again, this time on Ramrod 158, providing Forward Target Support to 12 Bostons bombing Schipol aerodrome. Crossing the Dutch coast at 22,000 feet between Noordwijk and Zandveert, the Spitfires then flew to Schipol, which was reached on time. Greycap's PCR relates what happened next:-

At 1957 I was flying on the east side of Schipol at 22,000 feet, when I saw an Me 109G, with underslung guns in wings, flying in the same direction about three miles ahead of the Wing. Enemy aircraft turned to port and was obviously positioning himself to attack the beehive, who were then crosing the coast. I instructed the Wing to remain at their height and took my Section down to attack this e/a. I closed in on e/a, then at 12,000 feet, and opened fire with cannon and m/g closing to 170 yards.

The 109 was flying directly into the sun and owing to this fact I could not see the result of my fire, but as I broke away he turned to port with glycol streaming from his starboard radiator. I saw him go down to about 6,000 feet and my No 2 saw him after this, diving vertically towards the ground. As I climbed away I saw an aircraft burning on the ground to the west of Schipol. As there were no Wing losses in the combat area I claim this Me 109 as destroyed on this evidence.

The Wing Leader was supported by Pilot Officer Isbister, flying Black 2:-

…Wing Leader opened fire, firing several bursts closing to point blank range. The enemy aircraft was pouring white smoke and taking no evasive action except medium turns. He then broke up and the last I saw of the E/A it was diving towards the ground at a very steep angle at 6,000 – 8,000 feet, pouring white smoke.

Flying Officer L Foster added:-

After the Wing Leader broke off his attack, I attempted to watch the E/A crash. I was able to see it still diving at about 3,000 feet but lost sight of it due to the thick ground haze. Shortly after I saw what could have been the E/A burning in the area I last saw said E/A diving.

The Me 109 concerned was probably from III/JG 54, based at Schipol, the pilot of which was killed.

After this combat, the Spitfires re-formed and headed for the Dutch coast. When south of Ijmuiden, at 15-16,000 feet, eight P-47 Thunderbolts were seen above and behind the Wing, flying the same course. The Americans misidentified the Spitfires and consequently one P-47 dived at Flying Officer Zary, White 4 of 421 Squadron. At 200 yards, the American pilot opened fire, but fortunately for White 4 his marksmanship was poor and Zary was unscathed. Yet again, an incident of so-called 'Friendly Fire' which, as I have said many times before and as the available evidence proves, was undoubtedly more frequent than many choose to accept. After this particular incident, the Thunderbolts were last seen heading towards Horsham. As the Kenley Wing Form 'F' later reported:-

Had this Section not been bounced by the Thunderbolts, they would probably have been able to engage two FW 190s which were seen below and to port.

Without further incident, the Kenley Wing landed back at Coltishall at 2055, returning to Kenley after the Spitfires had been re-fuelled. Four aircraft of 421 Squadron had been forced to return early from this sortie, having been unable to jettison their auxiliary fuel tanks. Red 1 of 403 Squadron, Squadron Leader Godefroy, had also returned early with a technical problem. By 2220, the Wing was safely back at Kenley, however, and as the 421 Squadron ORB reports, 'It was a long day'.

July 26th
Synthetic rubber factories in Hannover, and the Hamburg U-boat installations were the Eighth Air Force's targets for today. These locations, both in northern Germany, were beyond the range of escorting fighters, and so the B-17s went to Germany unprotected. In an effort to occupy as many German fighters as possible, however, raids and sweeps were mounted over the areas of France, Belgium and Holland that were within the Allied fighters' reach.

At 1035, Wing Commander Johnson led the Kenley Wing up on Ramrod 159, a sweep of St Omer, Bergues, Aire, and Berck. The Canadians' role was Forward Target Support to B-26 Marauders bombing St Omer. The sky was clear of both cloud and the enemy, and smoke soon rose from the marshalling yard target. Apart from heavy flak, which burst at 10,000 feet, the sortie was uneventful and the Spitfires were back at Kenley by 1200.

The next operation of the day for Johnnie's Spitfires was Rodeo 250, at 1555, in which the Kenley and Biggin Hill Wings together swept the Gravelines and Cassell areas. Although 25 FW 190s were sighted, the Germans would not engage and dived away. The Wing was down by 1730, with nothing further to report.

July 27th
At 1050, Wing Commander Johnson led the Kenley Wing up on Ramrod 162, in which the Spitfires were to provide the first wave of a fighter sweep in support of 12 Venturas bombing the coke ovens at Zeebrugge. Greycap led his Canadians out over Deal at zero feet, thence to Blankenburg at 22,000 feet. From there, the Spitfires swept Roulers and Guines but without meeting the enemy. Returning over Rye at 10,000 feet, the Wing returned to Kenley at 1220.

Next came Ramrod 164, a sweep of Harfleur, Londinieres and Le Touquet whilst bombers attacked the airfield at Tricqueville. Again, despite flying up the coast to the Abbeville area, no enemy aircraft were seen and the sortie passed otherwise without incident.

More of 403 Squadron's support staff left Kenley for 127 Airfield and in preparation for the Wing's forthcoming move.

July 28th

The previous day, although the weather had remained fine over England, over the Continent cloud persisted and thus interupted 'Blitz Week'. Although the weather remained slightly uncertain, July 28th would see the Americans mount their heaviest attack yet against the German aircraft industry. The 1st Bomber Wing's 182 B-17s crossed the North Sea and bombed the Fieseler works at Kassell-Bettenhausen, whilst the 4th Wing's 120 were to make the deepest penetration into Germany so far: the AGO fighter assembly plant at Ascherleben, near Magdeburg. Both works produced the FW 190 and were therefore top priority aircraft industry targets. The lead force of the latter Wing was the 94th Group based at Bury St Edmunds, led personally in the air by the Commanding Officer, Colonel Fred Castle who anticipated it being a 'hot' one.

First the B-17s feinted towards Hamburg before turning south-east towards Oschersleben. Over the Continent, however, bad weather again caused problems, dispersing the Fortresses. Over the Dutch coast, JG 1's FW 190s engaged the bombers, some of these fighters using, for the first time, aerial rockets. These were actually 21 cm mortars adapted to be underslung on both wings. Also, Me 109s of the Jever based II/JG 11, dropped 500-lb bombs onto the Fortress formations! This was a new concept, only practical against tight formations, but devastating when successful. These new and perhaps somewhat desperate measures indicate the resolve with which the Germans defied the Allied CBO. It also emphasises just how increasingly vulnerable the bombers were becoming without complete fighter support.

As the Americans battled onwards and further into Germany on yet another fateful summer's day in 1943, through a gap in the cloud Castle's bombardier in *Sour Puss* recognised a landmark, from which he was able to accurately calculate time from target. The majority of other B-17s in this formation followed suit. When reconnaissance photographs were taken later, a large concentration of bombs were found to have been dropped within the target area, this causing sufficient damage to write off a whole month's production: 50 FW 190s.

To extend range, the Kenley Wing operated from Manston on Ramrod 165. Greycap's brief had been to meet the homeward bound B-17s three miles north of the Hague, but the rendezvous was changed, in the air, to eight miles south of Rotterdam. By then the B-17s were protected by a gaggle of Allied fighters, so the Kenley Wing did a couple of orbits before sweeping south west along the Dutch and Belgian coast at 20,000 feet. A lone Fortress was seen coming out between Dunkirk and Nieuport, its crew no doubt being grateful for the escort provided by a couple of dozen Canadian Spitfires!

For Squadron Leader Buck McNair of 421 Squadron, however, it was to be a trip of high drama. At 1226, over the inhospitable North Sea just off Knocke, McNair's Spitfire developed engine trouble. Unable to keep up, he dropped behind the Wing, covered by Pilot Officer Parks. Slowly losing height from 20,000 to 10,000 feet, when 12 miles off Dunkirk and over the Channel, McNair's engine caught fire. Traumatically, the pilot lost control of his aircraft, which plunged seawards. At 5,000 feet, Squadron Leader McNair managed to break free of his doomed Spitfire. At 2,000 feet Pilot Officer Parks saw with relief his chief's parachute open. McNair splashed into the Channel, Parks immediately taking a fix and transmitting a Mayday signal. The young pilot then orbitted McNair's position for 1.30 hours, until eventually relieved by 411 Squadron. As the 421 Squadron ORB says of Park's effort, it was a 'good show'.

Immediately 421 Squadron landed at Manston and heard of their CO's predicament, the Spitfires were re-fuelled, the pilots taking off to participate in the ASR operation to rescue Squadron Leader McNair. A little while later, 421 Squadron watched a Walrus pick up McNair, the Spitfires then providing escort back to Hawkinge for the curious looking but life-saving seaplane flown by Squadron Leader Grove. As Greycap's PFLB relates, the ASR sortie had lasted 1.10 hours, and McNair's ordeal in the water had lasted two hours. He was one of the lucky ones, as the 421 ORB reports: 'The Chief was burned about the face and had a real close call, but is now resting satisfactorily in hospital and should be back in a few days.'

During this mission, the Eighth Air Force lost a total of 22 B-17s lost (and some 198 men, therefore), and four more so badly damaged that they only just reached England. It was hardly surprising that this period became known by the Americans as the 'Bloody Summer of 1943'.

At 1835, Squadron Leader Godefroy led the Wing on Ramrod 168, in which the 'Kenleys' were the first wave of a fighter sweep over Abbeville, Dieppe and the Somme Estuary. Neither enemy aircraft or ships were seen, and no flak, for once, greeted the Spitfires' arrival over France. By 2010 the Wing was back home.

Interestingly, on this day, P-47 Thunderbolts operated for the first time using auxiliary fuel tanks, which extended their range to Germany's western border. It was still not far enough, however, as Allied fighters were still only able to protect the bombers on the outward flight to the extent of their endurance, then return, re-fuel, and meet them likewise on the way home.

Following Ramrod 168, the Kenley Spitfires were re-fuelled and led by Greycap across to Coltishall. There the Canadians stayed the night in readiness for an early morning show. The morrow would be another long and even more dramatic day.

July 29th

A bright and virtually cloudless day, conditions were perfect for the Eighth Air Force's purposes. The target for today was the Arado plant at Warnemünde, another works producing the FW 190. For the RAF's No 2 Group, the task of providing diversionary attacks continued. The Kenley Wing was first to fly Ramrod 112 (12 Group Ramrod 22), providing Top Cover to American B-26 Marauders attacking Schipol aerodrome. The complexity of planning such an operation is evident from the details of 12 Group's Order No 12G/6:-

Bombers: 18 Marauders of No 3 Wing, No 323 Group USAAF.

Fighters:	Close Escort Cover	402 Sqn (LR Spitfires) (Digby)
		416 Sqn (LR Spitfires) (Digby)
		611 Sqn (LR Spitfires) (Coltishall)
		118 Sqn (LR Spitfires) (Coltishall)
	Escort Cover	302 Sqn (LR Spitfires) (Portreath)
		317 Sqn (LR Spitfires) (Portreath)
	Top Cover	303 Sqn (Spitfires IX) (Northolt)
		316 Sqn (Spitfires IX) (Northolt)
		403 Sqn (Spitfires IX) (Kenley)
		421 Sqn (Spitfires IX) (Kenley)

The Close Escort Spitfires took off from Ludham and Matlask at 0935, and rendezvoused with the Marauders 14 miles north of Southwold at 11,000 feet. The bombers, however, set off for the target a minute early and their formation became scattered. Some 20 miles off Ijmuiden, the Marauders turned south and flew parallel to the Dutch coast until reaching the Hook of Holland. Bombs were then jettisoned, after which the Americans turned west and headed home. The two Wing Leaders of the close cover escort Wings, Digby and Coltishall, were perplexed, however, as no enemy aircraft were in sight and visibility was unlimited, but tried in vain to contact the bombers over the R/T. The bombers had aborted due to a navigational error, having made landfall 18 miles further north than intended.

The Kenley Wing, however, continued to the target, crossing the Dutch coast at 22,000 feet over Zandvoort and sweeping between Ijmuiden and Schipol. Greycaps PCR:-

Enemy aircraft were seen below and I instructed various Sections of 421 Squadron to engage, leaving 403 Squadron as High Cover. I attacked the last aircraft of a pair of Me 109G with cannon and MG from 450-200 yards range, firing several short bursts from astern. Enemy aircraft gave off stream of black smoke and two de Wilde strikes were seen on the cockpit. As there were other enemy aircraft about I broke off this combat and last saw the 109 diving slowly down to 10,000 feet with a steady stream of black smoke coming away from the aircraft.

Johnnie had fired 134 rounds of 20mm, and 270 of .303. The 109 was claimed as damaged. His wingman, however, was more successful:-

Pilot Officer KR Linton:-

I was flying Black 2 on 12 Group Ramrod 22, behind Wing Commander Johnson. After crossing the Dutch coast I saw an Me 109 which Wing Commander Johnson immediately turned in and attacked. He could not get close enough, so pulled up and soon after this we saw one FW 190 chasing two 109s. Wing Commander Johnson's ammunition was getting low, so he told me to attack it whilst he covered me. It was 2,000 feet below and at 2 o'clock to me. I dived on him and when within 250 yards I gave several short squirts from dead astern. The top of his rudder was shot away and I could see strikes on the fuselage and wings, then he turned slightly to port and I got in a three second burst from 20 degrees. The whole of the FW 190 seemed to burst into flames and he half-rolled and dived straight into the deck just SW of Schipol aerodrome. At least four other pilots saw this. I claim this FW 190 as destroyed.

Whilst 403 Squadron provided top cover, 421 Squadron got stuck in, as the PCRs of the 'Red Indian' pilots testify.

Flying Officer WE Harten:-

On 12 Group Ramrod 22 I was flying Green 1. About 1035 hours I was about 10-12 miles west of Schipol when 3 Me 109s flew about 500 – 600 feet below me going north-east. They were turning to starboard, I followed them around and when we were about 500 yards away the centre one and the extreme starboard one half-rolled and went straight down. The third one continued on. I closed in and fired from about 250-300 yards, 30° off. He then turned slightly to port which brought me in line astern. I fired from 100-50 yards, observing strikes on cockpit and starboard wing. He turned over to left and went straight down, smoking. I circled the area then returned home.

Flying Officer LR Thorne:-

On 12 Group Ramrod 22 I was flying Green 2 to F/O Harten. About 10 miles west of Schipol we sighted 3 Me 109s. F/O Harten led the Section around, closing in on them. Two of them half-rolled straight down but a third continued straight on and seemed to be turning slightly to starboard. F/O Harten fired and the a/c streamed white smoke. F/O Harten then pulled away and I was in a position to see the enemy aircraft burst into flames on the starboard side. He (e/a) turned to the left and went straight down. I saw him fall 2-3,000 feet then we did a turn to starboard and on looking back I saw him burning on the ground, south of the lake just north of Leiden, about five miles. The a/c fired at by F/O Harten is definitely destroyed.

Flight Lieutenant NR Fowlow:-

I was flying White 1 on Ramrod 22 at 15,000 feet south-west of Amsterdam when I saw two Me 109s flying west in echelon port, 5,000 feet below. I turned and dived down to attack the No 1 in the formation, followed by my No 2 who attacked the port aircraft in the formation. The aircraft I attacked took violent evasive action, doing a quarter roll to starboard. I followed firing intermittently and closing from 300 yards to 200 yards. The aircraft rolled on its back at about 5,000 feet with smoke pouring from it and I saw it dive straight down into the deck. I claim this Me 109 as destroyed.

Sergeant NB Dixon:-

On 12 Group Ramrod 22 I was flying as White 2 to F/Lt Fowlow. When south of Amsterdam he sighted 2 Me 109s crossing to port at 18,000 feet. Turning sharply port he cut in behind as one Me 109 rolled over. He chased it down steeply and as the other Me turned starboard down after him, I gave him 3 squirts ranging from 300-50 yards, from 60° down to dead astern and above. With no reflector sight I hosepiped him and saw hits on the starboard wing. When he dived away he was turning and going down fast at a 70° angle. I pulled up and headed home, chased by 1 Me 109. I observed three fires caused by burning aircraft south of Amsterdam. Near a lake I saw another small fire caused by burning aircraft.

On this sortie, Pilot Officer JE Abbotts and Flight Lieutenant Golberg of 403 Squadron were flying White 3 and 4 respectively with 421 Squadron. South-west of Amsterdam, White Section was bounced and Abbotts simply disappeared. Fortunately the young pilot survived being shot down, but became a prisoner of war.

403 Squadron was about to attack three enemy fighters which appeared below, but then sighted a whole gaggle of bandits above. Upon climbing to investigate, Squadron Leader Godefroy confirmed these aircraft to be Spitfires before turning home. The Wing, fragmented after 421 Squadron's hectic and successful combat, crossed out over Noorwijerhout at various heights and times, pancaking back at Coltishall at 1115.

The 421 Squadron claims were as follows:-

Wing Commander Johnson: One Me 109 damaged.
Pilot Officer Linton: One FW 190 destroyed.
Flying Officer Harten: One Me 109 destroyed.
Flight Lieutenant Fowlow: One Me 109 destroyed.
Sergeant Dixon: One Me 109 damaged.

For one missing Spitfire pilot, it was an excellent result. Amongst the German losses was at least one experienced fighter pilot and leader, *Hauptmann* Karl Anton Waldemar, the *Staffelkapitän* of 7/JG 54 *Grun Herz*. The IIIrd *Gruppe* of this famous *Jagdgeschwader* had been brought to the west from Russia, and was now based at Oldenburg and Nordholtz on Heligoland Bight. JG 3 *Udet* was also moved from Russia to the west, and JG 26 was pulled away from the Channel coast to operate on a daily basis from bases on the lower Rhine and Holland, right on the American approach routes. The Me 109s of 2/JG 27 were

withdrawn from North Africa, these augmenting the strength of JG 11, at Jever, which had been formed in April 1943 out of JG 1. Hitler, however, had yet to consider that the Reich defence force was top priority, and still sent the bulk of fighters to both the Eastern and Mediterranean fronts. In the first eight months of 1943, in fact, the output of Me 109s and FW 190s soared to 7,477, but those available to the home defence force rose but slowly: 162 in May, 255 in June, and 300 in July.

After 421 Squadron's successful fight, Greycap led his Spitfires from Coltishall back to Kenley. At 1748, the Wing was up again, on Ramrod 171, a sweep of Dieppe, Neufchatel and the Somme Estuary in support of No 2 Group bombers attacking the airfield at Yanville. The sortie passed without incident, however, and the Spitfires were safely home by 1920. The day did not end there, however, as after re-fuelling the Kenley Wing flew back to Coltishall, where the pilots again stayed overnight, this being necessary for another early start.

July 30th

On this fine day, 186 B-17s struck out and again attacked Kassel. The resulting interception by German fighters signified the fiercest clash so far between the 'Mighty Eighth' and the *Luftwaffe*: 17 Fortresses were lost, 82 more were damaged, and two Thunderbolts also failed to return. After this trip, the Eighth Air Force were really in no position to fly another major mission to Germany without first making good losses in both men and machines. At the start of 'Blitz Week', the Americans had 330 aircraft and crews ready to go. Within a week that figure had been reduced to around170. Over 100 B-17s had been lost, and around 90 crews were either missing, killed or wounded. As Johnnie has said, 'They took some hard knocks'.

At Coltishall, the Kenley Wing's Canadians were amongst a number of fighter pilots briefed for 12 Group Ramrod 23, a raid by 13 Bostons, of No Group's 107 Squadron, on Schipol aerodrome. Close Escort Cover was to be provided by the Digby and Coltishall Wings, Top Cover by the Kenley Mk IXs, and Rear Cover by 609 Squadron's Typhoons (based at Coltishall).

The Kenley Wing was up at 1005, Greycap leading the Wing whilst Flight Lieutenants Dover and Fowlow led 403 and 421 Squadrons respectively. Rendezvous was made with the beehive over Coltishall at 1009, and a direct course was set for the target. At 1036, the Kenley Wing started to climb and crossed in over Ijmuiden with squadrons stepped up to 23,000 feet. The beehive thence proceeded inland to Schipol, the Bostons dropping their bombs on target. As the bombers crossed out over Noordwijerhoot, two aircraft were seen 6,000 feet below and about seven miles behind. Suspecting the presence of more bandits, Wing Commander Johnson took the whole of 403 Squadron down, leaving 421 as Top Cover, PCR:-

There were some six enemy aircraft in this area, and I attacked the starboard 109 of the original pair. I opened fire from 400 yards with cannon and MG but enemy aircraft turned to port and dived down. As he dived away, I gave him a burst from 450 yards. I watched enemy aircraft and was surprised to see him pull out and climb steeply up. I closed in and saw that both wheels were down. I gave him another burst but did not observe any results. The 109 was then stalling and I broke away to see Flying Officer Lambert destroy the second 109. I orbitted and saw a parachute descending from the combat area. This enemy aircraft is claimed as destroyed, shared with F/Sgt Shouldice (403 Squadron).

Flight Sergeant GM Shouldice was Greycap's wingman, Red 2:-

Red 1 led our Section down to attack in a very steep dive from approximately out of the sun. When we were about 600 yards from these two E/As the port a/c veered off to port while the starboard one turned and dived to the right. Red 1 attacked the E/A which turned to starboard and I followed Red 1. Red 1 took a squirt at the E/A and his wheels dropped down, and some black smoke was emitted. I took a short burst at about 400 yards after Red 1 broke off his attack. In the course of the scrap I had about four short bursts at the E/A but cannot definitely say that I saw strikes. At about 7,000 feet I took one short burst when the E/A had wheels and flaps down and was almost stalled – no results observed. After this Red 1 observed the pilot in his parachute from this a/c. Since it is not clear whose fire caused this, we claim one Me 109 destroyed (shared).

Flying Officer JF Lambert was Red 3 in Greycap's Section:-

Red 1 and Red 2 dived on the starboard E/A whilst I led Red 4 on the other which climbed inland to starboard. As I went after it, it dived steeply and rolled and then straightened out again. I was closing on it. At about 7,000 feet and at very high speed, it began to pull out. I shot a 2-3 second burst at about 10-15 degrees deflection at about 500 yards range and then since I was very low I pulled back hard out of the dive. Levelling out at about 2,000 feet I then climbed back up to the Squadron. I law saw the enemy aircraft at about 5,000 feet, diving away very steeply and at high speed, but I did not see the result of my shooting since I had to pull out very quickly. Because of what W/C saw, however, I claim this aircraft as destroyed.

Flight Lieutenant HJ Southwood was Yellow 2 of 403 Squadron:-

I was following Yellow 2 down when at about 12,000 feet the windscreen fluid tank discharged nearly all its contents over the cockpit and myself. At first, I presumed there was an engine glycol leak and by the time I had organised myself and cleaned off my windscreen I had somehow managed to lose the rest of my Section.

My height was about 10,000 feet and I was flying north when I recognised an Me 109 coming towards me, slightly below and about 500 yards ahead. The enemy aircraft turned in on my starboard and I turned in towards and dived straight down on him, at the same time taking a very short vertical burst at about 300 – 400 yards but there were no results. The enemy then turned starboard and I got astern of him. He then continued diving at 300-400 mph. I took a long burst at about 300 yards, then a much longer one closing to about 50 yards. I used up the cannon first and ended up using machine-guns. After the first long burst from astern the wheels fell down, and I saw black smoke over the tailplane but due to the fact that I was firing into the sun and the haze, I am not sure of seeing any strikes. My windscreen was still clouded up from the windscreen tank blowing up. I broke off my attack at about 4,000 feet, last seeing the e/a spiralling down to starboard with his wheels down and black smoke trailing. I claim this 109 as damaged.

After the combat, 403 Squadron re-formed and re-joined 421 Squadron. The Kenley Wing left Holland via Zandvoort, where two FW 190s were seen but were out of range. The Wing was safely back at Coltishall by 1140, re-fuelled and returned to Kenley at 1320. It had been another successful day for the Canadians, 403 Squadrons score being as follows:-

Wing Commander Johnson & Flight Sergeant Shouldice:	One Me 109 destroyed.
Flying Officer Lambert:	One Me 109 destroyed.
Flight Lieutenant Southwood:	One Me 109 damaged.

News was received this day that Squadron Leader McNair had received a Bar to his DFC, which the 421 Squadron ORB reported as being a 'Good show'.

By now, Johnnie was attracting an increasing amount of publicity, being hailed as Finucane's successor. The following article appeared in the 'Yorkshire Post' at about this time, headlined 'Hunts Huns in Foxes' Head Scarf':-

Wing Commander JE Johnson DSO DFC & bar, the Melton Mowbray fighter ace, now has 19 German planes to his credit.

I met Johnson a year ago when he was a Flight Lieutenant at a fighter station on the East Coast. In private life he was an assistant in the office of the Borough Surveyor at Melton Mowbray.

And appropriately enough for a man from hunting country, he never flies without a yellow scarf dotted with brown foxes' heads round his neck.

At that time he had shot down about seven Germans, and the Air Ministry would not then pass his name for publication. Today he has reached the amazing total of 19. It is amazing because nowadays fighter pilots have to go out and chase Huns. That is why sweeps are organised. In the Battle of Britain the Germans came here.

When I met Johnson he spoke confidently.

On the door of his little office was painted the words 'Flight Lieutenant Johnson and Pusher'. Pusher was the most peculiar looking mongrel I have ever seen. He waved a long tail and looked like a spaniel with a setter's legs. He was a strange puce colour. But he adored his master, and 'Johnnie', as the riggers of his Spitfire called him amongst themselves, seemed to return the worship.

When he went out to his plane to take part in a sweep over France that sunny April morning, Pusher followed.

Some six months later I met him again. He looked older and harder. He had a bar on his DFC. We talked about the previous meeting. Pusher was dead, he said, killed by a lorry. He changed the conversation.

July 31st

Although the Eighth Air Force's bombers remained stood down, the B-26 Marauders of Eighth Air Service Command were still active, and it was in support of 21 such bombers that the Kenley Wing took off at 1045 (Ramrod 179). The target was the aerodrome at Merville, and the Canadian Spitfires provided cover as the Marauders withdrew amidst the black puff-balls of a heavy flak barrage. South of Bergues, a dozen Me 109s were seen orbiting 6,000 feet below, so Greycap took 421 Squadron down to attack. Although Johnnie later wrote in his PFLB 'Me 109s bounced but e/a ducked', Pilot Officer Linton fired at a 109, on which strikes were seen around the cockpit area. The enemy fighter was last seen trailing a plume of black smoke, at 3,000 feet. After this inconclusive combat (in respect of which Linton was

awarded one Me 109 damaged), the Wing to Guines and Montreuil, between 22-29,000 feet. The remainder of the sortie was uneventful, however, and by 1225 hrs the Wing was back at Kenley.

The day's second operation was Ramrod 181, Forward Target Support to Marauders bombing Abbeville. The mission went according to plan but no enemy aircraft were seen, the sortie therefore passing without incident.

At the end of the month, the score of the Kenley Wing squadrons was as follows:-

403 'Wolf' Squadron: One FW 190 destroyed.
Six-and-a-half Me 109s destroyed.
One Me 109 damaged.

421 'Red Indian' Squadron: Four Me 109s destroyed.
Four Me 109s damaged.
One Me 109 probably destroyed.
One FW 190 destroyed.
One FW 190 damaged.

In total, the Kenley Wing had flown an impressive 935.53 hours on operations; as Dan Browne says, 'We were a keen bunch'.

August 1st

A cloudy morning gave way to heavy rain during the afternoon, as a consequence of which there was no operational flying. In the afternoon, both 403 and 421 Squadron were released, except for a Section from each for defensive purposes. Although there was one scramble, no enemy aircraft were seen. The Wing Leader himself flew up to Turnhouse in Scotland, but the reason for the trip, lasting 1.40, is unclear.

August 2nd

In Greycap's absence, Squadron Leader Godefroy led the Wing on Ramrod 184, a fighter sweep of the St Calais, St Omer and Boulogne areas, controlled by Appledore. Due to R/T problems, however, Squadron Leader Godefroy had to return early, the lead being taken by 421 Squadron's Flight Lieutenant Fowlow. Bombers were seen to accurately attack the airfield at St Omer, and the northern dispersal area in particular. No fighters were encountered, however, and so the sortie was once more an eventful one for the Canadians.

During the late afternoon, the Kenley Wing flew to Manston, from which airfield a sweep was planned, but due to 'duff' weather this was cancelled.

Good news from the Red Cross was received by the Wing's Medical Officer, Squadron Leader MacArthur: Squadron Leader Foss Boulton, formerly CO of 421 Squadron, was safe, although a prisoner of war.

August 3rd
A day of scattered cloud and light showers, there were no offensive operations caried out. The Kenley Spitfires flew a variety of training sorties, however, including air firing at Friston, and caliberation tests. Flight Lieutenant HD MacDonald DFC, of 403 Squadron, left for Canada and home leave.

August 4th
According to the 421 Squadron ORB, although the 'weather was very duff' the Squadron was on Readiness from 0830-1300. 421's pilots practised on the Link Trainer, and those of 403 trained in air-to-air firing at Shoreham. Squadron Leader Godefroy also used the opportunity to brief his pilots on the impending move to 126 Airfield.

Needless to say, Johnnie organised one last 'glorious thrash' in the Mess at Kenley, before the Wing moved into tents. Invitations were sent to all the Wing Leaders, the 'top brass' at RCAF HQ, and 2nd TAF. Needless to say, the 'Big Wing Ding' was a huge success!

August 5th
There was no flying at all today, the day being spent drawigs tents and other equipment in preparation for the imminent move to Lashenden. In the afternoon, the ground crews drew their tents and erected them around the airfield perimeter. These were later taken down and all slept in the Crew Rooms and at Dispersal, ready to go early in the morning.

August 6th
At 1000, pilots not flying aircraft joined ground crews and left Kenley in motor convoy for Lashenden. The ground crews were, in fact, formally posted to '127 Airfield HQ', only the pilots were actually assigned to 403 and 421 Squadrons.

The convoy reached its destination at 1430, at which time tents had to be erected and the whole Wing unpacked.

August 7th

At 1000, Wing Commander Johnson led his Spitfires off from Kenley for the last time, bound for 127 Airfield. It was the end of an era.

As the Canadians landed at Lashenden just 15 minutes later, a new and even more exciting time was just about to begin.

Chapter Five

127 Wing at War
August 7th – September 9th, 1943

"Can you get off quickly? The Forts are in trouble."

August 7th

At 1400, a briefing was held for the pilots in the Intelligence Section, after which the Wing practised formation flying and generally became familiar with the aerial view of their new surroundings. Officially, Johnnie's Spitfires were now No 17 Wing at No 127 Airfield of No 83 Group. Soon it would become simply '127 Wing', and for the purposes of clarity and continuity this reference is used hereafter.

Bob Middlemiss:-

We had left the luxuries of batmen, soft beds, hot showers, good food, nice bar and lounge, and a short ride by electric train to the lights and excitement of London. We traded all this for tents, canvas beds, canvas wash basins, cold water for shaving, damp, cool nights and the general mud and lack of amenities that we had become accustomed to. The 'Mess Hall' was a large tent, for example, where we ate off tin plates and sat at great wooden tables. The idea was to prepare and train us for the eventual landing in France and the mobile aerial and ground warfare that an eastward Allied advance would dictate. These primitive living and operating conditions were not exactly what we had bargained for, however!

I had two great tent mates, Harry Dowding and Dean Dover. We did not have the spacious rooms of Kenley, with places to hang your clothes and spread your kit. Everything was kept in your kit bag and became a jumble of things in no time. We were good buddies, though, and got along very well under the circumstances, so much so that we remain friends to this day.

The airmen, under our 'Chiefie', Flight Sergeant Champion, fared no better than we officers, in fact they were able to improve their lot by building stoves from half 45 gallon drums and having a trickle of oil dripping down for constant fire. They were able to heat and cook on these ingenious contraptions. Of course working conditions were far from ideal. The fuel was delivered in 45-gallon drums and the aircraft re-fuelled by pumping fuel from the drum through a chamois to trap any water or condensation that may have accumulated in the drums. The daily maintenance and repairs had to be carried out in the open and under varying weather conditions, not the easiest way of maintaining the aircraft.

The airfield had two runways of PSP, and a tent for our Operations Room, the telephones manned by LACs Batty and Bennett. The Spitfires were dispersed around the airfield. The main farmhouse, owned by the Palmer Family, is where Group Captain MacBrien and Wing Commander Johnson bunked. It was also the Wing Operations Centre.

August 8th

A clear, warm day of scattered cloud, Ramrod 190 was laid on, the Wing's first offensive sortie from Lashenden. The Spitfires' role was as the second fighter sweep in support of 36 Marauders bombing the airfield of II/JG 2 at Poix. Greycap led the Wing in at 20,000 feet, but was recalled whilst orbiting in the target area. The Canadians then swept back along the French coast from Le Treport to Cap-Gris-Nez. No enemy aircraft were sighted, and 127 Wing re-crossed the English coast high above Dover.

Over France the weather had been poor: 9/10ths cloud at 5,000 feet, and high cirrus cloud at 25,000 feet, although the weather was breaking between Boulogne and Dunkirk to 15 miles inland. Again, this emphasises how offensive operations during this particular era were influenced by the changeable weather over northwest Europe.

August 9th

In the morning and early afternoon, Johnnie flew EN398 on aerobatics, testing performance when fitted with the auxiliary fuel tank, and again on an 'Aircraft test'. It was then time for the day's offensive operation, Ramrod 191, high cover to 36 Marauders bombing St Omer.

The Wing was up at 1745, rendezvous being made with the Marauders according to plan. The Spitfires positioned themselves on the beehive's port side, crossing the French coast at 21,000 feet. Due to a complete covering of cloud over the target, no result could be seen after bombs were dropped. When 20 miles inland, Pilot Officer Heeney, of 421 Squadron, reported engine trouble. His motor cut, and the unfortunate pilot was last seen 'gliding into haze at 15,000 feet' (403 ORB) baled out at 2,000 feet. As the 421 Squadron ORB later reported 'Pilot Officer Heeney had just returned from a Fighter Leader's Course and will be greatly missed in the Squadron'. By 1745, the Wing was back at Lashenden, nothing else of note having occurred.

August 10ᵗʰ

Early in the morning, 127 Wing flew to Bradwell Bay, on the south coast, from where it was to participate in a sweep. Bad weather over the Continent led to the operation being scrubbed, the Spitfires returning to Lashenden just before noon. On this day, Sergeants Chevers and Cottrill reported back to 403 Squadron, having been detached to the Middle East for several months.

August 11ᵗʰ

Again due to the duff weather, there was no operational flying, although a number of training flights were made. 403 Squadron's proposed practise formation flight was called off at this last minute following an order for Godefroy's pilots to pack all their equipment ready for a practice move. Such short-notice mobility would soon be the order of the day, and practice was essential. The Squadron's ORB proudly states that 'It only takes one hour now to pack everything, including tents, ready to move'.

Squadron Leader McNair, recently discharged from hospital following his escapade which ended in the sea, returned to 421 Squadron and resumed his duties as CO. The ORB reported that 'He is quite recovered and in good spirits, anxious to get flying again.'

In the hope of improving weather, a sweep was planned for early the following day. Johnnie led 127 Wing down to the coastal airfield at Bradwell Bay, to extend the Spitfires' range, where the Canadians stayed overnight in readiness for the morrow.

August 12ᵗʰ

Having rested after the maximum effort of 'Blitz Week', the Eighth Air Force was once more ready to go. During that fortnight, staff officers had planned the greatest raid so far. The greatest priority was still destroying the enemy's capacity to produce fighter aircraft. The main production centres for Me 109s, and indeed nearly 50% of all German fighters, was at Regensburg and Wiener Neustadt, a long, long way from the American bases in East Anglia. If the bombers flew to those targets and returned to England, the enemy would literally have a field day. It was agreed, therefore, that instead, the bombers would fly out from England, bomb the target, but then fly on and land at Allied bases in North Africa. Such a route would undoubtedly confuse the enemy, in the process reducing casualties. Later it was decided that, as not all 1st Wing B-17s were fitted with long-range 'Tokyo' fuel tanks, Wiener Neustadt should not be attacked by the Eighth Air Force in England, but by the two B-24 Liberator Groups of the Ninth, based in North Africa, and those three of the Eighth currently on detachment in Libya. To cause maximum confusion, however, both targets were to be hit on the same day: August 7th. In the event, bad weather prevented this, dictating that the plan be changed to permit each force to attack its specified target as and when improved weather conditions allowed.

Whilst the Eighth Air Force planners anxiously awaited the opportunity to put their ambitious plans into action, the pressure was maintained on other targets. On August 12th, therefore, 330 B-17s attacked industrial targets in the Ruhr valley. Cloud caused problems over Germany, however, preventing the American bombardiers getting a clear sight of their targets. Consequently only two Bomb Groups bombed their objectives, the remainder seeking targets of opportunity. The Germans concentrated their fighters inland, beyond reach of the outward bound escorting P-47s. The result was devastating: at least 25 bombers were destroyed, with over 100 sustaining damage. It was a tattered and badly beaten up force, therefore, that droned back towards England, anxiously awaiting the arrival of 'Little Friends'.

The Canadians at Bradwell Bay found the early morning very cold with thick fog. The Wing was tasked with Ramrod 194, providing escort to the B-17s returning from Germany. The fog, however, delayed the Spitfires' take-off by 30 minutes.

Bob Middlemiss:-

A fine example of Johnnie's leadership concerns the events of August 12th, 1943. We were briefed for the trip, to escort B-17s withdrawing from Germany, but the fog was so thick that we thought the operation would be cancelled. The Wing Commander informed us of the desperate need for escorting the 'Forts' because of the pounding they had taken both on the way in to the target and equally out on return. He had us start up and taxi into position at the end of the runway. He finally said that he personally would take-off and test the weather, and if found suitable then the rest of the Wing was to follow. Johnnie took off, and was soon giving us the word to follow on and join him. We took off in absolutely zero zero weather, wingmen hanging on to their leader's wings, the latter having taken off blind, on instruments alone. Thankfully the fog was not actually too thick, and the Wing came through with flying colours.

Johnnie could have easily aborted this mission because of the bad weather conditions, but, knowing of the bombers' need for our help, he made the decision of a true leader.

Once airborne and formated on their leader, the Spitfire pilots headed for the Belgian coast, which was crossed at 22,000 feet. Shortly afterwards, the Hornchurch Wing was sighted to the north, covering a number of withdrawing Flying Fortresses. Greycap led his Wing to the Rotterdam area, making an orbit there before turning south. More bombers were then seen, escorted by Thunderbolts. Another box followed, without escort, with a single B-17 straggling some distance behind. Eight Me 109s, operating either singly or in pairs, were attacking these unprotected bombers. Kenley Control asked Greycap to protect this last box (PCR, JEJ):-

As I attacked a Me 109, who was nibbling at a straggling Fortress, I instructed my No 2, Flight Lieutenant Conrad, to engage another Me 109 in this vicinity. I opened fire on this e/a from 300-100 yards, firing several short bursts. Cannon strikes were seen on his wing roots and the e/a fell away in an exaggerated 'falling leaf', skidding and stalling from side to side. An aircraft was seen to crash by Flying Officer Browne (Yellow 3) and owing to the proximity of Flight Lieutenant Conrad's attack, one of these two e/a was undoubtedly destroyed.

Pending examination of cine film, these two e/a are claimed as one destroyed and one damaged, shared by Flight Lieutenant Conrad and myself.

Flight Lieutenant Phillip of 421 Squadron broke off to engage an Me 109, chasing and slightly damaging it. The Wing then re-formed and stayed with the bombers as the formation ponderously made its way back across the North Sea. When 15 miles off the Dutch coast, an Me 109 stalked 421 from astern. Flight Lieutenant Phillip and White Section crossed over to investigate, and when within range he opened fire, seriously damaging the German. It was the last combat during this trip, which saw the B-17s safely back to England.

It had been a long flight for the Spitfire pilots. 127 Wing had taken off from

Bradwell Bay at 0925, but had not landed, at various forward airfields, until 1130. After re-fuelling, the Spitfires headed back to Lashenden, all being back safely by 1220.

At 1800, the Wing was up again, on Ramrod 198, sweeping Dieppe, Amiens and Poix under Appledore Control. Flak spat forth from Abancourt, Amiens, Abbeville and Crecy, but the Spitfires were unscathed. Twenty Me 109s were seen but were beyond range and could not be engaged. By 1930, the Wing was back home without anything further of incident to report.

Having only just returned from hospital, it is to his great credit that the CO of 421 Squadron, Squadron Leader Buck McNair, flew on both of the day's offensive operations.

In 403 Squadron, there was a change of command. Squadron Leader Hugh Godefroy was posted to 127 Wing HQ, it being anticipated that he would return as Wing Leader when Johnnie was tour expired. Flying Officer NJ Ogilvie was promoted to Acting Flight Lieutenant, taking command of 'A' Flight, and Pilot Officer Dean Dover was likewise promoted and took command of 'B' Flight.

August 13th
Due to the worsening weather there was very little flying of any description. In the afternoon, both 403 and 421 Squadrons were released.

Although the Eighth Air Force's route to Regensburg was still obstructed by cloud, today the North African based B-24s successfully bombed Wiener Neustadt.

August 14th
Again there was no operational flying, but 127 Wing flew numerous training flights, mainly air firing at Shoreham. At 1115, 421 Squadron took off and practised an attack on 403 Squadron's dispersed Spitfires and Airfield HQ. According to the 421 ORB, the 'attack was very realistic'.

August 15th
By complete contrast, the weather on this day was 'exceptionally good' (ORB, 421). At 1015, Greycap led his Spitfires up on Ramrod 201, Forward Target Support to Marauders bombing Woensdricht. Although 127 Wing's Time On

Target (TOT) was correct, there was no sign of the bombers. South of Flushing the Spitfires clashed briefly with a gaggle of FW 190s, Flying Officer Johnson, of 421 Squadron, damaging one of these. After an otherwise uneventful sortie, 127 Wing was safely home by 1150.

The Wing's second and final operation of the day was Ramrod 202, providing escort to B-17s bombing the enemy airfields at Poix and Amiens. There was no enemy reaction. Poix airfield was not, in the event, hit but 'Amiens was well blanketed, causing a large number of fires. Lille and Vitry were also well hit. Heavy and accurate flak was experienced from Abbeville and Amiens, but all the bombers crossed back out over the French coast safely' (ORB, 403). By 2030, 127 Wing was back home.

There was a good reason for these frequent and heavy bombardments of German airfields in the Pas-de-Calais. Operation STARKEY had started at the beginning of this third week of August. This was aimed at deceiving the enemy into believing that an Allied invasion of the Pas-de-Calais was imminent, mainly in the hope of delaying German troop movements to both Italy and Russia.

August 16th
At last a sunny and cloudless day. 127 Wing was to fly on Ramrod 203, escorting Fortresses returning from STARKEY attacks in the Paris area. The Spitfires were off at 0940, meeting the B-17s over Bernay and bringing them safely back. The Wing was down by 1115 with nothing of incident to report.

Next came Ramrod 205, in which Johnnie's Spitfires provided Forward Target Support to Marauders bombing the JG 2 airfield at Beaumont-le-Roger. Notification of this operation was only given at 1600, there then being 'quite some panic' (ORB, 403) to get the Wing off by 1620. Nevertheless, the sweep went according to plan, although south of Rouen a gaggle of FW 190s were sighted. These rapidly 'ducked as usual' (PFLB, JEJ), however, and were not engaged.

Back at Lashenden, there was 'another panic for a while as all aircraft had to go to Bradwell Bay for an early morning sweep' (ORB, 403). Even a couple of spare Spitfires were flown down to Bradwell, where the Canadians again stayed overnight ready for an early morning operation. It would be the big one.

August 17th

This was the day that the Americans had been waiting for. With favourable weather over both Europe and the Mediterranean, the decision was made to go ahead with the Regensburg mission. The 4th Bomb Wing, equipped with Tokyo tanks, was to attack the famous Messerschmitt factory, then, instead of returning to England, fly on to and land in North Africa. As if this brilliant 'Shuttle' concept was not enough, the 1st Wing was to concurrently attack the Schweinfurt ball-bearing factory and then return to East Anglia.

The weather over England itself was still not that good, however, especially over East Anglia where the B-17s found themselves fog-bound. As so often in war, the best laid of plans became subject to hasty changes. As the 4th Bomb Wing needed to land at the unfamiliar North African airfields in daylight, take-off could only be delayed for an hour. The 1st Bomb Wing, however, had to wait three-and-a-half hours before take-off for the Regensburg fighter escorts to return and re-fuel. Fighter leaders were apparently not consulted regarding this change of plan which, however necessary, gave their ground crews one hour less than was required to turn their aircraft around. This meant that fighter cover would be significantly reduced. Circumstances, over which the planners had no control or influence, were beginning to suggest, in military parlance, that the mission would become a 'SNAFU', rather than executed with the precision that this innovative concept deserved.

Wing Commander Johnson briefed his pilots on their first task in connection with the day's major operations. This was to be Ramrod 206 Part I, on which 127 Wing was to be amongst the Allied fighters escorting the outward bound Regensburg force of 146 Fortresses. Having taken-off at 1315, Greycap rendezvoused with the B-17s as planned, just north of Walcheren Island. The Spitfires then escorted the Fortresses to Antwerp, the limit of their radius of action, where they were relieved by Thunderbolts of the 353rd Fighter Group. By this time, I & III/JG 26 were up, but although their FW 190s could be seen some way off, the Spitfires were unable to engage. Reluctantly, Greycap turned his Wing about and returned to Bradwell Bay, landing at 1457. Soon the Thunderbolts would also have to return, leaving the bombers to the mercy of the intercepting German fighters. Then, I/JG 1, I & II/JG 3 relieved I & III/JG 26, and were able to attack the B-17s unhindered.

Johnnie:-

After leaving the Regensburg Forts, we went back to Bradwell Bay and had a wad and a cuppa, and so on whilst the aircraft were turned around. About an hour-and-a-half later the Controller rang me and said "Can you get off quickly, the Forts are in trouble".

The Spitfires were up again, on Ramrod 206 Part II, at 1608, making haste to Antwerp. Crossing over the Belgian coast near Blankenburg, the B-17s were met at 24,000 feet over St Nicholas at 1647.

Johnnie:-

It was a devastating sight. This proud formation that we had escorted out was now very knocked about. There were great holes in the formation, and stragglers lagged well behind the main boxes. It was obvious that things had not gone well, as we anticipated would happen. I thought then and I still think now just how inexcusable it was that we had not been given the required range in the first place. Deplorable, wasn't it?

The 127 Wing Combat Report describes events:-

Dogfight seen in Antwerp area and one e/a seen to disintegrate. Three-four Me 109s seen in Antwerp area and six-seven Me 109s seen in Hulst area, following the bombers, but the Wing was unable to engage. Me 110 seen stooging around north of Ghent and attacked by 403 Squadron. W/C Johnson (Red 1), F/Lt Dover (Blue 1), F/O Foster (Blue 3), and F/O Preston (Blue 2), all making attacks and seeing strikes on e/a which resulted in silencing rear gunner and setting port engine on fire. This e/a was seen to go down in flames and crash, and is claimed as destroyed.

F/Lt Southwood (Yellow 2) attacked an Me 109G in this area without observing results. 421 Squadron escorted bombers to English coast, 403 Squadron leaving the bombers in Bruges area to investigate a/c that proved to be friendly. A lone FW 190 was seen near Bergues, and Yellow Section went down to investigate.

Squadron Leader Conrad, Red 3, and his wingman, Flight Sergeant Shouldice, Red 4, cut over the top of Yellow section, so keen were they both to attack. The 190 was subsequently hit by a veritable storm of shot and shell, and was last believed seen, by Flying Officer Dan Browne, Yellow 3, breaking up before piling straight in.

Disaster then struck Conrad and Shouldice, whose Spitfires collided. The former's tail unit and an aileron were seen to break off. Conrad's Spitfire was last seen tumbling earthwards from 3-4,000 feet over Bergues. The right aileron and wingtip of Shouldice's Spitfire was also damaged, as the Wing Leader remembered:-

That was a terrible shame as young Shouldice was a good pilot. He told me what happened over the R/T and I told him to climb up to 10,000 feet and bale out. The problem was that his hood had also been damaged during the collision, and was jammed. The only option was to try and get him back across the Channel, so I called up Kenley and got the controller to organise ASR. Having given Shouldice a course for Dover, we went looking and found him just off the French coast. It didn't look good. The aircraft kept trying to yaw to the right, and every time Shouldice had to struggle with the control column to pull the aircraft on course. We were half way home, with just 10 miles to go, when he lost the struggle. The Spitfire yawed right over, wings vertical. I could see Shouldice struggling with the hood, but he just couldn't open it and went straight in. There was a great splash and that was that.

Johnnie called up and fixed the position where the Spitfire had crashed, but nothing was ever seen again of Flight Sergeant Shouldice (who is now remembered on the Runnymede Memorial).

Having landed and re-fuelled at Bradwell Bay, by 1750 the Wing was back at Lashenden. There two now poignant items of news awaited the pilots' return: Walter Conrad had been promoted to Acting Squadron Leader and appointed to command 403 Squadron, and Flight Sergeant Shouldice commissioned.

On that winter's day in 1997, when Johnnie recounted this tale to me, there was moisture in the eyes of this tough old warrior, himself the victor of so many grim air battles and witness to countless violent deaths in those wartorn skies of yesteryear.

Walter Conrad was, however, more fortunate than his wingman, given that he managed to safely bale out. Landing in the Pas-de-Calais, assisted by the French Underground he successfully evaded and trekked over the Pyrenees into Spain. From there passage to England was arranged, the fortunate young pilot arriving on October 10th (for an account of Conrad's adventures, see *Winged Victory*, details in Bibliography).

The German pilot attacked by 403 Squadron in the action that led to Conrad and Shouldice being reported 'Missing' was *Leutnant* Helmut Hoppe, *Staffelkapitän* of 4/JG 26. Later he claimed the destruction of the two colliding Spitfires, but this was disallowed on the grounds that there were no witnesses. On that basis, however, it could not have been Hoppe who Flying Officer Browne had seen crash. Perhaps the speed of combat had once more deceived the human eye, and Dan actually saw Conrad's Spitfire impact?

At Regensburg, the Americans had bombed the target from 17-19,000 feet with great accuracy. Major damage was caused to two-thirds of the workshops. Included in that destruction were the fuselage jigs of the secret Me 262 jet fighter, which now faced a serious production delay. The cost, however, was high: 24 B-17s were missing, of which five had ditched in the Mediterranean due to fuel exhaustion and engine failure. Schweinfurt had also been successfully pranged, but 36 B-17s and over 370 airmen failed to return from that target. Furthermore, many other American fliers had returned either dead or wounded in damaged bombers. The dramatic events of this day represented the most awesome air battle that the world had seen so far in this global conflict.

Although the Germans were confused, as intended, by the Regensburg force's southern turn over Italy and onward flight to North Africa, the German controllers undoubtedly managed their forces extremely well. For JG 26, for example, the balance sheet represented one of the unit's most successful days of the whole war. Even so, it was not without cost. Amongst the *Geschwader's* five dead pilots was the popular Major Wilhelm-Ferdinand 'Wutz' Galland, *Kommandeur* of II/JG 26 and brother of General Adolf Galland.

Perhaps in war there are, after all, no victors?

August 18th
For the Allied fighter pilots there was no respite, as the STARKEY raids continued unabated. At 0945, Greycap led 127 Wing up on Ramrod 208, High Cover to Marauders bombing Lille/Vandeville airfield. After the rendezvous, the Spitfires took the Americans to within 10 miles of the French coast where 'towering black cloud and heavy rain' (ORB, 403) was encountered. Some of the bombers and the Close Escort flew straight through the weather, but 127 Wing remained above the cloud, picking up the beehive as it returned. No enemy aircraft were sighted and the Spitfires were back home by 1105.

In the afternoon, Johnnie flew EN398 over to Headcorn Airfield, another base similar to Lashenden, and undertook 'Runway Trials'. This would soon have significance.

August 19th
At 1245, Greycap and the Wing were up on Ramrod 209, a fighter sweep, under Appledore, in support of Marauders bombing Glisy. When southeast of Abbeville, the Spitfires of 421 Squadron engaged 12 Me 109s. Flying Officer AE Fleming and Flight Lieutenant AC Coles each destroyed an Me 109, but Pilot Officer Joyce failed to return. ORB, 421 Squadron: 'P/O Joyce had just been notified that his commission had come through just a few hours before taking off. He was a very promising pilot and had been with the Squadron for about five months'. Fortunately Joyce was not dead, but a prisoner of war.

Although weakened after the events of August 17th, during the early evening of August 19th, the Eighth Air Force B-17s attacked enemy airfields in Holland (Woensdrecht, Gilze-Rijen, and Soubourg). 127 Wing was to be amongst the Spitfire squadrons escorting the returning bombers. The bombers were met and seen safely off back towards England, at which point Greycap swept 127 Wing over Flushing and Ghent. A gaggle of 12 Me 109s were sighted and engaged by 403 Squadron. Two 109s were destroyed: one shared by Flying Officers Dowding and Brannagan, the other by Flight Lieutenant Dover. The Wing suffered no losses during the skirmish, and all were safely home by 1840.

August 20th
Today, 127 Airfield was changed from Lashenden to nearby Headcorn, bound for which location 16 Spitfires took off at 0755, pancaking 20 minutes later. The Wing's communications aircraft, a Tiger Moth, followed at 0815, the remainder of personnel moving by transport 45 minutes later. At Headcorn, the pilots busied themselves erecting tents and Dispersal marquees. According to the 403 Squadron ORB, 'Everybody was busy all day loading and unloading trucks, and then a sweep came off in the afternoon in the middle of the panic!' At 1450 the Wing took off on Ramrod 211, Forward Target Support, but no enemy opposition was encountered. By evening, 'everyone was pretty well settled' (ORB, 403).

Johnnie, however, had not flown on Ramrod 211 (contrary to the ORB of 403 Squadron). Instead he had taken off in a Spitfire Mk V, 'WH-M', bound for Bolt

Head, but for some unknown reason had to put down at Warmwell. From there he flew to the Sector Station at Middle Wallop, lunching with the Station Commander, Group Captain Hardy (PFLB, JEJ). Later that day Greycap flew up to Rearsby, in Leicestershire, and started a 48-hour leave. Of course there was great interest in his career back home, Meltonians in particular followed Johnnie's exploits with great pride. The following article was published in a county newspaper entitled 'Melton Ace in Over 200 Air Operations':-

When the Melton Mowbray air ace, Wing Commander Johnnie Johnson DSO DFC & bar, leader of Fighter Command" top scoring Canadian Wing, leads his men into battle, he wears on the shoulders on his flying tunic the 'Canada' name flash. The badge does not appear on his other tunics. He wears it as a token of fellowship and admiration for the Canadians with whom he has flown and fought for the past six months.

Under his leadership this Wing has destroyed more than 70 enemy aircraft and probably destroyed or damaged many more.

His own score is 23 enemy aircraft destroyed, the latest on Monday, which makes him next to Group Captain 'Sailor' Malan, the highest-scoring pilot still in service with Fighter Command.

He has taken part in more than 200 daylight operations.

Fourteen of his victories have been won in the same Spitfire, and though in it he led the Canadian Wing on more than 90 sweeps over enemy territory, it was never once touched by bullets or AA fire, states the Air Ministry News Service.

Some of his victories were won while flying as No 2 to Wing Commander Douglas Bader, the legless fighter ace now a prisoner of war. He was with Bader on his last flight.

Johnson was born at Loughborough in 1915, and his home is now in Melton Mowbray.

One reporter wrote that:-

Yesterday an RAF Spitfire pilot told me: "We reckon Johnnie is the 'find' of the year. In six months he has proved himself a great leader".

Like Malan, Johnson fights unselfishly, thinking always of the rawest youngster in his Wing, nursing his men, giving them a chance to destroy planes while he manoeuvres them to do it. But this did not stop him in one period of five days in May (1943) shooting down himself three FW 190s and sharing in the destruction of a fourth.

So Johnson's 23 victories have come almost in spite of himself. He is in no race to gather victims any more than other brilliant newcomers among the top rankers, including Wing Commander Bill Compton and Squadron Leader JM Checketts.

August 21st
A complete covering of cloud over England and the Continent dictated that no operations were flown today. Some local flying was carried out, but 403 Squadron was released from noon and until dawn the following day.

August 22nd
Today the cloud had thinned to 6/10ths. A sweep planned for 0800 was postponed and then cancelled. At 1500 a lecture on 'War Strategy' was given in the hangar At 1820, however, Squadron Leader McNair led 127 Wing off on Ramrod 213, in which the Canadians were to provide the first wave of a fighter sweep in support of medium bombers again attacking German airfields. East of Le Havre, the Wing sighted 16 FW 190s but could not close the gap to engage. By 1950 the Wing was safely back at Headcorn.

In the evening, Wing Commander Johnson flew his borrowed Spitfire Mk V from Rearsby to Headcorn, re-joining his pilots.

August 23rd
The cloud covering had now thinned to 3/10ths. At 0800, Greycap led the Wing off from Headcorn on Ramrod 214, Target Cover to Marauders bombing Gosnay. 403 Squadron was led by Flight Lieutenant Dean Dover, and 421 by Squadron Leader McNair. Halfway over the Channel, however, the bombers were re-called, but the Wing swept on, as described by Wing Commander Johnson's PCR:-

Appledore took over and after two vectors I sighted Huns in the Bethune area. There was 15 plus e/a with an up-sun cover of a further three e/a. I instructed one Section to shadow these three e/a until the remaining a/c were in a position to attack the main force, but unfortunately both Section Leaders misinterpreted this order and as a result only four a/c were left to deal with the 15 plus (421 Squadron top guard). E/A turned to port and climbed steeply. I selected a FW 190 in the middle of the gaggle and opened fire from 300-180 yards, with cannon and MG – angle off 5°.

Towards the end of the burst, several strikes were seen in the cockpit and wing roots and e/a caught fire and spun down enveloped in flame. This FW 190 is claimed as destroyed.

Most Wing pilots saw Greycap's victim to go down in flames, pouring heavy black smoke.

Flying Officer Bob Middlemiss was flying as Greycap's No 2:-

I fired a burst at the e/a flying on the starboard side of Red 1 (Wing Commander Johnson). The first burst I under-deflected and saw no results. I gave it another burst with less deflection and saw strikes on the port side about the wing roots. My attention was distracted by a large sheet of flame on my port side, which was evidently W/C Johnson's one. I therefore saw no further results on the e/a which I had fired at, and so I claim one FW 190 as damaged.

The Spitfires had clashed with 10/JG 26, and had, in fact, destroyed both FW 190s engaged; *Oberfeldwebel* Erich Borounick and *Gefrieter* Helmuth Ullman were both killed, their aircraft crashing in Artois.

127 Wing all landed safely at 0900. Interestingly, in his PFLB, Johnnie recorded the victory as an 'Me 109', which just goes to emphasise the difficulty of aircraft identification during combat.

After attending a meeting at Kenley, at 1720 Greycap was off at the head of his Spitfires again, on Ramrod 252. This operation was a sweep of the Somme, Abbeville and Amiens. Near the latter, five enemy fighters were sighted and chased, but the Germans dived towards Amiens and escaped. There was no other reaction and by 1840 the Spitfires were safely back at Headcorn.

August 24th

Heavy cloud during the morning and afternoon saw nothing doing operationally. According to the 403 Squadron ORB, however, 'In the afternoon six of our pilots were ordered to beat up the aerodrome and gun positions around it on a practice attack, which turned out very good indeed'.

By evening, the cloud had cleared sufficiently to permit B-17s to attack the enemy airfields at Evreux and Conches. 127 Wing consequently flew Ramrod 215, at 1755, proving Close Escort. East of Rouen a lone B-17 was seen heading north but was not in any trouble. Southwest of the city a fire was seen on the ground, possibly caused by a crashed aircraft. There was no enemy reaction, however, and the Spitfires were home by 1925.

August 25th

Although reportedly a day of scattered cloud and occasional showers, operations were still on.

At 1840, 127 Wing took off on Ramrod S2, High Cover to 18 Bostons bombing Beaumont-le-Roger. In the Caen area, the Bostons were attacked by elements of JG 2, 421 Squadron in turn bouncing a gaggle of FW 190s. Pilot Officer McLachlan promptly closed to 50 yards and destroyed one of them. There was nothing else of incident to report, but when the Spitfires landed back at Headcorn (2030) it was dusk. The lengthening shadows indicated that this particular 'fighter pilots' summer' was on the wane.

As from this day, 403 and 421 Squadron were to rotate always having four Spitfires on the runway at Readiness, for aerodrome defensive purposes.

August 26th

On this day, Johnnie received a visitor: Squadron Leader Wally 'Nip' Hepple DFC, a former 616 Squadron and Tangmere Wing comrade, now a successful fighter pilot having scored well over Malta. In the morning, Johnnie and 'Nip' flew up to Kenley in a Proctor, enjoying lunch in the Officers' Mess. The pair then returned to Headcorn, Squadron Leader Hepple waving his friend off at 1805 on Ramrod S5. Unusually, however, Greycap was not flying EN398, but 'KH-F'. 127 Wing was to be the fourth wave of a fighter sweep over Tricqueville, Rouen and Caen. Over France, a gaggle of 15 plus Me 109s and FW 190s were engaged in a running battle fought in and out of cloud from 12 – 5,000 feet. Several combats took place at close range but were inconclusive due to the cloud cover. Wing Commander Johnson, however, flying as Red 1 of 403 Squadron, destroyed a FW 190 over Caen. According to the 421 ORB, another 190 was 'frightened by Green Section into firing at and destroying an Me 109. This e/a is claimed as destroyed by P/O Cook'. All of our aircraft returned safely and were home by 1940.

August 27th

Today it was the turn of Beaumont-le-Roger to take another pounding from 18 Bostons. Greycap led 127 Wing on High Cover, taking off on Ramrod S6 at

0835. Over mid-Channel, however, the raid was aborted due to unsuitable weather, the bombers turning back. The Spitfires swept on over Rouen, Le Havre and the Somme, but there was no enemy reaction. By 1010, the Spitfires were back at Headcorn.

Next came Ramrod S8, at 1835. This time the Wing escorted 60 B-17s bombing an 'aeronautical facilities station' at Watten, located between Calais and St Omer. Allied Intelligence strongly, and as it turned out quite rightly, suspected that the site was connected with the enemy secret weapons programme. In total, 224 B-17s attacked this target, the force being divided into four smaller groups. This would be the first of many missions under the codename Operation CROSSBOW.

One minute before the Spitfire pilots started their mighty Merlin engines, however, word was received that the rendezvous time had been advanced by 15 minutes. By racing off at full throttle, the Spitfires managed to shave 10 minutes off that quarter-of-an-hour, and met the Fortresses over St Pol. The bombing had been fairly accurate, the target burning fiercely. Two B-17s were seen by 127 Wing to go down, one near St Omer, the other over St Pol. Many parachutes were seen amidst a whirling mass of fighters. In the confusion, only five enemy aircraft were positively identified, and although some of the Wing's pilots fired their guns it was without result. Flying Officer Foster of 403 Squadron crash-landed at Manston, although no reason is given, but otherwise the Wing returned safely, landing at various forward airfields.

Acting Squadron Leader FE Grant reported for duty as 403 Squadron's new CO.

August 28th
Due to bad weather there were no operations. 127 Airfield personnel were, however, kept busy digging slit trenches, and Squadron Leader Grant went aloft to familiarise himself with the local area.

August 29th
Again the weather was poor, forcing the cancellation of a Ramrod laid on for 0730.

The only sorties flown by 127 Wing were of a non-operational nature. Pilot Officer Wilson, of 403 Squadron, 'on landing broke his tail wheel on the wire netted runway. No blame was attached to him for the accident'. Greycap flew EN398 on a 30 minute air test following a 240 hour engine change and a 'general check at Hamble' (PFLB, JEJ).

August 30th

In the morning, Wing Commander Johnson flew over to 122 Airfield at Funtingdon, in Sussex, home of 19, 65 and 122 Squadrons. Flying Officer Peter 'Jock' Taylor was a young pilot with 65 Squadron at the time:-

I remember that. Johnnie Johnson came over to talk to us as his Wing was having more success than we were at lower altitude. He related to us his experience and returned for another operation.

That operation was Ramrod S14, Target Support to a bombing raid on St Omer airfield. 127 Wing swept the Armentieres area, covering the bombers. As the Pas-de-Calais was covered by scattered cloud, the bombers' results could not be seen. By 1958, the Canadians were back at Headcorn, ready to celebrate their leader's Bar to the DSO, news of which had been received that day and in recognition of yet more inspirational leadership. Even the AOC came down, so it must have been quite a party!

August 31st

Despite the party of the previous evening, Greycap was leading 127 Wing off at 0655 on Ramrod S16: Part 2, Top Cover to 36 Marauders bombing Maringarbe. Bombing was reportedly good, but although 12 Me 109s were seen over Lille, they could not be engaged. The operation passed otherwise without incident, the Wing landing at 0825.

The day's second and final trip was Ramrod S17: Part 2, at 1655, providing escort to B-17s attacking Brussells. When 10 miles south of Ghent, 421 Squadron bounced five Me 109s, out of the sun. Squadron Leader McNair and Flight Lieutenant Phillip subsequently claimed one each destroyed. Cloud, however, obscured the target, and so the mission was not a great success. In fact, it is fair to say that cloud had afforded the German aircraft industry the greatest protection of all throughout the summer of 1943.

After the brief engagement, 421 Squadron re-joined 403, which had provided cover, and returned to base via Dunkirk, landing at 1830.

This day's victories had brought the personal score of Squadron Leader McNair to 13 destroyed, five probables and eight damaged. Overall, during the month of August, 421 Squadron had destroyed four enemy aircraft and damaged four more. Two Spitfires had, however, been lost in return. 403 Squadron claimed five enemy aircraft destroyed and one damaged, but the balance sheet also recorded that Conrad and Shouldice were missing, and six other pilots had suffered injuries.

September 1ˢᵗ

As the 'weather over France was unserviceable' (ORB, 403), there were no operational flights made by 127 Wing. Squadron Leader Godefroy visited 403 Squadron, although he was officially still on leave, and in the evening Headcorn was also paid a visit by Wing Commander Hodgson DFC, Officer Commanding 126 Wing (Tangmere), and Wing Commander Dal Russell DFC, Wing Commander Flying at that aerodrome. The purpose of the 126 Wing officers' visit was to liaise with their counterparts in 127 regarding the following day's sortie.

September 2ⁿᵈ

At 0800, 127 Wing took off from Headcorn, led by Greycap, and flew down to Tangmere. At 1805, both 126 and 127 Wings were up, escorting 72 Marauders bombing Hesdin Woods, another CROSSBOW operation. Inland of Berck, 127 Wing left the beehive to investigate some aircraft, which turned out to be friendly. The Wing then swept to the target, thence to St Omer and back to Doullens/Berck. No enemy aircraft were seen but from the area southeast to southwest of St Omer 'some very intense, heavy, and unusually accurate flak was experienced'. By 1940, the Spitfires were back at Headcorn.

It was not all derring-do, however, as the 421 Squadron ORB relates, 'Some of our pilots have been shooting partridges during the past few days, and have met with some success'.

September 3ʳᵈ

Today the weather was good.

At 0917, Wing Commander Johnson led the Wing on Ramrod S26: Part III, Top Cover to 36 Marauders bombing Beaumont-le-Roger. North of Evereux, Greycap despatched a Section of 421 Squadron to engage four Me 109s, which could be seen attacking some B-17s returning from south of Paris. Flying Officer MC Love fired at one of the enemy fighters, which promptly blew up. Love's aircraft, however, was hit by debris from the explosion. The Spitfire's engine caught fire and the fighter streamed glycol. Greycap gave him the same orders that he had given Flight Sergeant Shouldice a few weeks previously: head inland and bale out. This Love did, last being seen flying towards Argentan, under control. Having acknowledged his instructions, the young Canadian's last words over the R/T were "See you in Gib".

Simultaneous to Love's attack, Squadron Leader McNair also destroyed a 109, which was seen to crash, so there was no question regarding the accuracy of either claim. The remainder of the Wing had stayed with the bombers and did not engage. By 1100, the Spitfires were back at Headcorn.

Later that day, there was to be another operation to bomb the V1 installations hidden within the Foret d'Eperlecques (as on August 27th). 127 Wing was to escort 24 B-25s on this raid, Ramrod S27, taking off at 1245. Having seen the bombers safely clear of the French coast, Greycap was vectored back into France. Except for two German fighters seen taking off from Merville, no enemy aircraft were sighted and there were no engagements, although flak, both intense and heavy, threatened the Spitfires over St Omer. By 1409, 127 Wing was home.

September 4th
Scattered cloud and sunny weather saw 127 Wing up at 0845, Greycap leading, on Ramrod S29, a fighter sweep of Poix, Amiens, Albert and Arras. Enemy aircraft were reported over France and nearby, by Appledore, but were not sighted by the Wing. Crossing out over the Somme Estuary, the Spitfires 'went down on the deck to see two pilots reported in the water but did not see anyone. A lone Spitfire with no markings was seen in the Amiens area and a red Very light was seen fired from this aircraft. Also one unidentified aircraft was seen to go down in flames in the Amiens area' (ORB, 403). Without further ado, the Wing was home by 1015.

Another operation was laid on for the afternoon, Ramrod S31, in which 127 Wing was to provide High Cover to 36 Marauders bombing Lille. In the target area, nine FW 190s of the *Geschwaderstab*, 8 & 10/JG 26, were seen approaching the bombers, so Wing Commander Johnson took a Section of 403 Squadron down to engage. The 'Wingco' fired at and hit *Oberfeldwebel*

Walter Grünlinger, who made off to the west before crashing in flames. Squadron Leader Grant, the new CO of 403, then shot down *Unteroffizier* Horst Schühl (8/JG 26); although the German baled out, his injuries were so horrendous that the Canadians could see blood on his parachute. Grant's luck then ran out, however, and he was shot down himself, probably by *Oberleutnant* Leuschel, *Staffelkapitän* of 10/JG 26.

The bombing had been accurate, many fires and explosions being seen a few minutes after the attack. Having safely escorted the bombers home, 127 Wing returned to Headcorn, landing at 1845.

Of the kills claimed by Wing Commander Johnson and Squadron Leader Grant, the ORB of 421 Squadron had this to say:-

Formed in November 1942, the Canadian Kenley Wing, which is now partly on 126 and the remainder on 127 Airfield, today scored their 99th and 100th successes…. A raffle had been held and the sum of £100 went to an airman in the Maintenance Section. Officers from 126 Airfield visited this airfield in the evening.

To mark this auspicious achievement, engraved silver tankards had been commissioned, one of which was presented to Wing Commander Johnson. Sadly Squadron Leader Grant would never receive his: the 28-year old, from Brockville, Ontario, was dead. Today, his grave can be found in Wevelgem Communal Cemetery.

September 5th
A sunny morning with scattered cloud saw operations on. At 0748, Greycap led 127 Wing up on Ramrod S33 Part I, High Cover to 72 Marauders bombing Mairelbeke, another STARKEY mission. In the Beynze area, five Me 109s were sighted trailing the bombers. Greycap and 421 Squadron's leading Section engaged four of these bandits. Two 109s were damaged, one by the 'Wingco', the other by Squadron Leader McNair. South of Gravelines, two FW 190s appeared and attacked 421 from 1,000 yards, but were 'soon chased off. Over Mardyk, three aircraft were seen on the aerodrome. Flak was experienced by our Wing from Dunkirk, Ostend, Ghent and the target' (ORB, 403). The Spitfires were all safely down by 0926.

Back at Headcorn, one flight of 403 Squadron was released, the other remaining at Readiness until dusk. The ORB of 421 Squadron observed that

'It is now practically a month since this Squadron went under canvas for the first time. The personnel have adapted themselves to this new life and seem quite at home in it'.

September 6th
The weather remained bright and sunny, with a near cloudless sky. It would be a busy day.

At 0700, Greycap and 127 Wing were up on Ramrod S35 Part V, Second Fighter Sweep to 72 Marauders bombing Rouen. One of the bombers was seen to crash in flames between Lydd and New Romney, but there was no reaction from the enemy. The operation was carried out according to plan, and the Spitfires were down by 0840.

Greycap then flew home to Leicestershire, landing his now famous Spitfire at Rearsby, for a 24-hour leave with his wife, Paula.

At 1125, however, 127 Wing was up again, this time on RamrodS35 Part II, escorting B-17s returning from Germany. Squadron Leader McNair led, and south of Bernay the Canadian Spitfires met a box of Fortresses which were escorted out to Coburg. There, 122 Wing took over so McNair wheeled his Spitfires back inland, bringing another 30 B-17s back to Coburg.

Over Beaumont, Squadron Leader McNair attacked and shot down a lone FW 190, which crashed in a wood some seven miles away from the enemy airfield. So bright was the aircraft's blue camouflage that the Spitfire pilots suspected it to be a reconnaissance machine.

By 1325, 127 Wing's Spitfires were all safely down but scattered at various forward landing fields along the south coast. There were also visitors at Headcorn, nine B-17s having landed, short of fuel. Two more Fortresses landed likewise at Lashenden. What a stir their arrival must have caused amongst the local schoolboys!

Squadron Leader McNair's kill was his 15th, and seventh since having joined 421 Squadron in mid-June. The ORB observed that this record was 'good going in any league'.

At 1720, Squadron Leader McNair led 127 Wing once more: Ramrod S36

Part III, High Cover to B-25s bombing the marshalling yards at Abbeville. The raid was carried out successfully and according to plan, after which the Spitfires swept south of Amiens. Three FW 190s were seen, and a Section of 421 Squadron attacked, Flight Lieutenant Phillip damaging one of the enemy fighters. Soon after, Yellow Section of 403 Squadron pounced on another three 190s, flying west at 24,000 feet. Flying Officer HJ Dowding, Yellow 3, shot down one of these 190s in flames, the aircraft being seen to crash. Flight Lieutenant HJ Southwood, Yellow 4, attacked another from underneath, this 190 also bursting into flames. Both German pilots were killed, *Feldwebel* Adolf Jörg and *Unteroffizier* Walter Berger, both of 6/JG 26. Flight Lieutenant Southwood then fired at another 190, damaging it.

By 1905, all of the Spitfires were safely back at Headcorn. A busy day, it had been the most successful so far for the Canadians whilst operating out of Headcorn. Back at base, however, there had been a mishap. Flight Lieutenants Peterson and Minton had taken off in 421 Squadron's Tiger Moth communications aircraft, failed to gain height quickly enough and crashed into some trees located at the right-hand side of the runway. Fortunately neither officer was injured, although the little biplane was wrecked.

Significantly, on this day the 403 Squadron ORB makes first mention of a legendary Canadian fighter pilot, Flying Officer George 'Screwball' Beurling DSO DFC DFM & Bar. Having started his career in 403 as a Sergeant Pilot, the maverick Beurling was back from Malta where he had enjoyed phenomenal success, his score now being 29 enemy aircraft destroyed with many others damaged.

Bob Middlemiss:-

One day, having had lunch in the Mess Tent at Headcorn, I was lying down on the ground sunning myself when I felt a kick at the bottom of my boot. I looked up and standing there as large as life was George Beurling, having just re-joined our Squadron. He looked fit, full of vim, vigour and vitality, and, if I knew 'Screwball', was ready to take on the whole *Luftwaffe*. When he had been with us previously, he would often fly the Tiger Moth locally, doing aerobatics and spins, disappearing below the treetops. On a number of occasions we thought he would crash, but he was a superb pilot and had full control of his aircraft, whether a Spitfire or a Tiger Moth. At times he would land in some field and talk the farmer into selling him some fresh eggs. Upon his return, we all then had a good feed in the Mess, courtesy of 'Screwball'.

Johnnie:-

As for 'Screwball' Beurling, I just couldn't do anything with him. I remember MacBrien coming to see me and saying "Canada House have been on and they want to put 'Screwball' Beurling into the Wing, what do you think?" Of course Beurling had a reputation, he had got a DSO and a DFC, and a DFM & Bar or something, he had more fucking gongs than I'd got at that time, but he also had this reputation of being very difficult to handle. Beurling came down, he didn't wear a tie, he was unshaven, and he had an old battered hat on. To all the youngsters he was God, you see, but he was a very, very bad example to them. He flew one show with me, towards the end of my tour, and suddenly we were at 25,000 feet and he half-rolled and disappeared down towards the ground. We got back and I sent for him. He said, "Well I saw a train, Wingco, so I thought that I'd go and give it a squirt".
I said, "Well nobody squirts anything unless I detach them to do so".
He said "Goddam it, Wingco, you've got to take a pot at these fucking Krauts".
I said "Well you do it once more and you're out, do you understand that? I don't know what you did in Malta or wherever but here we fly as a disciplined team, nobody breaks away unless I tell them to or unless we are bounced, and I just won't put up with this sort of stuff".

One day Beurling went off shooting, just took my gun and my dog, wearing his scruffy battledress, no tie, no hat, and he shot two of the rarest waterfowl on the fucking moat of Leeds Castle, great crested grebes or something! Not surprisingly the owner, some titled gent, went absolutely fucking barmy, and came down to see me, complaining bitterly.

There was a positive side, however. In an effort to make him a part of the team, Johnnie made Beurling the Wing Gunnery Officer, hoping that he could pass on some of his deflection shooting genius to the other pilots. Bob Middlemiss considered that 'Screwball' 'did very well in helping many of the pilots improve their shooting capabilities'.

September 7th
Again in Greycap's absence, 127 Wing was lead by Squadron Leader McNair, this time up at 0750, on Ramrod S32 Part IIA, escort to B-17s bombing the V-1 site at Watten, north of St Omer. The Canadians escorted the Fortresses out from the French coast, then swept inland to Lille. There was no enemy reaction, however, and the Spitfires were safely back at 0835.

The commander of 421 Squadron's 'A' Flight, Flight Lieutenant Norman Fowlow, was promoted today to Squadron Leader and posted to command the still-leaderless 403 Squadron. In turn, his place in 421 was taken by Flight Lieutenant RA Buckham DFC, who was posted in from 17 Wing.

Wing Commander Johnson returned from leave.

September 8th
Another sunny day with scattered cloud, Greycap was back in the lead for Ramrod S41 Part III, taking off at 1415. The Wing's role was to provide Top Cover to 24 Mitchells bombing the airfield at Vitry. Near the target, 15 FW 190s were seen manoeuvring to attack 421 Squadron. A brief clash ensued, also involving another Spitfire Wing, during which Flying Officer Dowding damaged a 190. Despite the Germans' efforts, bombing was accurate, explosions being seen in the centre and on the northern edge of Vitry. By 1100, 127 Wing was safely down without further incident.

The next operation was Ramrod S43, a sweep under Appledore in support of Venturas bombing Abbeville. Up at 1415, Greycap's Spitfires swept over St Pol, Amiens, Le Touquet and Boulogne, but without provoking any reaction. The Spitfires landed at 1535.

Back at base, something big was brewing, as indicated by Group Captain 'Iron Bill' MacBrien, Officer Commanding 17 Wing, who 'talked to everyone tonight at muster parade regarding an operation taking place tomorrow, an attempt to aid in the destruction of the German air force' (ORB, 403). The operation, said 'Tin Willie', was to begin during the night, continuing throughout the following day and probably longer. 'A special meeting was called for all pilots and further detail regarding the operation was given. It all sounds very interesting and everyone is looking forward to tomorrow' (ORB, 421).

September 9th
This was the climax of Operation STARKEY. Landing craft and other shipping were positioned in the Channel, and Allied air operations over the French coast and Pas-de-Calais were intensive. The intention was to deceive the Germans into believing that the invasion was actually being launched, and therefore provoke the enemy fighters into a massive reaction.

For 127 Wing, the day's first sortie was 'Beach Patrol No 1', Wing Commander Johnson leading the Spitfires off at 0715. The Spitfires patrolled over Cap-Gris-Nez, then south to Boulogne, but the enemy made no reaction. By 0830, the deflated Spitfire pilots were back at Headcorn.

Next came 'Beach Patrol No 2', a duplicate of the first sortie and with the same frustrating result.

Ramrod S43 Part II was then laid on, in which 127 Wing flew Top Cover to 18 Mitchells bombing Bryas Sud airfield. The only enemy fighters seen were two FW 190s diving away over Bethune. This trip was led not by Greycap but by Squadron Leader Hugh Godefroy, formerly CO of 403 Squadron.

The Wing's last show was at 1720, when Wing Commander Johnson led his Spitfires on Ramrod S44, High Cover to 12 Bostons bombing Courtrai aerodrome. However, when the Wing reached the English coast, poor weather over France dictated that the mission be aborted. The Spitfires returned to Headcorn, landing at 1750.

Given that the Germans had not reacted to what was supposedly an invasion attempt, Operation STARKEY was not, therefore, a success. Flying Officer Ken Wilkinson flew with 165 Squadron throughout that day, and many years commented that 'What was supposed to be the greatest air battle of all time was actually a damp squib'. 421 Squadron, nevertheless, acknowledged that 'much credit is due to the ground personnel for the hard way in which they worked to keep the aircraft serviceable' (ORB).

The day also marked a significant event at Headcorn: it was the end of Wing Commander Johnnie Johnson's first operational tour as a Wing Leader.

Johnnie:-

Yes, it was the right time to end that tour. Of course I had been on operations for three years, during which time I had flown, in total, 332 operational sorties, 127 or so with the Canadians, and my personal score was 24.

Was he tired?

Yes, yes I was, very tired, and I knew that. Things like flak were giving me more concern than previously, and instead of sending down appropriate Sections to attack, I had started going down myself, which was wrong.

Operational fatigue was something not to either overlook or take lightly. Wing Commander Douglas Bader, for example, had put so much energy and enthusiasm into leading the Tangmere Wing during 1941, but his press-on personality had not allowed him to admit that he was exhausted. The consequence was four years as a prisoner of war. Other Wing Leaders were even less fortunate: they were dead. Conversely, that great fighter pilot and leader 'Sailor' Malan, however, who had fought so courageously throughout the crucial early war years, had recognised the tell-tale signs in himself, and actually asked to come off operations. It was a brave move, but the man's huge experience was put to good use in the areas of fighter training and operational planning, rather than being wasted in the wreckage of a Spitfire in some foreign field.

Johnnie:-

Anyway, that was it. 'Iron Bill' MacBrien came over to Headcorn and told me that my tour was over. I had no objections, I knew that the time was right, and I also knew that Hugh Godefroy would succeed me, in whom I had every faith and confidence. There was nothing to be gained by staying on, but everything to be gained from having a rest. Also, we all suspected that the invasion would come off the following year, so I thought the likelihood was, given the timing, that if I went and rested now, I would be back for that long awaited event. It made sense.

On September 11th, Wing Commander JE Johnson, DSO & Bar, DFC & Bar, left for his new job, flying a desk on the Operational Planning Staff of No 11 Group, based at Uxbridge.

On September 18th, a dinner was prepared for a celebration that evening, the guest of honour being Wing Commander Johnson.

Bob Middlemiss:-

That afternoon, George Beurling and a number of us were outside our tent; 'Screwball' with shot gun in hand, when a low-flying Auster passed overhead. Beurling said casually "I will now demonstrate deflection shooting by giving the Auster a ring and-a-half". He fired. Unbeknown to us, flying in the Auster was Air Vice-Marshal Dickson, our No 83 Group AOC, who was attending the Wing Commander's farewell party. The Auster landed with buckshot in the elevator, and

the AOC was naturally extremely irate. Questions were asked, of course no one knew anything about a shooting, we all said that it must have been a local farmer.

The dinner was served in the Headcorn Mess Tent, starting at 1930, and was followed by after dinner speeches by Air Vice-Marshal Dickson and Group Captain MacBrien. Several senior officers from the Kenley Sector were also present, the occasion being a 'most enjoyable affair' (ORB, 421).

Bob Middlemiss:-

We gave Johnnie a very expensive gold watch as a token of our esteem for him as our Wing Leader. The Group Commander decided that because of the very late night and our condition, the Wing would be stood down next day.

Thereafter, Wing Commander Hugh Constance Godefroy DFC replaced 'Greycap' as 'Darkwood Leader'. He had big shoes to fill.

There is one final, short, story worth recounting. Hugh Godefroy:-

Before leaving the Wing, Johnnie decided that he needed a new car. After some dickering, I offered him £35 for his Morris Minor, on the understanding that he replaced the two back tyres. It was only after taking and accepting delivery I discovered that both 'new' replacement tyres had come off a 127 Wing starter battery cart, and the car had a *very* temperamental engine...

Chapter Six

Reflections
'Greycap' looks back

"A Marvellous life!"

Johnnie Johnson's leadership of the Canadians in 1943 was recognised by not one but *two* Distinguished Service Orders. Impressive by any standard, but anyone who knew Johnnie would appreciate the depth of his charisma and ability to lead, not 'manage', like many of today's so-called 'leaders', but really *lead*. It was a time when his natural ability to lead was not only honed, but matured.

As Bob Middlemiss has said, Johnnie appeared 'type cast' for his role as Wing Leader. So what did Johnnie himself think?

We just gelled together, the Canadians and me, but in any case the Squadrons themselves were first class. The whole thing went down the chain of command. If you've got a good man at the top then morale is better at the bottom. It didn't take me long to get the measure of them, don't forget that I was a pretty experienced chap, having flown 'Arse-end Charlie' myself and worked my way up. I had been a Squadron Commander for quite a time and I had led the Tangmere Wing once or twice as a Squadron Leader. The fact that I had previously been closely associated with Douglas Bader, who led a Canadian squadron during the Battle of Britain, may also have helped. There was, however, a bit of hostility from the senior chaps who used to come down from Canada House. They had a few guys under an Air Marshal and I remember one of them saying to me "Of course you're only a stop-gap until we find our own Wing Commander, you'll only be here for a month or so". As it happened I was there for seven!

And what of the Americans?

I think that the most exciting times of 1943 were escorting the Fortresses. They came over to drop it in a beer barrel with that Norden bomb sight, but all the RAF chiefs, Portal and Harris, told them that the only way to survive was to bomb at night and if the Yanks had any sense then they would as well. The Americans were adamant

that they were not going to bomb at night, though, and they took some hard knocks. Their bombers positively bristled with machine-guns, and they believed that the crossfire generated by large formations would save them.

With regard to operating procedures when protecting the Forts, you didn't get too close to them for a start because they fired at everybody! Consequently I never got nearer than a thousand yards, unless we were chasing somebody. I remember chasing some 190s making a head-on attack, which half-rolled. I was underneath them, and the Forts were firing at every fucker, every fucking gun was blazing away! So you never got within a thousand yards! In fairness, despite all their knocks, they kept going, and they did get knocked about a bit of course.

We had liaison, of course. I used to go and lecture them regarding enemy fighter tactics and that sort of thing. I went to the 8th Air Force HQ, where they got all their squadron commanders together on the outskirts of London. Sometimes I would go off to Bassingbourne and go to their de-briefings.

The great thing in war, remember, is to have an objective and stick to it, through thick and thin. This the Americans did regarding daylight bombing, and all credit to them for it.

And of German fighter tactics in 1943?

There wasn't much fighter-to-fighter combat in the true sense, as the Germans were just trying to get at the bombers. We were just an irritation. If they could avoid us they would. Most of our sorties were bomber protection or sweeps out to the flanks, sometimes as much as 100 miles away, which was Bomber Support. The *Luftwaffe* was very good at moving squadrons to threatened points and reinforcing and that kind of thing. More often than not the enemy would not react, certainly not in strength, which was frustrating as it meant that we only engaged every third or fourth sweep. Of course in taking on the Eighth Air Force the Germans had it easy at that time, given that we could only take them so far and then meet them on the way back out. All the German controller had to do was time his interception right and avoid our fighters.

And range?

As we have already said, the fact that efforts were not made to significantly and properly increase the range of our Spitfires was a disgrace, and that was down to the Chief of the Air Staff, Portal. He believed, wrongly, that to do so would impede the Spitfire's performance as a defensive fighter. If we had had the range in 1943, we could have prevented many American bomber losses.

The answer was, however, at hand in the shape of the North American P-51 Mustang, the so-called 'Cadillac of the Sky'. The Mustang had first flown in October 1940, and arose due to British requirements. The original Allison engine, however, provided only mediocre performance, and the Mustang was found wanting at high altitude. Consequently the first Mustangs received by the RAF, in April 1942, were assigned to army co-operation roles. The British, however, replaced the Allison with the potent Merlin engine, and the results were staggering. Mediocre no more, trials confirmed that the Mustang was superior to all comers and in all respects. The Mustang's range was awesome: P-51A – 2,200 miles; P-51B – 2,301 miles. This compared with the mere 980 miles of the Spitfire Mk IX. By early 1944, the P-51s were with the bombers all the way over the Reich and back. In August, the P-51s were over Berlin itself. The Mustang therefore became the long-range offensive fighter that the Allies had needed so badly from 1942 onwards.

Johnnie:-

The problem was that, right throughout the war, really, Fighter Command was not aggressive enough, never really fought as a proper offensive force. We became a Tactical Air Force, which was of short range, but we only had one Wing of Mustangs, for example. After the war, when I got onto the TSR2 programme, I kept saying that it had to be long range. They just said, "Look, it can't be long range if it is going to be an interceptor."
I said "I wrote the fucking requirement for this!" but of course it was botched up and never built in the end. *Not* good enough.

And what of the canvas experience?

Living under canvas and operating as a mobile, tactical, air force came as a bit of a shock to the system, I can tell you, after Kenley and putting on your nice blue uniform to get up to the West End for the odd night! But it was all good stuff, good training, and I actually enjoyed Lashenden and Headcorn very much. It was certainly essential experience for the events of the following year and beyond.

And of 'Screwball' Beurling?

Well as you know, shortly after he joined the Wing, I left and was succeeded by Hughie Godefroy who got rid of him. Beurling had taken up a Tiger Moth from Headcorn and beat the shit out of everybody at nought feet.

Bob Middlemiss:-

Beurling was not very happy just flying escort to B-17s, and sweeps, flying as one of 24 Spitfires. He wanted to obtain four Mustangs from the RAF and permission and freedom to roam deep into Germany to take on the *Luftwaffe*. As the existing Rhubarbs were closely routed and timed, the addition of four freelancing Mustangs flying hither and yon did not sit well with Fighter Command and his request was turned down.

After a couple of episodes of Beurling beating up the aerodrome and being warned by the Group Captain, he was transferred from 127 to 126 Wing. Rather than being offered what he thought was a useful role, he was repatriated to Canada and released from service before the war's end. Had he stayed on and gone onto the Continent, who knows how many more kills he would have made?

Beurling attended Hazel and my wedding in Montreal in May 1944, along with several 403 Squadron pilots. I still have the pearl handled fish forks and knives that he gave to us as a wedding present. I last saw 'Screwball' on St Catherine's Street, Montreal, and he suggested that I join him on his way to fight for the Israeli Air Force. On May 20th, 1948, he and his passenger were killed when their Norseman aircraft crashed whilst taking off from Rome. Sabotage was apparently expected.

They buried the maverick 'Screwball' in Israel, the Promised Land.

And, after leaving Headcorn, what did Johnnie make of enforced rest?

I left the Wing, going to HQ 11 Group on the Operational Staff, running the day to day operations. Once a month I used to get a light aircraft and fly to Tangmere, Hornchurch or Kenley, and then fly a Spitfire on ops with the various Wings. On reflection that was a mistake, really, there was I a very experienced chap, and they would say "You can fly with Flying Officer so-and-so, and stay out on the flank", so I had no control over what they were doing. It was sometimes frustrating for me and looking back I shouldn't have done it, it was foolish, but I wanted to keep my hand in and keep a good relationship with the various Wing Leaders, people like Ray Harries who got the first Griffon-engined Spits. Before that, we used to think that height was everything, Bader always used to say "Height, height, height!", but Harries, in the new Spitfire, the Mk XII, used to get underneath the 190s at 12,000 feet, to bring them down. The theory was that that Spitfire was superior at 12,000 feet, so Ray brought them down to that height, where he could hack them down. It was a hard way to learn a living, though, I always thought! But by then we were getting on top, and the German fighter pilot wasn't, by the end of '43, beginning of '44, the same animal that he had been in 1940 and after the Battle of Britain.

So what next?

After my rest I went back to ops with a new Canadian Wing, 144 Wing, leading up to the invasion. We had low-level IXBs. The 144 Wing story is actually more interesting, I suppose, as you are beating the fuckers, aren't you, keeping on the move, a kind of bucanneering, nomadic existence.

Johnnie took command of 144 Wing RCAF in March 1944, leading it during the D-Day and Normandy fighting. In August, 144 Wing was disbanded, so Johnnie returned to 127 Wing, which he led until early 1945. In April, he was given 125 Wing, by which time he was a Group Captain. The events of March 1944 – May 1945 will be related in the Part Two of this saga, *Johnnie Johnson: Spitfire Top Gun*, which will be released by Ramrod Publications in 2004.

To sum up the story so far? Johnnie:-

A marvellous life! Well, it was, wasn't it?

Index

D ue to the frequency that Johnnie Johnson is mentioned in this book, it was considered impractical to include those references in this index, which includes the personnel of both sides. Where initials are unknown, the unit with which the individual served is indicated.

The Johnnie Johnson Statue Appeal
Life-and-a-quarter bronze for the RAF Museum, Hendon!

Johnnie Johnson officially became the RAF's top scoring fighter pilot of WW2 with 38 ½ aerial victories. Following Johnnie's death in 2001, Dilip Sarkar felt strongly that a statue should be erected to permanently commemorate this great British hero. Of such projects Dilip already had some experience, his close friend, the sculptor Kenneth Potts ARBS having already created Goodwood Airfield's statue of Sir Douglas Bader, which was unveiled by Lady Bader on August 9th, 2001.

Having achieved the Johnson family's approval and support, Dilip contacted Dr Michael Fopp, Director of the RAF Museum, suggesting that Hendon would make a perfect site for this proposed tribute. Following a meeting with the Director and his staff, approval was granted, the intention being to locate the statue in what will become, under the Museum's significant expansion programme, a large open space outside the front entrance.

The Director's approval, however, was on the basis that the project would have to be funded by an Appeal, organised and overseen by Dilip Sarkar. The cost of the proposed life-and-a-quarter bronze, which Kenneth Potts will create, is estimated at some £60,000. This figure, therefore, is the Appeal target.

All donations, no matter how large or small, are much appreciated, and can be sent to the following address:-

Johnnie Johnson Statue Appeal
16 Kingfisher Close
St Peter's
Worcester WR5 3RY
ENGLAND

Please make cheques etc payable to 'Johnnie Johnson Statue Appeal'. For further information, please contact 01905 767735 (tel & fax), or dil@ramrodbooks.u-net.com

Did YOU Serve with Johnnie Johnson?
Would YOU like to contribute to Part Two?

Looking ahead, we need to trace as many veterans as possible who flew or served with Johnnie during his long and distinguished RAF career. Firstly such personalities would be on our VIP invitation list to the statue unveiling. Secondly, Dilip would be most interested to hear any recollections and/or see any relevant photographs that they may have, particularly regarding the period September 1943 – May 1945, which will be covered in *Johnnie Johnson: Spitfire Top Gun, Part Two* (release date May 2004). Please contact him at the above address.

Ramrod Publications Mailing List

If you have enjoyed this and other books by Dilip Sarkar, you can become a privileged customer through inclusion on our mailing list. This ensures automatic notification of new releases, in advance of both publication and availability to the general public. This provides the best opportunity of purchasing special limited edition copies, which always sell out very quickly and usually through our mailing list.

Please send your postal and/or email addresses to:-

Anita Sarkar
Ramrod Publications
16 Kingfisher Close
St Peter's
Worcester WR5 3RY

BADER BIKE CHALLENGE

The Bader Bike Challenge: Granada to Seville 2001

During the Year 2,000, a group of intrepid cyclists, some of them amputees, cycled 250 miles through Jordan to successfully complete the 'Bader Bike Challenge'. Each cyclist raised a minimum amount of £2,500 sponsorship for the benefit of the Douglas Bader Foundation. A small charity, founded by family and friends as a memorial to Group Captain Sir Douglas Bader, the Foundation, of which Lady Bader OBE is a most active President, provides a facility for amputee rehabbilitation and sport at Roehampton (The Douglas Bader Centre). Financial grants and a telephone advice line for the amputee disabled is an equally vital part of the Foundation's work.

In 2001, Anita Sarkar of Ramrod Publications (pictured right with Lady Bader and mascot!), completed the second Bader Bike Challenge by joining a group which rode a similar distance through the Spanish mountains. In 2003, a further Bader Bike Challenge will take place, in Cuba, and Anita will be taking part! If you would like to sponsor her in support of this most worthy cause, or take up the challenge yourself, please contact Anita at Ramrod Publications on (01905) 767735.